Latin Translation in the Renaissance

Latin translations of Greek works have received much less attention than vernacular translations of classical works. This book examines the work of three Latin translators of the Renaissance. The versions of Aristotle made by Leonardo Bruni (c.1370–1444) were among the most controversial translations of the fifteenth century and he defended his methods in the first modern treatise on translation, *De interpretatione recta*. Giannozzo Manetti (1396–1459) produced versions of Aristotle and the Bible and he too ultimately felt obliged to publish his own defence of the translator's art, *Apologeticus*. Desiderius Erasmus (c.1469–1536) chose to defend his own translation of the New Testament, one of the most controversial translations ever printed, with a substantial and expanding volume of annotations. This book attempts to provide a broad perspective on the development of Latin writing about translation by drawing together the ideas of these three very different translators.

PAUL BOTLEY is currently Research Associate in the Centre for the History of Science, Technology and Medicine at Imperial College, London.

CAMBRIDGE CLASSICAL STUDIES

LATIN TRANSLATION IN THE RENAISSANCE

The Theory and Practice of Leonardo Bruni, Giannozzo Manetti and Desiderius Erasmus

PAUL BOTLEY
Imperial College, London

 CAMBRIDGE
UNIVERSITY PRESS

PUBLISHED BY THE PRESS SYNDICATE OF THE UNIVERSITY OF CAMBRIDGE
The Pitt Building, Trumpington Street, Cambridge, United Kingdom

CAMBRIDGE UNIVERSITY PRESS
The Edinburgh Building, Cambridge, CB2 2RU, UK
40 West 20th Street, New York, NY 10011–4211, USA
477 Williamstown Road, Port Melbourne, VIC 3207, Australia
Ruiz de Alarcón 13, 28014 Madrid, Spain
Dock House, The Waterfront, Cape Town 8001, South Africa

http://www.cambridge.org

First published 2004

Printed in the United Kingdom at the University Press, Cambridge

Typeface Times 11/13 pt.   *System* LaTeX 2_ε [TB]

A catalogue record for this book is available from the British Library

ISBN 0 521 83717 0 hardback

CONTENTS

vii

FIGURE AND TABLES

ACKNOWLEDGEMENTS

This work has its origins in a doctoral thesis produced under the careful supervision of Dr Colin Burrow of Gonville and Caius College, Cambridge. It has been influenced by regular discussions with Dr Peter Stacey, also of Caius College, and it has benefited from the readings of Dr Jill Kraye of the Warburg Institute, and Professor Michael Reeve of Pembroke College, Cambridge. Because not all of their numerous contributions have been acknowledged *ad locum*, a general note of thanks is appropriate here.

I would also like to thank the Arts and Humanities Research Board for the studentship which made this research possible, and for contributing towards the expenses of my first visit to the Vatican Library in 1998. A scholarship and a further research grant from Caius College enabled me to return to the Vatican in 1999. My time as Munby Fellow in Bibliography at the University Library in Cambridge allowed me to recast my earlier research into this book.

ABBREVIATIONS

The abbreviations used for classical works and authors are those used in the third edition of the *Oxford Classical Dictionary*. In addition, the following abbreviations are used in this work:

CWE	*The Collected Works of Erasmus*, Toronto: University of Toronto Press, 1974–
EE	*Opus Epistolarum Des. Erasmi Roterodami*, ed. P. S. Allen, H. M. Allen and H. W. Garrod (12 vols.), Oxford: University Press, 1906–58
Iter Italicum	Kristeller, Paul Oskar. *Iter Italicum: A Finding List of Uncatalogued or Incompletely Catalogued Humanistic Manuscripts of the Renaissance in Italian and Other Libraries*, Leiden: Brill, 1963
LB	*Omnia Opera Desiderii Erasmi Roterodami*. ed. J. LeClerc (10 vols.), Leiden, 1703–6, facsimile: Hildesheim: Olms, 1961
PG	*Patrologiae Cursus Completus: Series Graeca* (161 vols.), ed. Jean-Pierre Migne, Paris: Migne, 1857–66
PL	*Patrologiae Cursus Completus: Series Latina* (221 vols.), ed. Jean-Pierre Migne, Paris: Migne, 1844–90

INTRODUCTION

This book is a contribution to the exploration of the extensive but relatively neglected body of Latin writing about translation which was produced during the fifteenth and early sixteenth centuries. The subject was first suggested to me by the observation that Bolgar's appendix of translations in *The Classical Heritage* does not detail Latin translations of Greek texts.[1] In fact, works of synthesis have tended to pass over the productions of these translators. Gilbert Highet's study of the classical tradition, for example, specifically excludes Latin literature.[2] Wilamowitz-Moellendorff too places translations beyond the scope of his study, because, he argues, the Humanist translators were more often *littérateurs* than scholars.[3] Latin translations have thus fallen between two stools: they are too scholarly to receive the attention of literary historians, and too literary to interest the historians of scholarship.

This work emerged from an attempt to compile a survey of the Latin translators of the Renaissance touched upon in the histories of Sandys and Pfeiffer.[4] It is particularly indebted to the modern scholarship characterised by the work on the transmission of ancient Latin texts brought together by Reynolds in *Texts and Transmission*, and by similar studies of Greek texts by Wilson.[5] Yet although the *fortuna* of a number of Greek texts in the Renaissance is clarified in this book, my principal aim is to study what the fifteenth and sixteenth centuries thought of the translations of their predecessors, and how these ideas informed their own translations. It is an attempt to examine the ways Renaissance scholars thought about the transmission of the ancient works. The material for this study is scattered widely, in the prefaces of translations and editions of Greek authors, in occasional letters, and in

[1] Bolgar (1954).   [2] Highet (1949).   [3] Wilamowitz-Moellendorff (1921) 2, 10.
[4] Sandys (1908); Pfeiffer (1976).
[5] L. D. Reynolds (1983); Reynolds and Wilson (1974); Wilson (1992).

I

commentaries and annotations. I have chosen to focus on the work of three translators: Leonardo Bruni (c.1370–1444), Giannozzo Manetti (1396–1459) and Desiderius Erasmus (c.1469–1536). The work of these three figures spans the entire period under investigation. All three translators made translations of the central texts of their day, Aristotle and the Scriptures; all encountered criticism of their versions; and all wrote in defence of their methods of translation.

The translations of Leonardo Bruni mark the start of a process of translation which eventually transferred into Latin most of the literature salvaged from the Greek world. With the recent publication of the first volume of the *Repertorium Brunianum*, Bruni scholarship is gathering pace.[6] Much of the preparatory work for the long-meditated and much-needed edition of Bruni's correspondence has been completed.[7] Bruni's work as a translator constitutes a substantial portion of his writing, and some parts of this work have been carefully explored: James Hankins' work on his translations from Plato, for example, places their study on a new foundation.[8] However, not a few of Bruni's translations are still in manuscript, and most of the rest have not been edited since the sixteenth century. In particular, his translations from Plutarch and the Greek historians, and consequently his debt to Greek biography and historiography, remain poorly documented. While there is much more to be done in this area than can be achieved within the scope of this book, it is hoped that the contextualisation of some of his versions attempted here may lead to a reassessment of their significance. Although Bruni's essay on translation, *De interpretatione recta*, was edited by Hans Baron in 1927, it has attracted surprisingly little attention from modern scholars, perhaps because it attracted very little attention from Bruni's contemporaries. Here it is located, as Bruni conceived it, amongst the controversies surrounding his Aristotelian translations.

One Florentine translator certainly studied Bruni's essay on translation. Giannozzo Manetti is the least known of the three translators examined in this book. Recent editorial work is at last bringing some of Manetti's rarer works to light, but Manetti's

---

[6] Hankins (1997).   [7] See Baron (1981); Viti (1992).   [8] Hankins (1990).

translations have received little attention.[9] This is remarkable considering his position among the Latin translators of the fifteenth century. Manetti is an important link between the Florentine translators of the early fifteenth century and the Greek scholars who gathered around Pope Nicholas V in the middle years of the century. He was translating Aristotle at Rome during the great wave of Aristotelian translations produced during Nicholas' pontificate. If his translations of Aristotle's *Libri morales* look back to Bruni's *Ethics* controversy, then his work on a new translation of the Bible anticipates the New Testament scholarship of Erasmus. Not only was he translating the New Testament while Lorenzo Valla was preparing his influential annotations on the New Testament, he was also a Hebrew scholar of the first rank at a time when the language was almost unknown among Christian scholars in Italy. Here, I attempt to clarify the obscure history of his translations. His treatise on translation, *Apologeticus*, more substantial than either Jerome's or Bruni's comments on the matter, remained almost unknown from Manetti's day until it was edited by De Petris in 1981. It is a document of central importance to the history of fifteenth-century ideas about translation.

Manetti did not publish his New Testament translation, perhaps because he anticipated that it would involve him in controversy. Erasmus' New Testament translation, first printed in 1516, was one of the most controversial translations ever made. Although a number of aspects of Erasmus' work on the Scriptures have been explored, his *Annotations* on the New Testament have received less attention.[10] In fact, until the recent editorial work of Anne Reeve on the *Annotations*, finally completed in 1993, the systematic study of the development of Erasmus' ideas on translation was a laborious process.[11] The successive revisions and expansions of the *Annotations* revealed in Reeve's edition allow the accumulation of factors which informed Erasmus' renderings to be traced. His

---

[9] Recent editions include: *Vita Socratis* (1974), *Vita Senecae* (1976), *Apologeticus* (1981), *Dialogus consolatorius* (1983), *Apologia Nunni* and *Laudatio Dominae Agnetis Numantinae* (1989). I am preparing an edition of the *Exhortatio ad Calistum III*. Manetti's *De illustribus longevis*, and his *Adversus Iudeos et Gentes* remain in manuscript, as do all his translations.

[10] See, for example, Rabil (1972); Bentley (1983). I am indebted to Rummel (1986).

[11] A. Reeve (1986), (1990), (1993).

debt to Valla, and to Valla's concept of *Elegantiae*, has been well advertised, not least by Erasmus himself. Here, I stress that although Erasmus had very real doubts about the application of Valla's methods to the text of the New Testament, his citation of Valla's work in the *Annotations* is often tactical as well as philological. By repeatedly pointing out Valla's excesses, Erasmus attempts to make his own work appear more conservative than it really is.

If the advocates of Greek studies are to be believed, most students of Greek did not learn Greek to read Greek texts. It certainly appears that most Latinists acquired only a little Greek, and that they remained dependent on the translations made by other scholars. The final chapter suggests that the translations created by these scholars can be placed in several categories. Medieval versions tended to function as replacements for the original Greek text, partly because very few contemporaries could read any Greek, and partly because most medieval translations were of works of Greek science, the technical manuals of medicine and philosophy. In the fifteenth century different varieties of translation emerged. A new type of translation developed in the language schools as a supplement to Greek texts, to help students of Greek to learn the language. At the same time, Bruni revived an ancient conception of translation, touched on by Cicero and Quintilian, and produced his translations to compete with the original Greek texts, and with the Latin versions of his fellow translators. This method of translation was most appropriate for the literary works of Greek rhetoric and poetry, and Bruni justified its application to the works of Aristotle by redefining Aristotle as a rhetorical author. Subsequently, Manetti outlined the position that ancient translations of the Bible had been produced for specific reasons, and that new translations of Scriptural texts could also be justified in terms of the purposes they were created to serve. Erasmus, with the backing of his friend Thomas More, later developed this line of thought when he argued that it was better to have several versions of a difficult text than to have a single authoritative translation. In their different ways, the approaches of the teachers of Greek, and of Bruni, Manetti and Erasmus, encouraged readers to regard translations as temporary and replaceable accommodations with the Greek text. This development is described in the following pages.

4

LEONARDO BRUNI

Introduction

Leonardo Bruni was the most illustrious pupil of the famous Byzantine teacher Manuel Chrysoloras. He went on to become one of the most prolific translators of the fifteenth century. Bruni's development as a biographer and as an historian was stimulated and punctuated by his contact with a succession of Greek authors. This chapter attempts to assess Bruni's role in reorienting Latin thought in the light of these contacts with Greek texts. It is worth making this attempt because although several valuable studies of a number of Bruni's translations try to reconstruct his Greek manuscript sources, they are often uninterested in his attitudes to the texts he translates.[1] In the manuscript collections of Florence he had access to a large portion of the surviving corpus of Greek works; he also had a grasp of the Greek language rare among his contemporaries. He could have chosen to translate any number of authors. In this chapter, I shall examine the availability of Greek authors in Florence in the early years of the fifteenth century and attempt to identify some of the factors which led him to them.

To this end, I examine his apprenticeship as a biographer through his translations of Plutarch's *Lives*. Latin prejudices often made contact with Greek culture productive, and Bruni's own Latin biographies of Cicero and Demosthenes grew out of his dissatisfaction with this Greek source. Bruni also did a great deal to reshape the Latin historical tradition in the light of newly available Greek sources. Although his work as an historian has been the subject of a number of essays, his very real debt to Livy has often overshadowed the contributions made by Greek historians to

---

[1] See, for example, Accame Lanzillotta (1986); Berti (1978); Naldini (1984).

the development of his thought.[2] He applied his ideas about classical historiography to the problems of assessing Greek historical sources. To find out how he treated his Greek sources, I concentrate on three of his historical works: his *Commentaries* on the First Punic War, a work based on the early books of Polybius; his *Commentarium rerum Graecarum*, drawn from Xenophon's *Hellenica*; and his *De bello italico adversus Gothos gesto*, which he compiled from Procopius.

Bruni's rhetorical training also influenced his treatment of Greek texts. His most popular and most controversial translation, of Aristotle's *Nicomachean Ethics*, replaced the literal medieval translations with a more classical Latin prose. In defence of his methods of translating Bruni wrote the treatise *De interpretatione recta*, a more extensive treatment of translation than anything which has survived from antiquity. I consider these works in the context of the criticisms of Bruni's translation put forward by his contemporary Alfonso, Bishop of Burgos, who takes issue with Bruni's conception of Aristotelian eloquence. In some modern criticism, Bruni's insistence on the philosopher's eloquence has been rather summarily treated. I hope to demonstrate the coherence of Bruni's ideas about Aristotle's *eloquentia*, and to show that they reopened an ancient debate about the relationship between rhetoric and philosophy.

Bruni's early Greek studies

Some time in the 1370s, the Archbishop of Thebes, Simon Atumano, translated Plutarch's *De remediis irae* into Latin.[3] Twenty years later Coluccio Salutati, Florentine Chancellor and patron of the young Leonardo Bruni, revised Atumano's translation of the treatise. Salutati was no Greek scholar and simply recast his predecessor's rendering into more elegant Latin. This marriage of Atumano's Greek learning and Salutati's Latinity was the best compromise possible at the time. As he wrote in the preface to his version,

---

[2] See, for example, Santini (1910); Santini's introduction to his edition of Bruni's history, Santini (1914–26); Ullman (1946).

[3] For the date of the version, see Mercati (1916) addendum.

Non sunt hoc tempore Cicerones, Hieronymi, Rufini, Ambrosii vel Chalcidii, non Cassiodori, non Evagrii, non Boetii, quorum translationes tante sunt venustatis atque dulcedinis, quod nichil possit ornatus vel perspicuitatis in his que transtulerunt desiderari.[4]

[Today there are no Ciceros, Jeromes, Rufinuses, Ambroses or Chalcidiuses, no Cassiodoruses, no Evagriuses, no Boethiuses, whose translations are so attractive and pleasant that no refinement or clarity is lacking in what they have translated.]

This list pointedly excludes medieval translators, whose techniques Salutati identified with Atumano's. Bruni's early career as a translator was constructed to fill a gap which Salutati perceived. Having brought the Byzantine scholar Chrysoloras to Florence in 1397 the Chancellor encouraged Bruni, then a promising law student, to study Greek under him.[5] Bruni, who later provided alternatives to some of these medieval versions, shared the older man's opinions about medieval Greek learning. Clearly Salutati felt that he knew what a good translation ought to look like, even though he never mastered enough Greek to produce one himself.[6] It is likely that the essential elements of Bruni's ideas about translation were established under the influence of a man who knew no Greek, and before he himself had learnt any.

Salutati's interests can be discerned in many of Bruni's early translations. Bruni's Latin translation of St Basil's treatise *De studiis secularibus* was completed by May 1403, and dedicated to the Chancellor.[7] A letter of Salutati's uses Bruni's recent translation to vindicate his position on the study of pagan authors.[8] Through Bruni, Salutati was able to cite authorities that opponents had to respect, even if they could not read them. This was to be Bruni's only translation of a patristic work, and its purpose was to legitimise the study of pagan literature by Christians. It was chosen, he writes, 'quod maxime eum conducere ad studia nostra

---

[4] Novati (1891–1911) II: 482. Cited in Setton (1956) 50. I have modernised the punctuation of quotations throughout. All translations are my own.

[5] Bruni says, 'ego per id tempus Juri Civili operam dabam, non rudis tamen ceterorum studiorum' (Di Pierro (1914–26) 431).

[6] For Salutati's Greek, see Ullman (1963) 118–21. For four other fifteenth-century translations of the treatise, see Resta (1959) 237–41. Erasmus' version was published in 1525. See *EE* VI: 70–2.

[7] Baron (1928) 160–1.

[8] To Giovanni da Samminiato. Novati (1891–1911) IV: 170–205, 25 January 1405–1406?

arbitrati sumus'[9] [because I thought it contributed a great deal to our studies]. Its keynote – *non omnia nobis recipienda sunt, sed tantum utilia* – was to provide the standard justification for the study of pagan antiquity.[10] Under Chrysoloras, Bruni studied with Roberto Rossi, Pier Paolo Vergerio, Jacopo Angeli and Palla Strozzi. All of these students produced translations from the Greek, but none of these versions were as numerous, as ambitious or as elegant as Bruni's. To judge from the prefatory letter to this version of Basil, Bruni was excited by the extent of the Greek literature which he was beginning to uncover:

Ego tibi hunc librum, Colucci, ex media (ut aiunt) Graecia delegi, ubi eiuscemodi rerum magna copia est et infinita paene multitudo. Nec veritus sum ne abs te ut parum liberalis ac sane ingratus accusarer, si ex tanta abundantia hoc tam parvum munus ad te mitterem.[11]

[I have chosen this book for you, Coluccio, from the midst of Greece (as they say), where there is a great supply, a near-infinite multitude, of this sort of thing. And I was not afraid that you would reproach me for being ungenerous and ungrateful, if from such abundance I were to send to you such a small gift as this.]

This is an understandable reaction to the essay: Basil's work makes a point of quoting interesting passages from a large number of Greek authors. By the time he made this translation, Bruni was in a remarkable position. He had been given the key to a field almost entirely unexplored by western scholars. His grasp of the language was improving steadily, and many of the surviving works of classical Greek literature were available to him through Chrysoloras and the manuscript collections of his fellow students. The reasons which led Bruni to translate certain works cannot be evaluated without first attempting to discover which works were available to him before the important manuscript collections of Guarino, Aurispa and Filelfo reached Italy. Here, I shall piece together some of the scattered notices of Greek manuscripts to establish which Greek authors were used by this circle of students in Florence in the final years of the fourteenth century and the first years of the fifteenth.

No doubt one of the first texts they met was Chrysoloras' own grammar, *Erotemata*, produced by him for his western pupils.[12]

---

[9] Baron (1928) 99.   [10] Naldini (1984) 241.   [11] Baron (1928) 99.
[12] For Chrysoloras' grammar, see Pertusi (1962).

Chrysoloras himself seems to have introduced his students to a very wide range of authors. We know that he used several of Lucian's dialogues with his students, and a surviving manuscript made by one of his Florentine pupils throws some light on his teaching methods.[13] In the fourteenth century Boccaccio had begun his Greek studies with Homer, and throughout the fifteenth century he remained among the first authors encountered by students.[14] Vergerio certainly had a Greek manuscript of the *Odyssey* from Palla Strozzi in the winter of 1400–01.[15] A lost translation of Homer made by Vergerio has been tentatively assigned to this period.[16] Bruni's own prose translations from Homer were published in his maturity, but it seems likely that he too first met the poet under Chrysoloras' supervision.[17] He is able to cite the poet in his *Laudatio* of Florence, which was produced by 1404.[18] The *Laudatio* itself is modelled on Aristides' *Panathenaicus*, which must therefore have been available to Bruni in some form before this date.[19]

There are also good reasons to believe that many, if not all, of the works of another writer popular with students were in Florence at the time. Some time before 1403, Bruni translated Xenophon's *Hiero* and dedicated it to Niccolò Niccoli. In the preface he says that he translated the treatise 'ingenii exercendi gratia'[20] [to train my ability]. Bruni would have known that Cicero had translated Xenophon's *Oeconomicus* in his youth, and perhaps he was deliberately following Cicero's lead in choosing Xenophon to sharpen his Greek on.[21] Some remarks in the preface to his version of *Hiero* suggest that Bruni already knew another work of Xenophon, the

[13] Chrysoloras owned Vat.gr.87, from which Urb.gr.121 was made. An interlinear Latin gloss was added by an anonymous pupil. An anonymous Latin translation of Lucian was made from this copy before 26 May 1403. See Berti (1987).
[14] See Coulter (1926) and Boccaccio, *Genealogiae*, XV: 6–7.
[15] Smith (1934) Ep. 95.   [16] Pertusi (1964) 522.
[17] Baron places the publication of Bruni's Homeric versions after 1421 (Baron (1928) 172); Pertusi dates them to 1405 (Pertusi (1964) 522). They have been edited by Thiermann who dates them c. 1438 ((1993) 126–9).
[18] Baron (1968) 237; *Iliad* XII: 278–86. The *Laudatio* was probably produced late summer 1404 (Hankins (1990) II: 377).
[19] For Bruni's use of Aristides in the *Laudatio*, see Santosuosso (1986). Palla Strozzi owned Urb.gr.123 of Aristides (Diller (1961) 316).
[20] Baron (1928) 100, 161. Bruni's version of *Hiero* was often reprinted until Erasmus' rendering replaced it in 1530.
[21] See *De officiis* II. 24. Cicero's translations are listed by Bruni in a letter of 1435 (Mehus (1741) VII: 4; Luiso (1980) VII: 4). This letter is edited in Birkenmaier (1922) 129–210.

Anabasis.[22] Bruni's interest in Xenophon continued. In a letter of 15 March 1407, Bruni writes from Rome that Pietro Miani has promised to send him some manuscripts: 'Habet enim . . . Plutarchi et Xenophontis quaedam volumina'[23] [For he has some volumes of Plutarch and Xenophon]. In the autumn he writes to Miani with a request for a Greek manuscript of the *Cyropaedia*.[24] In the same year Bruni paraphrased Xenophon's *Apologia Socratis*.[25] Xenophon's *Agesilaus* was perhaps known to Bruni by 1408.[26] Other, less common, authors can also be located in this period. Angeli owned a Greek manuscript of Dionysius of Halicarnassus, which he may have had before 1400.[27] We also know that when, in August 1401, Salutati requested from Angeli a copy of a passage from the *Heroicus* of Philostratus, Angeli responded by sending him the entire Greek manuscript.[28] It was presumably from this manuscript that Bruni translated for Salutati that part of the *Heroicus* which deals with Hector.[29] An extant Latin version of the so-called *Letter of Aristeas*, an account of the production of the Septuagint Greek translation of the Pentateuch, has been wrongly attributed to Angeli. The *Letter* will be considered in more detail in the next chapter, but for the moment it is enough to observe that the work can be situated within this Florentine context.[30]

We have already noticed Xenophon; of the other Greek historians, we know that at least some of Diodorus Siculus' work was available in Florence, because Bruni translated a passage from the

---

[22] Xenophon 'qui bellum difficillimum ac periculosissimum ita gessit, ut plurimis ex hoste victoriis summa cum gloria potiretur exercitumque victorem ex intimis Babyloniae finibus per infestissimas atque barbaras gentes ad patrias sedes reportaret incolumem' (Baron (1928) 101).

[23] Luiso (1980) II: 6. This passage is not in Mehus (1741).

[24] Luiso (1980) II: 16, October–November 1407.

[25] Marsh (1992) 109; Baron (1928) 187.

[26] On 17 September 1408 Bruni wrote to Niccoli 'Agesilaum tibi remittam propediem, ut opinor, si tamen per curas et dolorem mihi illum expolire licebit' (Luiso (1980) III: 3). This appears to refer to a translation rather than to an edited Greek text, but no version by Bruni of Xenophon's *Agesilaus* or Plutarch's biography of Agesilaus has come to light.

[27] Now Vatican Library Urb.gr.105. See Weiss (1955c) 261–2, described in Stornaiolo (1895) 161–2. This manuscript was later owned by Palla Strozzi (Diller (1961) 316).

[28] Weiss (1955c) 264–5. See Novati (1891–1911) III: 522–3, III: 547 and note.

[29] Novati (1891–1911) 547.

[30] Laur. 25. Sin.9, fols 3^r–27^r, dated 26 May 1403 and dedicated to 'Frater Thedaldus'. See chapter 2, 105–6. For the suggestion that this translation is Bruni's, see Weiss (1977b) 244–5.

first book for Salutati.[31] Another ambitious project first floated in the early Florentine Renaissance has received very little attention. About 1406, in the preface to his version of the *Posterior Analytics*, Rossi talked in vague terms of translating Plato and Thucydides at some time in the future.[32] It seems that neither of these versions was ever made, but he did have a copy of Plato, and this comment suggests that he had, or had access to, a manuscript of Thucydides.[33] In the autumn of 1407 Pietro Miani sent Bruni a manuscript of Thucydides.[34] Niccolò Niccoli presumably had this manuscript in mind when, in December 1407, he asked Bruni to make a translation of the history.[35] Bruni was unwilling to undertake such a large and difficult text: 'Non tibi venit in mentem quam multis vigiliis opus sit ad tantum opus conficiendum?' [Do you not realise how many sleepless nights would be needed to produce such a work?] Lorenzo Valla, who later translated Thucydides, would no doubt have sympathised with Bruni.[36]

As will be seen below, Bruni's latest estimate of Plato's work emerged from a comparison with Aristotle. Bruni's first version of a Platonic dialogue, *Phaedo*, was the most ambitious project of his apprenticeship, and once again it seems that Salutati provided the inspiration.[37] Salutati had been interested in Greek texts of Plato since at least 1396 when he wrote to Angeli in Constantinople asking him to look out for manuscripts.[38] We may also suppose that Bruni was introduced to the Greek text of Plato by Chrysoloras:

---

[31] For this passage in Salutati's *De laboribus Herculis*, see Ullman (1963) 227.

[32] Edited in Manetti (1951) 54.

[33] For Rossi's manuscript of Plato, see Sabbadini (1905–14) 50–1 and n. 55.

[34] Luiso (1980) II: 16, October–November 1407. Not in Mehus (1741).

[35] Luiso identifies this Greek manuscript with one sent by Pietro Miani from Venice (Luiso (1980) 42 n. 77). Vergerio owned a manuscript of Thucydides about 1400 which he obtained at Padua from Miani (Smith (1934) 240–2, letter to Demetrius [Chrysoloras]). Vergerio left Florence soon after Manuel Chrysoloras: he was in Padua by 30 April 1400 (McManamon (1996) 87).

[36] See Luiso (1980) II: 18, not in Mehus (1741). Bruni's letter to Niccoli is also edited in Sabbadini (1891) 223–6. For Valla's version of the historian, completed in 1452, see chapter 2, 89.

[37] Bruni was translating it in a letter of 5 September 1400 (Mehus (1741) I: 8; Luiso (1980) I: 1). The finished work was dedicated between October 1404 and March 1405 (Baron (1928) 161).

[38] 'Platonica velim cuncta tecum portes et vocabulorum auctores quot haberi possunt, ex quibus pendet omnis huius perceptionis difficultas' (Novati (1891–1911) III: 131; Oliver (1940) 318 n. 17).

the translation of Plato's *Republic* which was finally published in 1440 had originated with that Greek scholar.[39] Salutati seems to have had some access to a translation of the *Republic*, and when he quotes from Plato's *Cratylus* we may guess that it was Bruni who supplied him with the text.[40] Salutati had also read the medieval Latin translation of the *Phaedo* made by Henricus Aristippus and he sent it on to Bruni, encouraging him to make a new translation of the work.[41] Most of Bruni's translations would make his chosen Greek authors available in Latin for the first time, but here he could take advantage of the efforts of an earlier scholar. Near the beginning of his career as a translator, he probably appreciated his predecessor's help. Perhaps he was mindful of this debt when he came to dedicate the translation several years later: he was much less critical of its Latinity than he would be of the medieval translation of the *Ethics*, which shared its faults.[42]

The timing of the publication of this version of the *Phaedo* was intended to help Bruni secure the next stage of his career: it was dedicated to Pope Innocent VII at a time when he was hoping for a position in the papal court. The careful piety with which he prefaces the translation is particularly noticeable: he describes the book as 'valde utilis cum ad doctrinam et intelligentiam tum ad rectae fidei confirmationem'[43] [very useful for doctrine and understanding, and also for the strengthening of proper faith]. Bruni attached another pious preface to his version of another Platonic dialogue dedicated

---

[39] The translation begun by Chrysoloras was completed by his pupil Uberto Decembrio and by Uberto's son, Pier Candido. See Garin (1955) 341–57.

[40] For the *Republic*, see Ullman (1963) 245–6 and Novati (1891–1911) IV: 84. For *Cratylus*, see Ullman (1963) 245. Bruni had a Greek manuscript of this work with him in Viterbo in August 1405 (Mehus (1741) I: 6; Luiso (1980) I: 8).

[41] Neither man seems to have known the name of the earlier translator, 'qui bene et graviter nomen suum suppressit' (Bruni to Niccoli, 5 September 1400). Mehus' text of the letter ((1741) I: 8; Luiso (1980) I: 1) is revised by Garin (1955) 361–3. Bruni probably wrote 'gnaviter': see Cicero, *Ad fam.* V: xii, 3. 'Maximas igitur Colucio patri ac preceptori meo gratias ago, qui iniungendo hoc munere tantum mihi beneficium attulit' (Garin (1955)). Salutati's manuscript of Aristippus survives: Vatican Library Vat.lat.2063. A translation of the seventh chapter of Plutarch's *De profectibus in virtute* was written by Salutati in the margin of this manuscript (fol. 68ᵛ). Bruni may have made this version for him. See Weiss (1977b) 254 and Ullman (1963) 186–7. Aristippus' version is in Minio-Paluello (1950).

[42] A description of Aristippus' methods of translation is in Minio-Paluello and Klos (1972) 95.

[43] Baron (1928) 4.

to another Pope. The translation of the *Gorgias* belongs among his early works because it was begun in 1405, although it was completed in 1409, and dedicated to the antipope John XXIII some time after his election in May 1410.[44] Bruni probably met this dialogue too while Chrysoloras was in Florence. Two of Chrysoloras' students knew it in Greek: Jacopo Angeli had acquired a copy of the text before 1400, and Vergerio borrowed it from him.[45] Bruni may have been inspired by the knowledge that Cicero had translated a brief passage from the *Gorgias*.[46] He probably also knew that Aulus Gellius quoted a long passage from the dialogue, which he declined to translate. Gellius said of Plato's words 'ad proprietates eorum nequaquam possit Latina oratio adspirare'[47] [Latin cannot possibly hope to represent them accurately]. Bruni, now confident of his command of the Greek language, was eager to take up this sort of challenge.

Greek biography

In October 1405, in a letter to Niccoli from the papal court at Viterbo, Bruni recorded his intention to prepare a version of

---

[44] For the beginning of the translation, see Hankins (1990) I: 53. For its completion, see Baron (1928) 163. The dedicatory letter to this translation is printed in Bertalot (1975b) 268–9. Bruni had a Greek manuscript of the *Gorgias* with him at Viterbo in 1405. See Mehus (1741) I: 6; Luiso (1980) I: 8.

[45] Weiss (1955c) 261. Sabbadini (1905–14) 44 n. 5. Angeli lent Vergerio a manuscript of the *Gorgias* which Vergerio had in the winter of 1400–1. Vergerio says that he read the *Gorgias* in Greek twice at Padua after he left Florence: 'Gorgiam bis ex integro evolvi' (McManamon (1996) 87; Smith (1934) 240–2). He quoted *Gorgias* 526a in Latin in his *De ingenuis moribus* of c.1402–3 (ed. Kallendorf (2002) 26). Kallendorf says that Vergerio translated *Gorgias* ((2002) 323 n. 55). I have not come across this translation.

[46] *Gorg.* 470d is at *Tusc.* V: 34–5. See Jones (1959) 24.

[47] *Gorg.* 485a ff. is at *Noctes atticae* X: 22. Gellius also translated a passage from *Symposium* (*Noctes atticae* XVII: 20). Bruni translated *Symposium* 215a–222a in a letter to Cosimo de' Medici, perhaps in 1435 (Mehus (1741) VII: 1; Luiso (1980) VII: 1). The surviving portions of the Latin text of the *Attic Nights* were first reunited in a Florentine manuscript produced in 1418. Niccoli and Traversari subsequently worked together to reconstruct the Greek elements of the text. The result of their labours survives in a manuscript of 1431. See Baron (1968) 204–5 and n. 15. On 15 September 1428 Poggio wrote to Niccoli asking to borrow Bruni's manuscript of Gellius (Harth (1984–7) I: 182; Gordan (1991) 130). Sabbadini suggests that Bruni drew his meaning of the word *traducere* from *Noctes atticae* I: 18 (Sabbadini (1916a) 222). Bruni also seems to have borrowed *discerniculum* from Gellius in a letter of 1438 (*Noctes atticae* XVII: 15; Mehus (1741) X: 24; Luiso (1980) VIII: 2).

Ptolemy's *Geographia*.[48] He asked Niccoli to send him the Greek text and that part – *eam particulam* – which Chrysoloras had already translated.[49] In fact Jacopo Angeli, who had had a Greek manuscript of the work since 1400, eventually completed the translation.[50] Exactly why Bruni abandoned the project is unclear, although Angeli's presence at Viterbo at the time of the letter to Niccoli must have had something to do with it. The letter does show that shortly after taking up his new position in the papal court, and with his command of Greek now assured, Bruni was looking for a substantial text to Latinise. However, Bruni's interest in Plutarch did not emerge from the frustration of his designs on Ptolemy. In the same letter to Niccoli he mentions that his version of the life of the younger Cato is already complete, although it was not yet ready for publication.[51] He dedicated his first published translation of Plutarch, the *Life of Antony*, to Salutati, probably before he left Florence for Rome in March 1405.[52] In the preface to this version, Bruni announced an ambitious new project: the translation of all the surviving biographies of Plutarch.[53] Although Bruni did not complete this task, his *Antonius* was to be the first of nine Plutarchan biographies which he translated over the next six years.[54]

It is possible to identify a number of influences which guided his choice of Plutarch. Of primary importance was the availability of the Greek text. In March 1396 Salutati wrote to Angeli in

---

[48] Luiso (1980) I: 10; not in Mehus (1741). The letter is also in Baron (1928) 104–5. See Weiss (1955c) 262 n. 50.

[49] Chrysoloras brought the famous Urb.gr.82 of the *Geographia* to Florence in 1397, and seems to have bequeathed it to his former pupil Palla Strozzi on his death in 1415. See Diller (1961) 315–16 and Fiocco (1964) 301.

[50] No later than 1409. See M. D. Reeve (1991) 137; Novati (1891–1911) Ep. IX: 16 and Ep. XII: 14; Weiss (1955c) 262.

[51] '*Catonis Vitam* propter has turbationes expolire nondum potui; cito tamen, ut spero, absolvam et ad te mittam' (Baron (1928) 105). In a letter of August 1406 Bruni explains that it still needs polishing (Mehus (1741) X: 19; Luiso (1980) I: 20).

[52] For the date of Bruni's *Antonius*, see Baron (1928) 161; Gualdo Rosa (1994) 122; Hankins (1990) II: 374, 377. Salutati died on 4 May 1406.

[53] 'habemus quidem in animo hos omnes Plutarchi viros, si per occupationes nostras licebit, in Latinum convertere' (Baron (1928) 102). See also Fryde (1983a) 37 and Bertalot (1975c) 287.

[54] They are: *Antonius* (perhaps 1405, before May 1406), *Cato minor* (late 1407–8), *Sertorius* (1408–9), *The Gracchi* (1410), *Aemilius Paulus* (before December 1410), *Demosthenes*, *Cicero*, *Pyrrhus* (all by 1412). These dates are from Baron (1928) 161–3, but for the dating of the lives of Sertorius and Pyrrhus, see Bertalot (1975d) 383.

Constantinople asking him to get hold of a manuscript of Plutarch.[55] By 1400, both Angeli and Vergerio owned Greek manuscripts of Plutarch's *Lives*.[56] Second, Chrysoloras had recommended the study of Plutarch to his western students because the *Lives* placed the Greek world beside the Latin.[57] Some of the versions of Bruni and Angeli may have originated in studies begun under the Byzantine scholar. It is easy to imagine that some of Plutarch's straightforward narratives found favour with beginners. A fragment survives of a version of the *Life of Antony* made by Bruni's classmate Vergerio;[58] Bruni's dedication of his translation of the *Life* to Salutati may have owed more to its use as a classroom text than to its appropriateness for its recipient. Third, despite Bruni's growing confidence with the Greek language, he probably benefited from a handy prop. Bruni owned an anonymous Italian version of the *Lives*, made about 1396–7.[59] This version would certainly have allowed him to make rapid progress. By 1408 the long-meditated *Life of Cato* was published, and four more Roman lives were published during the next two years: *Aemilius Paulus*, *Sertorius*, and *Tiberius and Caius Gracchus*. The last of these was finished before the end of 1410.[60] There followed a busy eighteen months in Bruni's life: in November 1410 he assumed the Florentine Chancellorship for the first time; only six months later, in April 1411, he resigned this post to take up a position in the papal court again; and early in 1412, at the age of forty-two, he married.[61] The decisions as to which of Plutarch's *Lives* to translate were informed by the preoccupations of Italian students of Greek in the early fifteenth century. There were certainly good Roman reasons for making many of the Greek *Lives* Latin. Here I want

---

55 Weiss (1953c) 223; Novati (1891–1911) III: 131–2.
56 Weiss (1955c) 262; Smith (1934) 241; Sabbadini (1905–14) 62.
57 See Chrysoloras' Greek letter to Salutati: 'παρ' ἐκείνου [Πλουτάρχου] ἐστὶ δήπου καλῶς ἰδεῖν, ὁπόση κοινωνία πρὶν ἐν ἅπασιν ἦν τῷ τε τῶν Ἑλλήνων γένει καὶ τῷ τῶν Ἰταλῶν' (Novati (1891–1911) IV: 333–44, 341).
58 For Vergerio's effort, see Smith (1934) 451–2.
59 This anonymous Italian version was in fact made from an Aragonese version of a lost demotic Greek translation. Salutati had hoped to translate the Aragonese version into Latin, or have it translated for him. See Weiss (1953c) 218–22.
60 Baron observes that it was complete before December 1410 (Baron (1928) 163). It is probable that it was completed before he assumed the Chancellorship in November.
61 Bruni's marriage had been planned since at least 1410, when he had secured the permission necessary for one working in the Curia. See Baron (1967) 31.

to concentrate on Bruni's translations of three important works of Plutarch which punctuate Bruni's development as an historian: the lives of Pyrrhus, Demosthenes and Cicero.

One reason for Bruni's interest in Plutarch's *Pyrrhus* will be examined in the next section of this chapter. Here, I want to locate Bruni's version of this biography in the context of a contemporary debate which was increasingly fought out among Greek texts.[62] The title of *maximus imperator* had been contested since antiquity. Livy seems to be the earliest extant author to raise the *topos* for Latin readers: he relates a conversation between Scipio Africanus and Hannibal on the subject.[63] The Renaissance debate begins with Petrarch's *Collatio* of the generals, and in his *Africa* Scipio is awarded first place amongst the generals.[64] Angeli contributed to Alexander's reputation with his translation of Plutarch's orations *De Alexandri fortuna et virtute* some time between June 1405 and June 1409.[65] In the preface to this work, Angeli refers to a contemporary debate at Florence regarding the merits of Caesar and Alexander.[66] In Plutarch's *Life of Sertorius*, translated by Bruni about 1408–9, the Roman general is compared to Hannibal, and Mithridates is compared to Pyrrhus. The companion biography of *Pyrrhus*, the *Life of Marius*, was translated by Angeli in 1409–10, and about 1411 his version of *Pompey* was published.[67] In the *Life of Flamininus*, translated by Guarino in 1411, Plutarch recounted Livy's story that Hannibal placed Alexander first, then Pyrrhus, then himself, an entirely non-Roman cast. With Guarino's translation of the lives of Caesar and Alexander, published together in 1412, all the lives of the important figures of the late Republic had been translated into Latin.[68] The debate was picked up again by

---

[62] Bruni's *Pyrrhus* was produced between autumn 1408 and March 1412 (Baron (1966) Appendices, 614ff.).

[63] The most relevant *loci* are: Livy xxxv: 14; ix: 17ff.

[64] Edited by Martellotti (1964) 145–68; *Africa* viii: 42–232.

[65] Cardinal Peter Philargus, later Alexander V, gave Angeli a Greek manuscript containing this essay and Plutarch's *De fortuna Romanorum* between these dates (Weiss (1955c) 269 and n. 84). This manuscript may have contained more of Plutarch's *Moralia*.

[66] Bevegni (1994) 82–3 n. 38.

[67] Weiss (1955c) 273–4. Bruni cites the *Life of Marius* in a letter to Salutati of November–December 1405 (Mehus (1741) x: 5; Luiso (1980) i: 12).

[68] These versions are both sometimes wrongly assigned to Angeli (Weiss (1955c) 273 n. 121).

Aurispa in 1425, the year of his arrival in Florence, in the translation of another Greek text, Lucian's *Comparatio*. Whilst Lucian's
sketch had placed Alexander first, and Scipio before Hannibal,
Aurispa's version put Scipio before Alexander.[69] Ten years later,
Poggio defended Scipio Africanus for his virtue and the preser-
vation of the Republic, Guarino spoke up for Caesar, and Poggio
responded with his *Defensiuncula*.[70]

Bruni's *Life of Pyrrhus* contributed to this debate. In this biography, Plutarch writes that Hannibal, when asked for his opinion,
had named Pyrrhus the best general, Scipio second, and himself
third; that Appius Claudius recalled to the Senate their boast that
they would have defeated Alexander had he turned his armies west-
wards; and that Cineas reported to Pyrrhus that the Roman Senate
was an assembly of kings.[71] The political allegiances of all the great
generals of antiquity were involved in fifteenth-century assessments of their reputations. More fundamentally, there were two
sets of oppositions at work in all these reworkings of ancient judgements: the Romans versus the Greeks, and the Republicans versus
the Monarchists. Brilliant generals like Alexander or Pyrrhus were
most dangerous when they wielded absolute political control. The
best defences against such enemies lay in a robust and stable constitution. It may have taken a Scipio to defeat Hannibal, but it was –
at least in Livy's opinion – the strength of republican institu-
tions which enabled Rome to survive Trasimene and Cannae. The
story of the defeat of Pyrrhus was important to Bruni because it
demonstrated the military strength of Roman republican institu-
tions when threatened by the genius of a single man, equipped
with all the advantages which Greek military science could
bestow.

Bruni's translation of Plutarch's *Demosthenes* was published late
in 1412. Bruni's interest in Demosthenes' biography focussed on

[69] Aurispa (wrongly) claimed the authority of Libanius for this innovation: see Cast (1974)
159–60. Few people were in a position to check such statements: see chapter 4. The
debate had an echo in England: Dublin, Trinity College D.4.24 has Aurispa's expanded
comparatio further extended to include Henry V's claims to superiority. This work may
have been produced by Frulovisi, no later than 1440 (Weiss (1967) 196–7).

[70] For Poggio's contribution, see Fubini (1964–9) III: 357ff. For Guarino, see Sabbadini
(1915–19) II: 221–54. See also Holmes (1992) 145–6.

[71] The tradition that Alexander was going to turn west is in Livy IX: 17–19, and in Pliny,
Nat. Hist. III: 57.

his roles as a politician and as a rhetorician. Here too the influence of Chrysoloras is discernible: during his stay in Florence he gave Bruni and Roberto Rossi a copy of some speeches of Demosthenes. In 1405 Bruni, convalescing from an illness at Viterbo, wrote to Niccoli to ask whether they were still at Florence.[72] He may well have got hold of this manuscript or manuscripts, because by the end of 1406 he had translated two speeches of Demosthenes: *Pro Diopithe* and *De corona*.[73] In 1406, four years after the death of Giangaleazzo Visconti, the importance of the speech *Pro Diopithe* for Bruni lay in Demosthenes' response to Macedonian expansion. Bruni's *Laudatio* of Florence was based on Aristides' panegyric of Athens, and the parallel between Philip and Giangaleazzo and the identification of Athens with Florence would accompany Bruni throughout his political career. To defend Athens' wayward but effective general, Demosthenes invokes the fundamental difference between Athens and her enemy. Philip, he says, intended to destroy Athenian power:

Ex omnibus tamen nichil est quod ille magis oderit quam reipublicae nomen, nec quicquam magis conatur evertere. Nec inmerito quodammodo id agit. Scit enim certissime nichil in tuto sibi fore, nec si ceterorum omnium fiat dominus, donec vos liberi estis . . . Itaque nequaquam vult, nec est consilii, ut suis temporibus immineat libertas vestra.[74]

[But there is nothing in the world that he hates more than the word *Republic*; nothing does he try harder to destroy. And this policy is in some way proper for him. He knows perfectly well that even if he makes himself master of everything

---

[72] Baron (1928) 104–5; Luiso (1980) I: 10, to Niccoli, 12 October 1405: 'Orationes Demosthenis, quas Manuel mihi et Roberto nostro donavit, certior fieri cupio an Florentiae sint.' This letter is not in Mehus (1741).

[73] *Pro Diopithe* was completed between 6 and 30 November 1406 (Hankins (1990) II: 376–7). See Accame-Lanzillotta (1986) 14. *De corona* was begun in the second half of August 1406 (Mehus (1741) X: 19; Luiso (1980) I: 20). It seems to have been complete but unrevised by 23 December 1406 (Mehus (1741) II: 4; Luiso (1980) II: 3). On 31 December 1406 Bruni sent Niccoli an *argumentum* for the speech (Mehus (1741) II: 5; Luiso (1980) II: 4), but he was still not happy with his version on 15 March 1407 (Luiso (1980) II: 6; not in Mehus). The translation was completed by 25 April 1407, at Rome, as appears from a manuscript colophon (Luiso (1980) 33 n. 38). Bruni then sent it to Niccoli some time before 9 August 1407 (Luiso (1980) 33 n. 36). It was dedicated to Francesco Pizolpasso according to Baron (1928) 108–9, 162; it was dedicated to Bartolomeo Capra according to Accame-Lanzillotta (1986) 15.

[74] *De Chersoneso* 40–2. Bruni's translation has not been printed. This extract is from Cambridge University Library, Ii.I.38, fol. 90ʳ. His Latin is more pointed than the Greek: 'οὐδενὶ μέντοι μᾶλλον ἢ τῇ πολιτείᾳ πολεμεῖ οὐδ' ἐπιβουλεύει . . .'

18

else, he can hold nothing securely while you are free . . . And so he certainly does not want, and he does not intend to permit, your freedom to threaten his every moment.]

Bruni felt that Demosthenes shared his conviction that a tyrant must always fear a free republic. Many years later he introduced a similar idea into his *History of the Florentine People*. In the ninth book of this work, in a set speech assigned to the year 1389, Johannes Riccius talks of the steady advance of Giangaleazzo:

Illud praeterea considerandum est: non eadem mente contra vos illum venire qua contra civitates alias. Cogitat enim servitutem vos pati non posse, qui, libera in civitate nati, non modo non servire, sed dominari aliis consuestis. Itaque nec vos sub iugo tenere, nec caeteras vicinas urbes firmiter possidere posse existimat, nisi Florentiam magna plaga prosternat.[75]

[Moreover you must consider this: he does not come against you with the same intention as he does against other cities. This is because he thinks that you cannot bear slavery, for you are natives of a free city, and accustomed not only not to serve, but to rule over others. And so he does not think that he can keep you under his power, or securely hold other neighbouring cities, unless he lays Florence low with a great blow.]

Giangaleazzo's enmity is assured because Florence poses a unique threat to his ambitions. Bruni's interest in Demosthenes was due in part to the parallels he cultivated between the Athenian and Florentine republics.

Bruni's interest in Demosthenes was also inspired by the fact that both Cicero and Livy had thought highly of his oratory.[76] Bruni must have begun his translation of Demosthenes' defence of Ctesiphon, *De corona*, not long after finishing his version of *Pro Diopithe*; by the summer of 1412 he had also translated Aeschines' speech for the prosecution.[77] Bruni would no doubt have known St Jerome's claim in the preface to the Pentateuch that Cicero had made versions of both these speeches. He seems

[75] Santini (1914–26) 242.
[76] In a lost letter to his son, Livy recommended the study of Demosthenes and Cicero. See Quintilian, *Inst. orat.* x: i,39.
[77] For *De corona*, see above, n. 73. For other Latin versions of this speech in the fifteenth century, see chapter 4, 170–1. Bruni's version of Aeschines' speech was made at Arezzo in 1412, certainly before 1 September (Mehus (1741) III: 20; Luiso (1980) III: 29).

also to have known the pseudo-Ciceronian *De optimo genere oratorum*. This short essay claims to be Cicero's preface to his Latin translations of these famous examples of Greek forensic oratory.[78] Although *De optimo genere oratorum* is not listed among Cicero's works in the *Cicero novus*, Bruni knew the preface – or at least knew of it – before the dedication of his biography to Niccolò Niccoli in 1415.[79] In a letter addressed to Niccoli in 1412 he writes:

Cicero cum has orationes quas ego latinas feci convertisset, addidit proemium, quod perditis orationibus extare nunc etiam credo, et si non erro videor me meminisse. Hoc ego velim diligenter quaesitum ad me mittas, ut quantum valeam me summo viro propinquum afferam.[80]

[When Cicero had translated these speeches which I have put into Latin, he added a preface which is, I believe, still extant, although the speeches themselves have been lost; and if I am right, I seem to remember seeing it. Please look carefully for this preface and send it to me, so that, as far as I can, I may measure myself against the great man.]

Niccoli, of course, had a remarkable library and, as Vespasiano da Bisticci says, 'era Nicolaio liberalissimo et prestava libri a chi gliene domandava'[81] [Niccolò was very generous and lent books to whoever asked]. Bruni certainly got hold of a copy somehow. Writing to Pizolpasso in 1435 he describes it as 'praefatiuncula . . . quae est in manibus omnium'[82] [the brief preface which everyone is reading]. Some manuscripts put the two modern translations together with the ancient preface. Bruni's critic, Alfonso,

---

[78] It is now thought to be spurious. See Dihle (1955).

[79] For Cicero's works listed in the *Cicero novus*, see Baron (1928) 115–17.

[80] To Niccoli. Mehus (1741) III: 20; Luiso (1980) III: 29, from Arezzo, 1 September 1412. For the *fortuna* of this *proemium*, see Reeve in L. D. Reynolds (1983) 100–1. Reeve is mistaken when he says that Bruni did not know the work before the publication of his *Cicero novus* in 1415. Reeve notices a copy of the preface added to a text dated at Florence, 13 January 1412, *stylo florentino* (Bodl.Lat.class.d.37). See Watson (1984) I: 88. This date is four months after Bruni made this request to Niccoli. A photograph of the first page of *De opt. gen. orat.* (fol. 34ᵛ) from this manuscript is in Alexander (1977) 13.

[81] Greco (1970–6) II: 231.

[82] Mehus (1741) VII: 4; Luiso (1980) VII: 4; Birkenmajer (1922) 187. Ambrogio Traversari wrote to Niccoli on 8 July 1431 mentioning an inventory of lost classical works which Niccoli had given to the Cardinals Cesarini and Albergati in the hope that they might come across them on their travels. All of Cicero's translations are listed as *desiderata*. Alongside the translations of Aeschines and Demosthenes the words 'prologus invenitur' have been written (Robinson (1921) 255).

LEONARDO BRUNI

seems to have known one such confection in the 1430s.[83] Bruni's
words to Niccoli, quoted above, probably mean simply that he
wanted to compare his efforts with the declarations of the preface, but it is possible that the manuscript tradition that joined
his translations and this preface originated with Bruni himself.
In support of this suggestion, we may note that, although the
translation of *De corona* was published separately with a preface, Bruni never provided his version of Aeschines' speech with
its own preface. We may infer that he published it alongside some
other work or works. In the *Cicero novus* Bruni makes it clear that
he made these two versions in imitation of the lost translations of
Cicero.[84]

Bruni says that he began a new translation of Plutarch's *Life
of Cicero* because he felt that the earlier Latin version was inadequate. That version was made, he says, by a good but not a learned
man.[85] This man was Jacopo Angeli, who was responsible for the
first ever Latin versions of Plutarch's *Lives*: the *Life of Brutus* had
been published in 1400, the same year in which Chrysoloras left
Florence; Angeli's Latin *Life of Cicero* emerged a year later.[86] We
have already seen Bruni's intention to translate the *Geographia*, a
translation which Angeli later made, and the relationship between
their versions of other Roman *Lives*. His older rival did not live
to see Bruni attempt to retranslate Plutarch's treatise, and perhaps
Bruni would not have done so had he still been alive. Despite professional rivalry, their personal relations seem to have been cordial.
Bruni's version was probably not completed: his reaction against
the work of his predecessor led directly to his extension and redi-
rection of Plutarch's biography. If Bruni's version of the *Life of*

[83] Birkenmajer (1922) 163. *Repertorium Brunianum* lists forty-four manuscripts containing both translations. The earliest dated manuscript among these, now at Florence
(Naz.II.II.65), was made at Milan in 1417 (Hankins (1997) no. 823).
[84] 'Demosthenis et Aeschinis orationes ... cum apud nostros negligenter custoditae iampridem ex Italia tamquam peregrinae alienaeque aufugissent, nos Ciceronem imitati eas ex
Graecia in Latinum nostra manu reduximus' (Baron (1928) 116).
[85] 'bonum quidem virum, sed non satis eruditum' (Baron (1928) 113).
[86] Between late 1400 and June 1401 (Weiss (1955c) 273). Weiss records a claim that
Angeli's *Brutus* was later revised by Guarino Veronese (Weiss (1955c) 272 and n. 110).
In a letter of 1414 Guarino noted that he was about to translate the life of Brutus when
he realised that there was an earlier version extant (Sabbadini (1916a) 222; Giustiniani
(1961) 37 n. 3).

21

Cicero had been intended to remedy the inaccuracies and inelegancies of Angeli's translation, his *Cicero novus* was produced to supplement the deficiencies of Plutarch himself. Bruni had, in fact, already felt the tension between his own views and those of his Greek sources. His confidence in his ability as a translator was also growing. In a letter to Niccoli about his translation of the *Phaedo* he had warned that his readers were not reading Plato but 'meas ineptias'.[87] In contrast, a few years later, in the preface to the *Life of Antony*, he complained that translating is a thankless task: readers are so willing to think well of an ancient author that they will attribute all the virtues of his version to his Greek source, and all its vices to the Latin translator.[88]

Bruni's response to Plutarch's *Cicero* must be gathered from the preface to his *Cicero novus*, produced some years later.[89] Here, he talks with some reserve of Plutarch's *Life* as one 'in quo Ciceronis vita contineri dicebatur' [which was said to contain Cicero's biography]. He describes his growing dissatisfaction as his translation proceeded:

Mox vero ut progredior, et ad convertendi diligentiam singula quaeque magis considero, ne ipse quidem Plutarchus desiderium mei animi penitus adimplevit; quippe multis praetermissis quae ad illustrationem summi viri vel maxime pertinebant, cetera sic narrat ut magis ad comparationem suam, in qua Demosthenem praeferre nititur, quam ad sincerum narrandi iudicium accommodari videantur.[90]

[And now as I go on, and the more carefully I consider every word so that I can make a good translation, I see that even Plutarch has not entirely satisfied me. He has omitted many things very proper to the depiction of a great man, and he recounts the other matters in such a way that they seem to be more adapted to his comparison (in which he tries to favour Demosthenes) than to an honest and judicious narrative.]

These words suggest a fairly acute criticism of Plutarch and of previous historiography. That Plutarch omitted many things which would have told in Cicero's favour is a judgement that

---

[87] Mehus (1741) I: 8; Luiso (1980) I: 1, 5 September 1400. Quoted at length in Garin (1955) 361–3.
[88] Baron (1928) 102–3. Dated 1404/5 in Baron (1966) 568.
[89] Addressed to Niccoli, edited in Baron (1928) 113–14, and dated no later than October 1415 (ibid. 163).
[90] Baron (1928) 113.

many might have made. More subtle is Bruni's suggestion that the need to put both lives into comparable forms has distorted Plutarch's judgement. The structure of the *comparatio* dictates the historian's selection and disposition of his material. As indicated above, earlier translations of Plutarch had often contributed to a broader *comparatio* between the generals of antiquity. It must have occurred to many, and it certainly occurred to Bruni, that in many ways Caesar and Alexander were too different to be profitably compared. Like must be compared with like. Instead, Bruni proposes another sort of *comparatio*. At the end of the preface he invites others to write upon Cicero:

mihi tanti est Ciceronis honor, ut vehementer exoptem a multis de hoc ipso scribentibus superari.

[Cicero's honour is so important to me that I fervently hope to be surpassed by others who write on this subject.]

Instead of comparing Caesar with Alexander, why not compare Bruni's Cicero with Plutarch's, and his successors' with them both? Bruni seems to have found the element of emulation implicit in Plutarch's comparisons very provoking.

Greek history

In 1400, Bruni's fellow student, Jacopo Angeli, completed his Latin translation of Plutarch's life of Marcus Brutus.[91] According to Plutarch, Brutus was making an epitome of Polybius' histories on the eve of the battle of Pharsalus.[92] In 1419, Bruni published his *Commentaria primi belli punici*, an abbreviation of Polybius' early books.[93] As noticed above, Bruni translated the speeches of Demosthenes and Aeschines for and against Ctesiphon in emulation of Cicero, and it is tempting to speculate that Bruni took some satisfaction from the knowledge that he was following in the footsteps of another great Roman republican hero. It is more likely, however, that Bruni was more interested in using the newly

[91] For Jacopo's version, see chapter 1, 21 and n. 86. [92] *Brutus* 4.
[93] Baron revised the date of December 1421 which he gave in Baron (1928) 167, in Baron (1966) Appendices, 611 n. 16, and in Baron (1981) 835–6.

available Greek histories to fill some of the gaps in Latin historiography. Thus, in 1439, towards the end of his life, he produced
the *Commentarium rerum graecarum*, drawn from Xenophon's
Hellenica and dedicated to Angelo Acciaiuoli; and in 1441 he
dedicated *De bello italico adversus Gothos gesto libri IV*, based
on Procopius' books on the Gothic Wars, to Cardinal Giuliano
Cesarini.[94]

Bruni's treatment of these Greek historians requires some explanation. In the prefaces to these works Bruni presents them as com-
pilations of historical material from a variety of sources, but each
is in fact heavily dependent on a single Greek source. They are
sometimes translations, and often paraphrases, of these sources.
Bruni's integrity as a scholar has often been questioned in connection with his translations. In 1435 Bruni had to defend himself against the insinuation that he has stolen his translations of
Aeschines and Demosthenes from Cicero.[95] Bruni's dedication of
his *Politics* translation to Eugenius IV caused controversy because
some believed it had been promised to and commissioned by the
duke of Gloucester.[96] It has often been maintained that Bruni fraud-
ulently claimed to have translated the third book of Aristotle's
Economics from the Greek, when in fact he only rewrote the extant
medieval version of the lost Greek original.[97] For three hundred
years after his death, it was a common judgement that Bruni took
advantage of his audience's ignorance of Greek to publish the
works of Greek authors as if they were his own. Many of these
attacks focussed on Bruni's treatment of the Greek historians. In
the final chapter of this book I shall look at some of the factors
which informed this hostile critical tradition. Here, I shall examine Bruni's treatment of these three Greek authors and the role he
intended for his Latin historical works.

First, it is as well to deal with a more general criticism of the
way Bruni acknowledged his debts. I believe that he thought that
his relationship with his Greek sources was as clearly indicated as

---

[94] The prefaces to these works are in Baron (1928) 146–9. For the dates, see Luiso (1980)
144 n. 25 and 151 n. 11.
[95] Mehus (1741) VII: 4; Luiso (1980) VII: 4, 15 October.
[96] For an account of the misunderstanding, see Weiss (1967) 46–9.
[97] Baron has demonstrated that Bruni made no such claim (Baron (1955b) 166–72).

it needed to be in the prefaces to his historical works. For Bruni, the primary purpose of the preface was to establish a relationship between the writer and the recipient of the work, not to map out the relationship between the writer and his material. The information about sources which later critics wanted to see would have seemed outlandish and irrelevant to most contemporaries. For a rhetorician, the audience's ignorance of Greek is itself sufficient reason not to expand upon the treatment of texts found only in the rarest manuscripts and in an unknown language. In the preface to the work from the *Hellenica*, Bruni briefly summarises the position of Athens towards the end of the Peloponnesian War, but does not refer his reader to Thucydides: those who could read that historian would not have needed the notice and those who could not did not yet have a Latin version to turn to. Some of the criticism subsequently directed at Bruni's work with Greek writers has been founded upon his failure to observe a scholarly etiquette which had not yet evolved.

This examination of Bruni's use of his Greek sources begins with his account of the First Punic War. In the preface to his commentaries on the First Punic War he does mention his principal authority, Polybius, but this is a name he could have expected his audience to know from Livy and Cicero. In this preface he stresses his role as a compiler who has taken his material 'non ab uno . . . ut interpres, sed a multis' [not from a single source, like a translator, but from many]. The rediscovery of Greek historical works raised the possibility that some of the holes in western historiography might be repaired. As early as 1405, Bruni had seen that the Greek biographies of Plutarch could be used to supplement the defective Latin tradition. In the dedicatory letter to the *Life of Antony* he wrote

doluimus profecto, animadvertentes tantam apud nos scriptorum factam esse iacturam ut nec facta maiorum nostrorum, nec nomina iam eorum teneremus, per quos Italia in universo orbe gloriosissime nominata esset.[98]

[We were certainly sad when we saw that there had been such great loss of our own Latin writers that now we know neither the deeds nor the names of our ancestors, who made Italy so renowned throughout the whole world.]

[98] Baron (1928) 102.

Bruni's version of Plutarch's *Life of Pyrrhus* has already been located in the context of the fifteenth-century debate on the best general of antiquity. No doubt he was aware that Livy's lost second decade had covered some of the same ground as Plutarch in this biography.[99] He can hardly have failed to notice that Polybius' history conveniently picks up where Plutarch's biography leaves off. Moreover, Bruni was translating this portion of Polybius at a time when searches for the lost books of Livy were intensifying. Interest in Livy had been heightened in 1413 when a body thought to be that of the historian was unearthed at Padua. Bruni was present when Sicco Polenton's account of the discovery was read to Pope Martin.[100] His response to this pagan relic was cautious. In March 1419 he wrote to Polenton to ask him for the length of the skeleton's tibia: the height of the man could be estimated from this measurement, and it was known that Livy had been very short.[101]

In such circumstances, Bruni's treatment of Polybius was inevitably defined by its relationship with Livy's books. The possibility that Bruni's translation of Polybius was an attempt to reconstruct Livy's lost second decade has been voiced before.[102] Vespasiano da Bisticci clearly saw it as a supplement to Livy. In the list of Bruni's works which the bookseller appends to his life of Bruni, this work is described as 'De primo bello punicho, che è in luogo della seconda decha de Tito Livio, libri tre.'[103] In fact, Bruni suggested this interpretation of his project himself. In the preface, he wrote that the work is justified by the loss of the second decade:

Cuius libri si extarent nihil opus erat novo labore. Cum vero haec pars operis eius interierit nullaque fere huius belli notitia nostros apud homines haberetur . . . quantum solerti lectione Polybii ceterorumque Graecorum consequi potui, commentaria huius belli pro communi utilitate suffeci.[104]

---

99 The second half of book 12, and books 13–14 dealt with Pyrrhus, as is clear from the extant epitomes of these books.
100 Apparently after Martin's arrival in Florence in February 1419. The letter read to Martin, addressed to Niccoli, is in Segarizzi (1899) 77–84. For another account of the discovery, see Ullman (1928) 183. See also Ullman (1973) 53–77.
101 Bruni's letter is in Bertalot (1975d) 419–20; Polenton's reply is in Segarizzi (1899) 92–7; neither is in Mehus (1741) or Luiso (1980).
102 See Momigliano (1977) 84.   103 Greco (1970–6) I: 481.   104 Baron (1928) 123.

[If his books were extant there would have been no need for a new work. But since this part of his work has perished and very little information about this war is available to us Latins . . . I have supplied commentaries on this war for the use of all, as far as I could from a careful reading of Polybius and other Greeks.]

In this connection, it is worth noting the terms in which Giovanni Aurispa advertised his manuscript of another Greek historian, Dio Cassius, to a Latin readership in 1421: 'Dio Nicensis omnes res Romanas centum libris descripsit, in quo sunt plurime orationes; quem qui habet Livium non desideret.'[105] [Dio of Nicaea wrote all about Roman affairs in one hundred books, in which work there are very many speeches; he who has Dio would not miss Livy.] Dio can be quarried for examples of ancient rhetoric, and used as an alternative to Livy's lost narrative. Similarly, Bruni seems to have felt that because the third decade of Livy had survived there was no need to take his treatment of Polybius beyond the end of the First Punic War.

Bruni's *Historiae florentini populi* was well under way during the production of his work with Polybius.[106] His own attempts to produce Latin history benefited from a new understanding of the way that Livy had used his sources. Bruni knew that Livy had followed Polybius in the surviving third and fourth decades of his history. No doubt he read the first five books of Polybius – all that were then known – with a keen eye to the ways in which Livy had handled this source.[107] Bruni's new understanding of Livy's use of source material would have allowed him to guess what Livy might have done with it in the lost second decade. The mention of other Greek authors besides Polybius in the preface does suggest that some sort of reconstruction is being attempted. Moreover, it is worth remembering that the results of Bruni's efforts with Polybius have been mistaken for Livy's work in the past. In 1783 a reader

---

[105] Omont (1887) 186–7. Aurispa translated one such speech from Dio (XXXVIII: 18–29) and dedicated it in 1425 to Battista Capodiferro (Sabbadini (1931) 174; Sabbadini (1898) 400, 404–6).

[106] Bruni had completed book 1 by January 1416 (Fryde (1983a) 34); book 2 by 1419 (Griffiths, Hankins and Thompson (1987) 36); book 3 by 1420 (Ullman (1946) 325–6); and book 4 after 1422 (Hankins (2001) xi). The entire work was complete by 1442 (ibid.).

[107] It has not been demonstrated that any other part of Polybius' work was known before the early sixteenth century. See Momigliano (1977) 87.

in Bergamo found a Latin manuscript containing a history of the First Punic War. Thinking that he had stumbled on part of the lost decade, he began to transcribe it. He had gone some way with his copy before a learned friend pointed out that it was Bruni's work.[108] If Bruni had intended to reconstruct some of the lost Livy, he had clearly managed to create something quite plausible.

However, the thesis that Bruni attempted to do to Polybius what Livy would have done to him should be treated with caution. Although Bruni does seem to have regarded his translations as supplements to the defective Latin tradition, this is not to say that he saw himself as reconstructing the lost Livy. At least one contemporary did not think that Bruni's work was sufficiently Livian. In a lost letter, Giovanni Tortelli seems to have suggested to Bruni that he improve *De primo bello punico* by making it more like a Livian history.[109] The key to Bruni's intentions seems to lie in the claim of the title, repeated in the preface, that he is writing *commentaria*. In his long career, Bruni produced three *commentaria*: the works drawn from Polybius and Xenophon, and the *Commentaria rerum suo tempore gestarum* of 1440. It is worth observing here that about a year after the *commentaria* from Polybius, Bruni retranslated and annotated the pseudo-Aristotelian *Economics*. In his preface, he called these annotations an *explanatio* where he might have been expected to call them a *commentarius*.[110] It seems that he deliberately avoided the medieval sense of the word in favour of a more classical usage.

Fortunately, this usage does not need to be inferred from Bruni's works alone, for he is clearly aware of the generic distinction. In his reply to Tortelli's lost letter, Bruni explained his practice and his terminology in *De primo bello punico*:

---

[108] Ullman (1973) 70.

[109] Tortelli's letter is implied by Bruni's reply, Mehus (1741) IV: 20; Luiso (1980) IV: 26. Luiso dates this letter after Bruni's letter of 31 January 1422 (n.s.) with which Bruni sends his *Commentaria* to Tortelli (Mehus (1741) IV: 18; Luiso (1980) IV: 24). Luiso supplies the terminus of 1424 from the letter's position in the manuscripts. Baron disputes this latter terminus (Baron (1971) 69ff.). For Tortelli's later criticism of Bruni's work see Pace (1988) n. 2, n. 35. For Perotti's criticism of Bruni's *De bello italico*, see below.

[110] Griffiths, Hankins and Thompson (1987) 390 n. 8; Baron (1928) 121.

Ego quae scivi, quaeque memoratu digna aestimavi, in eos libros congessi, neque veto quominus, si qui plura teneat, plura conscribat. Commentaria tamen ab historia multum differunt. Illa enim amplior ac diligentior est, haec contractiora et minus explicata.[111]

[I have brought together in those books what I knew and what I thought worth recording, and if anyone knows more, then let him write more. Commentaries, however, are very different from history. The latter is written at greater length and with greater effort; the former are briefer and less elaborate.]

Bruni's sense of the ancient application of the word must have owed a great deal to Caesar's commentaries on the Gallic War. He would have known Aulus Hirtius' remark in the preface to his conclusion of these commentaries. They are written, said Hirtius,

ne scientia tantarum rerum scriptoribus deesset; adeoque probantur omnium iudicio, ut praerepta, non praebita facultas scriptoribus videatur.[112]

[so that writers might have knowledge of these important events. And yet they are so highly regarded by everyone that rather than supplying writers with material, they seem to have deprived them of the ability to write at all.]

Bruni's response to Tortelli has been roughly dated between 1422 and 1424. This uncertainty is frustrating because these are the years during which Cicero's newly recovered *Brutus* found its way to Florence. Bruni's sense of *commentaria* does seem to have been firmly established before the recovery of the treatise. Still, when he finally got his hands on Cicero's work he must have read his description of Caesar's commentaries with some satisfaction:

Atque etiam commentarios quosdam scripsit rerum suarum. Valde quidem, inquam, probandos. Nudi enim sunt, recti et venusti, omni ornatu orationis tamquam veste detracta. Sed dum voluit alios habere parata unde sumerent qui vellent scribere historiam, ineptis gratum fortasse fecit, qui volent illa calamistris inurere: sanos quidem homines a scribendo deterruit.[113]

['And he has also written some commentaries on his own affairs.' 'And they are very good,' I said, 'for they are plain, accurate, elegant, and stripped bare of all

---

[111] Mehus (1741) IV: 20; Luiso (1980) IV: 26, 1422–4. Mehus reads 'neque vero quominus'.
[112] *De bello gallico*, VIII, proem.
[113] *Brutus* 75: 262. Cicero's work was written while Caesar was still alive; Hirtius' preface was written after his assassination. Cicero's words may have inspired Hirtius' preface. Compare Cicero's description of the 'subtilis oratio' in *Orator* 78, also available only after 1421.

the ornaments of language. He wanted to provide material for those inclined to write history proper: instead, although he may possibly have pleased such fools as will want to prettify Lady History, he has certainly discouraged sensible men from writing at all.]

It seems that the highest praise that can be bestowed on a commentary is that it comes close to being a history. Still, although commentaries may have their own excellence, they are intended to provide material for others to make into history. Bruni may have felt that he was producing documents which could form the basis of another scholar's historical writing. This was not a unique procedure. A few years later, another Florentine, Vespasiano da Bisticci, expressed the desire that his plain Italian *Lives* be written up by some elegant Latinist.[114] More certainly, Bruni's awareness of the classical genres had emerged from, and been stimulated by, his development as an historian. Bruni was keenly aware – as some of his predecessors had not been – of the difference between historical analysis and material on which it was exercised; that is, of the distinction between primary and secondary sources.[115] The title of his work on the First Punic War is intended to indicate the extent and nature of Bruni's interest in Polybius in this work.

What, then, did Bruni do to Polybius' histories in order to make them *commentaria*? First of all, he omitted Polybius' preface.[116] This was natural enough: the preface discussed the purpose of history, and Bruni was not writing a history. For obvious reasons, Bruni eliminated Polybius' description of the broader plan of the work, and his summary of earlier events.[117] Bruni also inserted material from other sources. Thus, the description of Sicily in the first book of *De primo bello punico* is compiled, as Beatrice Reynolds points out, from elements of Polybius, Strabo and Thucydides, with a few of Bruni's own clarifications.[118] Bruni included incidents in his work which are not to be found in Polybius. He seems, for example, to have taken from Gellius the story of the great African serpent which was killed by the Romans under

[114] Greco (1970–6) I: 34; George and Waters (1963) 15.
[115] Discussed by Ullman (1946).
[116] Polybius I: 1–4. For Bruni's work, I consulted *Polybius historicus de primo bello punico et Plutarchi paralelia* [sic]. Brixiae: J. Britannicus, 1498.
[117] Polybius I: 5–6, 12.5–13.   [118] B. Reynolds (1954) 112.

Regulus.[119] He includes in his history the story of Regulus' embassy to Rome after his capture, and his voluntary return to execution at the hands of the Carthaginians.[120] Both of these incidents are part of a well-established Latin tradition, and both reflect well on the Romans. Curiously, Bruni does not include one telling Roman anecdote which had certainly appeared in Livy. Gellius recounts an incident from the First Punic War, drawn from Cato's lost *Origines*, about the heroism of a Roman tribune.[121] Cato comments that this tribune has not been made as famous as Leonidas at Thermopylae, although his actions were just as brave, and the outcome more successful. This omission is more puzzling because Cato shared Bruni's view that to write Latin history was an expression of Roman patriotism. Perhaps Bruni did not insert the incident because he found it difficult to know where to place it in his narrative.

Some light is shed on Bruni's practices in *De primo bello punico* by another of his omissions. Bruni excluded Polybius' digression on the value and interpretation of two of his principal sources: the Greek history of Philinus the Carthaginian, and the Latin account of Fabius Pictor.[122] The names of both writers appear in the preface to *De primo bello punico*, where Bruni writes:

uterque patriae affectu suae ac studio partium inductus, etsi non circa rei gestae seriem, circa belli tamen causas iustitiamque excessisse modum putatur.[123]

[each of these men favouring his native country and guided by a partisan spirit, is thought to have distorted, not the order of events, but the causes of the war and its justice.]

---

[119] *De primo bello punico* I (sig. b1ᵛ) corresponds to *Noctes atticae* III: 6. The story is also in Valerius Maximus I: 8,19; it is mentioned briefly in Florus I: 18 and in the epitome of Livy's eighteenth book; it is recounted at length in the sixth book of Silius Italicus' *Punica*. Poggio rediscovered the *Punica* in 1417, and a copy of the poem was soon in Florence. See M. D. Reeve in L. D. Reynolds (1983) 389–91. Bruni, however, does not seem to have made use of the *Punica*.

[120] *De primo bello punico* II (sig. b4ᵛ). Bruni's account is drawn from Gellius, *Noctes atticae* VI: 4, although he doubtless knew Cicero, *De officiis* III: 26–7 and Horace, *Carm.* III: 5. The incident is noticed in the epitome of Livy's eighteenth book, in Florus II: 2, and in Cicero, *Paradox.* II.

[121] *Noctes atticae* III: 7, where Cato's words are quoted. The incident is recounted in Florus II: 2, and noticed in the epitome of Livy's seventeenth book. It is referred to in Frontinus IV: 5, and Seneca, Ep. 82.

[122] Polybius I: 14–15.

[123] Baron (1928) 123. Quintilian says that *historia* is 'gestae rei expositio' (*Inst. orat.* II: iv, 2).

This response to Polybius' reservations marks the beginning of modern criticism of Livy's lost sources, but it must be said that it does Polybius no justice at all. Bruni says in this preface that Polybius, a Greek, followed Philinus and that Livy followed his fellow Latin. Yet, in the passage removed by Bruni, Polybius stresses that the national allegiances of these sources must be weighed when they are interpreted by the historian; he even uses a refutation of one of Philinus' claims to illustrate his point.[124] Still, this perception of partisanship in the sources is the basis of Bruni's treatment of Polybius' history. Only the *rei gestae series* is untainted by this patriotic distortion. The analysis of causes and the determination of justice is the work of the historian. By removing this sort of analysis from Polybius, Bruni hopes to reveal the facts *nudi, recti, venusti*. Perhaps he felt that sorting out the tangle of ancient loyalties was beyond the capacities of the modern historian. In these circumstances, *commentaria* were a way to clarify the sources of Latin history.

Reynolds claims that Bruni did not insert speeches into *De primo bello punico* because 'this technique was beginning to receive unfavourable attention'.[125] This is simply untrue. Bruni's model for *historia*, Livy, included speeches in his history; Bruni included speeches in his *historia* of Florence; if he had regarded his *De primo bello punico* as *historia* it would certainly have contained speeches. Bruni was well aware of what *historia* should look like. Cicero had described it, even if he had not produced any himself. History, wrote Cicero, is a form of speech:

Huic generi [orationis] historia finitima est, in qua et narratur ornate et regio saepe aut pugna describitur; interponuntur etiam conciones et hortationes. Sed in his tracta quaedam et fluens expetitur, non haec contorta et acris oratio.[126]

[History is related to this sort of speech: it is given rhetorical trimmings, and it often describes a location or a battle; it also contains public addresses and exhortations. However, the historian looks for a certain coherence and fluency in these speeches, not the sharp and controversial tone of the forum.]

---

[124] For Bruni's use of an account by Philinus which Polybius criticises, see Pace (1988) 330–1.

[125] B. Reynolds (1954) 114.

[126] *Orator* 20: 66, a passage only available to Bruni after 1421.

Sempronius Asellio, quoted by Gellius, had also written that the writer of *historia* had to do more than simply record events:

Nobis non modo satis esse video quod factum esset id pronunciare, sed etiam quo consilio quaque ratione gesta essent demonstrare.[127]

[I do not think it is enough for us historians to state what happened: we must show the intent and the motivation behind the actions.]

In the preface to his history of Florence, Bruni says that *historia* demands three things: an account of events (*rerum ratio habenda*), an examination of causes (*causae explicandae*), and a pronouncement of judgement (*iudicium proferendum*).[128] It is useful to examine Bruni's other history, of the Gothic Wars, to see whether it conforms to these criteria.

Bruni's treatment of Procopius in his work on the Gothic Wars has been the subject of many attacks.[129] Some of these contemporary attacks obliged Bruni to state his position on the matter. Criticism focussed on the grander claim for this work implied by the fact that he called it *historia*. Bruni insists on this status for the work. In 1441, not long after its publication, Bruni called his work *historia mea* in a letter to Ciriaco of Ancona. He explains:

Est autem haec non translatio sed opus a me compositum, quemadmodum Livius a Valerio Antiate vel a Polybio Megalopolitano sumpsit et arbitratu suo disposuit.[130]

[This work is not a translation, but a work which I myself have compiled, just as Livy drew material from Valerius Antias or Polybius and ordered it according to his own judgement.]

This is Livian history, claims Bruni, a work differently conceived from his reworking of Polybius, and from the account of Procopius. In the preface to this work, Bruni does not name Procopius as his source, but says that he has taken his material 'ex graecorum commentariis' [from the commentaries of the Greeks]. By calling Procopius' work *commentaria* he appears to suggest that the Greek work is not *historia* proper, but the stuff from which *historia* is made. Bruni's low opinion of Procopius' work seems to have been

---

[127] *Noctes atticae* V: 18.   [128] Hankins (2001) I: 4.
[129] For Bruni's work I consulted *Leonardi Aretini de bello italico apud Gothos gesto historia* (Paris, 1534). For Procopius' *Gothic Wars* I used Dewing (1914–40).
[130] Mehus (1741) IX: 5; Luiso (1980) IX: 6, 31 August.

formed on the basis of the Gothic Wars alone: his sole manuscript of Procopius – which called the Greek work ἱστορία – did not contain the first four books of the history, the *De aedificiis*, or the *Historia arcana*.[131] In 1442 he wrote to Giovanni Tortelli about his books on the Gothic Wars:

Scripsi vero illos non ut interpres sed ut genitor et auctor; quemadmodum enim, si de praesenti bello scriberem, noticia quidem rerum gestarum ex auditu foret, ordo vero ac dispositio et verba mea essent, ac meo arbitratu excogitata et posita; eodem item modo ipse, noticiam tantum rerum gestarum de illo sumens, in ceteris omnibus ab eo recessi, utpote qui hoc unum habeat boni, quod bello interfuit. Cetera illius sunt spernenda.[132]

[I have written them not as a translator but as a creator and author. If I were to write on the present war I would hear of events from others, but the plan and arrangement and the words would be my own, and they would be carefully set down according to my own judgement. I have taken only the events from Procopius in just this way and left everything else behind, since his only virtue is that he was present during this war: in every other way he is a contemptible writer.]

In the preface to *De primo bello punico* Bruni talks of the *rei gestae series* as the foundation on which the historian builds. Here, he stresses that what he has taken from Procopius is simply *notitia rerum gestarum*. Bruni never saw Procopius' preface to his history, but the Greek author's presence at many of the events he narrates is easily discerned from the pages of the Gothic Wars.[133] Some months before the dedication of *De bello italico* Bruni had published his own *notitia*, a bald commentary on events during his own lifetime, under the title *Commentaria rerum suo tempore gestarum*.[134] In 1443 Bruni wrote to Francesco Barbaro

[131] Laur.69.8, fol. 1ʳ. This seems to have been the manuscript which Aurispa received from the Greek Emperor at Constantinople c.1420, and which he brought to Italy in 1423 (Sabbadini (1931) ep. 7); it has a distinctive *lacuna* covering the account of Totila's death. For this manuscript, see Comparetti (1895) xxviii and Haury (1962–4) xlv.

[132] Mehus (1741) IX: 9; Luiso (1980) IX: 10. Tortelli's criticism of *De primo bello punico* has been noticed above. After Bruni's death, Tortelli encouraged Lianoro de' Lianori to translate Procopius and sent him a manuscript of the Greek text. Some pages of this version were ready by November 1449, but the project was subsequently abandoned. See Frati (1933) 166–7.

[133] Procopius' name appears in Bruni's work as a participant in events (*De bello italico*, 62).

[134] Dated between mid-1440 and mid-1441 (Baron (1966) 502 n. 10).

with a defence of his use of Procopius which was becoming well practised:

Ab hoc ego scriptore sumpsi non ut interpres, sed ita ut notitiam rerum ab illo susceptam meo arbitratu disponerem meisque verbis non illius referrem.[135]

[I have not taken material from this writer as a translator would do, but in such a way as to set down the information about events which he supplies at my own discretion, and to retell it in my words, not in his.]

Bruni's protests at the end of his life – 'non ut interpres' – echo his description of how he had handled Polybius in his earliest *Commentaria*. It is significant that all these defences were scholarly notes to fellow translators and students of Greek letters; that is, to people who were equipped to assess the relationship between his Latin work and his Greek source. It is also significant that Bruni felt obliged to justify his treatment of Procopius at least three times. These early criticisms or reservations grew to a chorus over the following centuries. Lorenzo Mehus began the long counter-offensive against Bruni's detractors when he gathered together some of the critics of his use of Procopius in *De bello italico*:

Tradit Jovius, Cuspinianus, Freherus, Crescimbenius, Baelius, Placcius, Jacob. Thomasius, Almeloveenius, Menagius, Fabricius, aliique omnes, Leonardum omisso Procopii nomine libros hos pro suis venditasse, nullique ejus aetatis furtum suboluisse, quoad post Arretini mortem plagium detexerit Christophorus Persona.[136]

[Jovius, Cuspinianus, Freherus, Crescimbenius, Baelius, Placcius, Jacobus Thomasius, Almeloveenius, Menagius, Fabricius, and others, all say that Leonardo left out Procopius' name and passed these books off as his own, and that none of his contemporaries suspected the deceit, until Cristoforo Persona uncovered the theft after his death.]

More recently, a modern student of Procopius, Averil Cameron, has repeated the old charge that Bruni passed the Gothic Wars off as his own work.[137] However, in a remark that would appear to mitigate such criticisms of Bruni's work, she observes elsewhere

---

[135] Dated 23 August, and edited in Griggio (1986) 48–50.
[136] Mehus (1741) I: liv. See chapter 4 for another slanderous anecdote.
[137] Cameron (1985) 261 n. 2.

that 'modern histories of the period still tend to paraphrase large sections of the *Wars*'.[138]

What does Bruni do to Procopius' narrative which might justify his claims for his work? He omits a great deal, freely reorders Procopius' narrative, and adds many of his own judgements, the *iudicia* which are his third criterion for *historia*. Bruni's attitude to Procopius' work emerges from what he refused to admit into his own. He omits all of Procopius' digressions on matters of antiquarian interest: on the Via Appia; on the temple of Janus in Rome and the attempt by anonymous pagans to open its doors; on the history of the Eruli; on Scylla and on names.[139] Bruni also eliminates all of Procopius' fantastic anecdotes: the anecdote of the pigs, the prophetic incident of the Samnite boys, the story of the crumbling mosaic at Naples and the Sibylline oracles, the child nourished by a goat, and the story of the cannibal women are all omitted.[140] It is likely that such asides contributed to Bruni's low opinion of Procopius as an historian. As with the work from Polybius, Bruni created a new work by radically narrowing the focus of the original Greek text. This narrower interest appears in his decision, announced in the title, to concentrate exclusively on affairs in Italy. Even the Gothic conquest of Corsica and Sardinia is passed over.[141] Thus he omits all of Procopius' digressions on geography, such as that on the sea at Ravenna, or the account of Vesuvius.[142] Italian geography was well known to his readers and was, besides, best described by Italians. To this end, he sometimes clarifies Procopius' account.[143] Elsewhere, he corrects and expands upon Procopius' geographical notices.[144] One consequence of this decision to deal only with events in Italy is to remove the Gothic Wars from the political context which Procopius attempts to provide.

---

[138] Cameron (1985) 4.

[139] See Procopius V: xiv, xxv; VI: xiv–xv; and VII: xxviii.

[140] Procopius V: ix, 1–7; V: xx, 1–4; V: xxiv, 22–37; VI: xvii, 1–11; VI: xx, 27–33. Bruni also omits most of Procopius VII: xxix, which recounts marvels.

[141] Procopius VII: xxiv.

[142] Procopius V: i, 16–23; VI: iv, 21–30; *De bello italico*, 203.

[143] E.g. 'Petrum, oppidum, quod hodie corrupto in vulgus nomine Brentanorum appellant' (*De bello italico*, 124).

[144] *De bello italico*, 168; Procopius VII: xxiv, 31–3.

He omits all discussion of the wider world;[145] he omits the negotiations between the Franks and the Emperor;[146] he omits Procopius' account of the political situation in Constantinople, and of events in Constantinople and eastern Europe.[147] These omissions diminish Bruni's scope for historical analysis of the Italian wars.

Bruni's additions, though not infrequent, are far less prominent than his omissions. Sometimes he does no more than spell out the implications of Procopius' account. Bruni says, for example, that the intrigues of the Goths caused Belisarius to regard the truce as broken. This is Bruni's inference: it is not in his source.[148] In a similar vein, Bruni offers a concluding judgement on the loss of Verona which is only implied by Procopius.[149] Sometimes his contribution is more definite. Thus, he offers his own assessment of the value of Totila's victory in enhancing his own reputation;[150] he exaggerates the stoicism of the besieged Romans;[151] and he expands upon the desolation of Rome before the arrival of Narses.[152] Some of Bruni's additions are clearly intended to provide the rhetorical finish which *historia* required. Procopius describes how the desperate imperial troops garrisoning Rome repelled a determined Gothic attack on Hadrian's mausoleum by using as missiles the marble statues which adorned the tomb. Bruni records his dismay at the destruction of these statues:

Ita praeclara artificum opera, ac multorum annorum labores, maximaque eius sepulchri ornamenta militum sive rusticitas sive malignitas paucis horis absumsit.[153]

[And so the rusticity or the malice of the soldiers consumed in a few hours the remarkable works of the sculptors, the labours of many years, the great ornaments of that tomb.]

This is another example of the historian's *iudicium*, added in accordance with Bruni's principles as a writer of *historia*. Later, after

---

[145] E.g. of the Sclaveni in Greece (Procopius VII: xl, 30ff.). He omits Procopius VIII: i–xx, which are of events outside Italy.
[146] Procopius VIII: xxiv.
[147] Procopius VI: xxii; VII: xxxi–xxxv.
[148] *De bello italico*, 70.
[149] Ibid. 119.   [150] Ibid. 121.   [151] Ibid. 144–5.
[152] Ibid. 199–200.   [153] Ibid. 47; Procopius V: xxii, 12–25.

Rome falls to Totila, a number of imperial troops are besieged in this same tomb. Bruni dramatises this scene by giving their leader, Paulus, a speech in which he urges his comrades to die gloriously in battle.[154] This speech is Bruni's largest single addition to Procopius, but his usual practice is to abbreviate or omit the speeches which he found in Procopius. This is not surprising, given that in his letter to Barbaro, quoted above, Bruni is particularly critical of the speeches which Procopius inserted into his narrative.[155] Where Bruni adds to his source, his intervention is usually brief. He expands, for example, the taunts of the Goth Vacis to the besieged Romans. This passage contains a traditional insult that Greeks are 'τραγῳδούς τε καὶ μίμους καὶ ναύτας λωποδύτας' [tragic actors and mimes and thieving sailors], an insult which Bruni renders as 'histriones' and good-for-nothings.[156] Bruni's emphasis on this passage is consistent with one of his clear additions. Following Totila's seizure of Rome both historians show the Gothic leader upbraiding the Roman aristocracy. Bruni has him say:

Dicite . . . si quid boni a Graeculis istis accepistis unquam . . . genus vitiosum, ac maleficum, et in nulla re magis quam in mentiendo efficax.[157]

[Tell me if you have ever received anything good from these Greeklings . . . a vicious and wicked race, better at lying than at anything else.]

The ethnic slur is Bruni's own, although it is consistent with the contemptuous tone of Totila's language and his insistence that the imperial troops are foreigners. Procopius always styles these soldiers 'Ρωμαῖοι; Bruni several times calls them *Graeci*.[158] Procopius' sympathy for Totila's doomed resistance seems to have acquired a new patriotic element in Bruni's account. Taken as a proportion of the entire *historia*, these judgements constitute a very small part of Bruni's new work. Moreover, he adds no conclusion to his history: his ending is starker than even Procopius' bald

---

[154] *De bello italico*, 182–3; Procopius VII: xxxvi, 16–28.
[155] 'Scripsit enim hanc historiam . . . Procopius Caesariensis . . . sed admodum ineptus et eloquentie hostis ut apparet maxime in contionibus suis, quamquam Thucydidem imitari vult' (Griggio (1986) 49–50).
[156] *De bello italico*, 39; Procopius V: xviii, 40. *Vacis* is called *Bacchius* by Bruni.
[157] *De bello italico*, 159–60; Procopius VII: xxi; cf. Juvenal III: 78; X: 174–5.
[158] *De bello italico*, 175, 178, 193.

statement, and it is distorted by the fact that Bruni was unable to supply the *lacuna* in his manuscript surrounding Totila's death.[159] To one who had Procopius' account to hand, many of Bruni's additions must have seemed a little perfunctory. His achievement in *De bello italico* lies rather in the clarity which he brings to Procopius' account of affairs in Italy.

I have emphasised Bruni's originality in his treatment of Greek history. This originality has its limitations. In *De bello italico*, when Belisarius exposes himself recklessly to danger in battle Bruni's judgement expands on Procopius' gentle censure. Had Belisarius been killed, he writes,

interitus cuncta simul secum in ruinam traxisset, Gothique eodem die rerum domini efficiebantur. Sed non permisit dei benignitas tanta mala contingere.[160]

[his death would have brought everything to ruin with him, and the Goths would have been made masters that very day. But the favour of God did not allow such terrible things to happen.]

This is a strikingly conventional reflection from the great Florentine historian, and one which brings me finally to the much shorter Latin work which Bruni extracted from Xenophon's *Hellenica*, the *Commentarium rerum graecarum*. Bruni's familiarity with Xenophon's works has already been noticed.[161] Late in 1439 Bruni sent Giacomo Foscari a copy of this new work. In an accompanying letter he explained its purpose:

Scripsi noviter commentarium quoddam rerum Graecarum, ut nobis aliorum pericula forent exemplo, quam sint bellorum contentionumque discrimina formidanda.[162]

[I have recently written a certain *commentarium* on Greek affairs, so that the trials of others might be an example to us of how greatly the divisions of wars and factions are to be feared.]

Bruni used Xenophon's work to illustrate the fall of three powerful states of ancient Greece: Athens, Sparta and Thebes. He does not eliminate the long speeches of his source: the speech at Athens of

---

[159] Bruni left a gap in his Latin history at this point. In his letter to Francesco Barbaro, quoted above, he asks Barbaro to look out for a more complete manuscript of Procopius. See Griggio (1986) 49–50 and n. 2.

[160] *De bello italico*, 69.   [161] See above, 9–10.

[162] Mehus (1741) VIII: 3; Luiso (1980) VIII: 10, 25 December 1439.

Critias and the response of Theramenes are both largely reproduced in the Latin work. In fact their confrontation is retold at length in Bruni, even down to Theramenes' bitter last jokes.[163] Bruni passes over books three and four, which deal with affairs in Asia Minor, and he picks up Xenophon's account with the imminent decline of Sparta in book five, culminating in the expulsion of the Spartan garrison from Thebes. Bruni uses a very traditional image at this point:

Cum igitur florere Lacedaemonii viderentur, et imperii gloriam firmiter obtinere, convertit fortuna orbem suum, mirabilique casu omnem eorum potentiam, autoritatemque prostravit . . .[164]

[So when the Spartans seemed to flourish and to hold firmly the glory of their empire, Fortune turned her wheel and prostrated all their power and authority with a remarkable event . . .]

These words indicate that his interest in this new source was bounded by some very conventional limits. He looked to Xenophon for ancient *exempla* of the dangers of war and civil disunity.

The genre of this late work poses some problems. The pains Bruni takes to insist on the genres of his works show that he felt it was important. In the 1440s he defended the liberties he takes in his *Laudatio* of the city of Florence by claiming that he handled his material in accordance with a classically formulated genre.[165] Bruni insists that his work on the First Punic War is original because he has translated Polybius' history not simply into a different language, but into a different genre. Similarly, Bruni seems genuinely to have believed that Procopius' work hardly merited the name *historia*, and that his own more disciplined approach granted it

---

[163] *Hellenica* II: 3, 24–49; II: 3, 56.

[164] For Bruni's *Commentarium rerum graecarum* I consulted: *Leonardi Aretini Rerum suo tempore in Italia gestarum commentarius. Eiusdem De rebus graecis liber* (Lyons, 1539) 64–123. This passage is at 100–11. For Fortune's wheel, see Boethius, *Cons.* II: i.

[165] 'Aliud enim est historia, aliud laudatio. Historia quidem veritatem sequi debet, laudatio vero multa supra veritatem extollit'. Letter to Pizolpasso. Mehus (1741) VIII: 4; Luiso (1980) VIII: 11, first half of 1440. Baron suggests that Bruni took the distinction between ἐγκώμιον and ἱστορία from Polybius X: 21, 8 where a similar distinction is made (Baron (1966) 508 n. 14). If this were true Bruni would have to have seen portions of Polybius not certainly available until the early sixteenth century. See Momigliano (1977) 87. Bruni knew Aristotle's distinction between ἐγκώμιον and ἔπαινος at *Nic. eth.* I: xii, 6; cf. *Eud. eth.* II: i, 12; *Rhet.* I: ix, 1367b. After 1421, Bruni had Cicero, *Brutus*, 62 for the difference between *laudatio* and *historia*.

that title. However, Bruni ends his letter to Foscari with a comment which neatly confuses the two categories I have been trying to distinguish:

Commentarium illud lege quaeso diligenter; continet enim luculentam historiam.

[Please read that *commentarium* carefully, for it contains an illuminating *historia*.]

Bruni's treatment of the *Hellenica* throws some light on this statement. In this instance at least, Bruni's usage allows some flexibility in the application of the terms. Bruni does seem to have believed that commentaries were a lesser genre than history. Thus, the work from Xenophon may carry the title simply because of the modesty of its conception. Another explanation for Bruni's statement is that his new work is a *commentarium* in so far as it is an abbreviation of a much larger *historia*, and an *historia* in so far as it has a moral purpose. Bruni certainly believed that *historia* has such a purpose. In the preface to his work on the Gothic Wars, the elderly chancellor surveyed the destruction of Italy: 'et sapientiores et modestiores nos historia efficit,' he says[166] [history makes us wiser and more temperate]. Even if remarks such as that made to Foscari throw doubt on the clarity with which he maintained such distinctions, Bruni's awareness of the ancient genres did allow an original approach to the ancient historians.

Eloquentia and *Interpretatio recta*

All of Bruni's Aristotelian translations were retranslations of texts available in medieval versions. This was not a new procedure: Salutati's 'translation' of Plutarch and Bruni's use of Aristippus for his version of the *Phaedo* have already been noticed. Nor was he the first to apply this procedure to Aristotle: his fellow student Roberto Rossi had retranslated the *Posterior Analytics* about 1406, although this version did not have a wide circulation;[167] Ciriaco

---

[166] Baron (1928) 149.

[167] See Garin (1949–50) 59–60. He says 'non è, in sostanza, che una minuta revisione della versio communis, con l'evidente preoccupazione di raggiungere, soprattutto, una forma più elegante' (Garin (1949–50) 61). A limited circulation is inferred from the fact that it survives in a single manuscript: Marc.lat.Z.231. Rossi's preface to this version is edited by Manetti (1951) 52–5. He used a Greek manuscript now at Venice, given to Francesco Barbaro from Rossi's library (Weiss (1977b) 247).

of Ancona had made a new translation of the pseudo-Aristotelian *De virtutibus* some time before 1420.[168] Bruni's attentions as a translator focussed on three works of Aristotle from the *Libri morales*. These works were a traditional triad, which dealt with *Mores*, *Res familiaris* and *Res publica* – or as the Greeks put it Ethics, Economics and Politics.[169] His version of the *Nicomachean Ethics*, the first and most popular of his Aristotelian translations, was substantially complete by 1416.[170] His translation of, and commentary on, the pseudo-Aristotelian *Economics* was dedicated in 1420.[171] Bruni's version of the *Politics* was under way by 1435, although it was not finally dedicated until March 1437.[172] Subsequently Bruni wrote in defence of his translations and of his methods as a translator. This work, *De interpretatione recta*, was the first treatise on translation produced in western Europe since antiquity.[173]

Bruni insisted that Aristotle was an eloquent author who approached his material as a rhetorician. This belief had a number of consequences for Bruni's ideas about translation. His conception of Aristotle's eloquence seems to have been at least as old as

---

[168] Garin (1949–50) 69.

[169] In the preface to his *Economics* translation he writes of the divisions of that part of philosophy which deals with action: 'Ea vero praecepta dividuntur trifariam: aut enim circa mores nos instruunt aut circa rem familiarem aut circa rem publicam. Harum primam *ethicam*, secundam *oeconomicam*, tertiam *politicam* Graeci appellant. Nos, ut opinor, nostris vocabulis uti magis decet quam alienis' (Baron (1928) 121).

[170] It was probably dedicated to Pope Martin V in March 1419 (Baron (1966) 553 n. 19). On 30 March 1408 Bruni wrote: 'Nam cum in ethicis [Aristotelis] per hoc tempus satis bonam operam posuerim et mirifice eorum lectio studiumque delectarit, cupio iam et physica legere et Aristotele duce naturam perscrutari' (an extension to Mehus (1741) II: 1, first published in Luiso (1980) 47 n. 9).

[171] See Baron (1928) 163–4; Baron (1966) 171; Baron (1955b).

[172] For the date of the publication of the *Politics* translation, see Zaccaria (1959) 190–1. According to Vespasiano, Bruni used Palla Strozzi's Greek manuscript for this translation (Greco (1970–6) II: 141). If this is true, then he may have first met the Greek text in his early days when they studied together under Chrysoloras. Palla took a Greek manuscript of the *Politics* with him into exile in Padua in 1434 (Sabbadini (1905–14) 62). See also Diller (1961) 313ff.

[173] I have adopted Thiermann's chronology ((1993) 118–29). It is dated between 1424 and 1426 according to Baron (1966) 554 n. 25. *De interpretatione recta* is one of the rarest of Bruni's works: nine copies survive from the fifteenth century. See Hankins (1997). Giannozzo Manetti owned one of these. See chapter 2, 70 and n. 43. It was not printed until this century. A partial edition is in Baron (1928) 81–96. This text is corrected in Bertalot (1975d) 378–9. A parallel Latin–Italian text is in Viti (1996) 150–93. An English translation is in Griffiths, Hankins and Thompson (1987) 217–29.

his acquaintance with the Greek language, and, like some of his ideas about translation, may have been acquired before the arrival of Chrysoloras in Florence. That Aristotle is eloquent is a notion that recurs throughout Bruni's career. He had been convinced of it since at least 1401, when he put a speech to that effect into the mouth of Niccolò Niccoli in the first of the *Dialogues to Pier Paolo Vergerio*.[174] In the *Dialogue* he writes:

studiosum eloquentiae fuisse Aristotelem atque incredibili quadam cum suavitate scripsisse, Ciceronis sententia est.[175]

[Cicero states that Aristotle was devoted to eloquence, and that he wrote in an extraordinarily attractive way.]

In 1416, in the preface to his translation of the *Ethics*, he repeats the claim in very similar words:

studiosum eloquentiae fuisse Aristotelem et dicendi artem cum sapientia con-iunxisse, et Cicero ipse in multis locis testatur, et libri eius summo cum eloquentiae studio luculentissime scripti declarant.[176]

[Cicero himself declares in many places that Aristotle was devoted to eloquence, and that he combined wisdom with the orator's art; and Aristotle's own books, written very lucidly and with the greatest attention to eloquence, demonstrate it.]

In the *Vita Aristotelis* of 1429, written after the objections aroused by the *Ethics* translation, he observes that his claims for Aristotle's eloquence have encountered some opposition:

Expertus sum apud quosdam doctos viros graecarum tamen litterarum ignaros fidem non fieri assertione mea dum Aristotelis eloquentiam commendo. Quippe adulterinas huius philosophiae translationes lectitare soliti intricatum quendam et obscurum et inconcinnum arbitrantur.[177]

[Among certain learned men – men, however, who do not know Greek – I have come across some scepticism when I commend Aristotle's eloquence. In fact, accustomed as they are to pore over the so-called translations of this philosopher, they think that he is knotty and unclear and writes awkwardly.]

---

[174] Ed. and tr. Garin (1952) 44–99.   [175] Garin (1952) 58.
[176] Baron (1928) 77. Bruni is alluding to Cicero's definition of *eloquentia* as 'copiose loquens sapientia' (Cicero, *De partitione oratoria*, 79, 2).
[177] Baron (1928) 46.

Bruni's claims for Aristotle are still disputed today: eloquence is not one of the virtues commonly attributed to Aristotle's surviving works by modern scholars. One modern explanation for Bruni's attitude has been repeated a number of times. Jerrold Seigel has argued that when Cicero talks of Aristotle's eloquence he is actually referring to his earlier published works which were extant in Cicero's day, but have since been lost; he says that Bruni mistakenly applied Cicero's comments to the Aristotelian works which were extant in the fifteenth century. Consequently, says Seigel, in applying Cicero's praise to Aristotle's less polished writings, Bruni was 'the victim of a complicated trick of fate'.[178]

Yet this trick of fate was not an illusion that deeper knowledge of Aristotle's style dispelled. Seigel's argument emphasises Bruni's dependence on, and acceptance of, Cicero's opinions. It also assumes that the belief that Aristotle is eloquent is such a remarkable departure that it requires an explanation. A closer examination of Bruni's conception of Aristotelian eloquence may save Bruni from these judgements. First, it is worth noting that Bruni's belief in Aristotle's eloquence became stronger as he became more familiar with Aristotle's work. In the mid-1420s, an unidentified correspondent named Demetrius criticised Bruni's translation of the *Ethics*.[179] Demetrius' attack is lost, but it seems to have been a flat denial of Aristotle's eloquence. A man with a name like Demetrius probably knew enough Greek to put up some interesting arguments, but there is no evidence of this in Bruni's reply.[180] In his response to this critic, Bruni acknowledges that some of Aristotle's works are more eloquent than others; he writes that he is aware of the possibility that Aristotle may teach eloquence without practising it in his works;[181] but he does insist that

---

[178] Seigel (1968) 110. Stinger (1977) 105–6, follows Seigel.

[179] Demetrius' criticisms can be reconstructed from Bruni's reply, Mehus (1741) IV: 22; Luiso (1980) IV: 29, 1424–6. This letter is edited in Marchesi (1904) 50–3.

[180] There have been several attempts to identify him. See, for example, Franceschini (1955) 302 n. 9. Demetrio Scarano, amanuensis to Ambrogio Traversari, has also been suggested as a possible candidate (Griffiths, Hankins and Thompson (1987) 370 n. 9). Giannozzo Manetti, whose translation of the *Nicomachean Ethics* is considered in the next chapter, had a Greek named Demetrius in his household in Florence at about this time (Vespasiano da Bisticci, *Commentario della vita di Giannozzo Manetti*, in Greco (1970–6) II: 513–627, 525).

[181] 'fieri potest, ut curaverit quidem, nec tamen sit eloquentiam consecutus.' Mehus (1741) IV: 22; Luiso (1980) IV: 29.

Aristotle is not only eloquent in the *Libri morales*, where it might be expected, but also in the *Physics* and *Metaphysics*:

Invenies locos nullius eloquentiae capaces eloquentissime ab eo tractatos, rebusque obscurissimis splendorem et claritatem per eloquentiam attulisse.[182]

[You will find that he has written very eloquently about subjects which seemed incapable of eloquence, and that he has brought brilliance and clarity through his eloquence to the most obscure matters.]

By 1438, after forty years as a translator and student of Greek, Bruni seems to have become even more certain of Aristotle's rhetorical orientation. In a preface to his translation of the *Politics*, he writes:

Aristoteles certe tanta facundia, tanta varietate et copia, tanta historiarum exemplorumque cumulatione hos libros refersit, ut oratorio paene stilo scripti videantur . . . Nec est in his libris quaestio ulla paulo uberior, quae tractata ab illo sit absque rhetorico pigmento atque colore . . . Fuit enim Aristoteles studiosissimus eloquentiae.[183]

[Aristotle packed these books with such eloquence, with such variety and *copia*, with such a great number of examples and historical illustrations, that they seem written in the style almost of an orator . . . And in these books he conducts none of his more extended inquiries without rhetorical colouring and complexion . . . For Aristotle was devoted to eloquence.]

It must be granted, as Seigel points out, that Bruni's arguments for Aristotle's eloquence sometimes take the form of deductions: Cicero is a good judge of eloquence; Cicero thinks that Aristotle is eloquent; *ergo* Aristotle is eloquent. But to suggest that Bruni maintained Cicero's opinion despite all contemporary evidence to the contrary pays Bruni's command of the Greek language no compliments. We should note that Bruni spent his whole life studying *eloquentia*. It was a word he used more reverently than we now use its English equivalent. It is better to ask, what did Bruni think *eloquentia* was that he could attribute it to Aristotle?

One factor in changing perceptions of the philosopher in the fifteenth century was the introduction of new works to the Aristotelian

---

[182] Mehus (1741) IV: 22; Luiso (1980) IV: 29. In *De interpretatione recta* Bruni cites as examples of Aristotelian eloquence *Nic. eth.* X: viii, 7, *Nic. eth.* II: i, 4, *Nic. eth.* II: iv, 3–6, *Politics* VII: i, 3 and *Politics* VI: viii. See Viti (1996) 170–4. For Bruni's version of *Nic. eth.* II: iv, 3, see Table 2.1.

[183] Baron (1928) 74.

corpus available to Latin scholars. In 1423 – after Bruni's *Ethics* translation – Giovanni Aurispa returned to Italy with the substantial collection of Greek manuscripts which he had been accumulating during his stay in the East. One of these is of particular interest. It contained a text of the *Eudemian Ethics*, and a copy of the *Rhetorica ad Alexandrum*, a work which was then attributed to Aristotle. This Greek manuscript was in the possession of Niccoli in Florence by 1425 at the latest.[184] The *Eudemian Ethics* will be considered in the next chapter; the *Rhetorica ad Alexandrum* was translated by Francesco Filelfo in 1428, and he sent this version to Ambrogio Traversari in Florence the same year.[185] Bruni – and others – could have taken the work as further evidence that Aristotle had been more interested in practical rhetoric than the texts commonly studied in the universities suggested.[186] Other works attributed to Aristotle may also have suggested a different type of writer. The short treatise *De mundo ad Alexandrum*, for example, is carefully put together and its compiler clearly had rhetorical training.[187] In 1429 Bruni published his *Life of Aristotle*. In this biography he describes a fourfold division for the philosopher's works. These are Rhetoric, Conduct, Logic and Natural Science:

---

[184] Aurispa arrived in Venice in December 1423. He informed Traversari of this manuscript in 1424. Niccoli probably received it either about December 1424, or at the beginning of September 1425 when Aurispa arrived in Florence (Baron (1971) 66). See Sabbadini (1931) 30, no. xii (1 Dec. 1424) and Ullman and Stadter (1972) 73 and 256 (no. 1130).

[185] For the *Eudemian Ethics*, see chapter 2, 73–8. Filelfo's translation of the *Rhetorica ad Alexandrum* was reprinted in the Berlin Aristotle (Aristotle (1831–70) III: 727–42). It is available in a modern facsimile: Aristotle (1962) II, fols 157ʳ–183ʳ.

[186] Bruni's letter to Demetrius, written in the mid-1420s, talks of Aristotle's *artes rhetoricae* (edited in Marchesi (1904) 51). Here, however, Bruni is probably referring to the lost rhetorical works listed by Diogenes Laertius. In 1531 Erasmus found in the rhetorical cast of the *Rhetorica ad Alexandrum* a reason to question its attribution to Aristotle: 'quod oratorum more praefatur, id quod alibi nunquam, sed semper ad rem festinat' (Ep. 2432. *EE* IX: 138).

[187] It remains to be established that Bruni knew this work. The earliest use of the Greek text in Italy known to me is in a miscellany apparently made by Nicholas Secundinus at Florence in 1441 (Cambridge University Library Dd.IV.16, fol. 87ʳ). As regards its Aristotelian authorship, it is worth noting that it is not clearly referred to in the list of Aristotle's works recorded by Diogenes Laertius, and that Rinuccio Aretino, who translated it in 1449, recorded his suspicions. See Lockwood (1913) 76–8. For a full discussion, see Kraye (1988) 171–97 and Kraye (1990b) 339–58.

Eorum una pars eloquentiae suasionisque rationem complectitur, altera ad civilem moralemque pertinet disciplinam, tertia disserendi praecepta continet, quarta vero secreta naturae ac rerum occultissimarum causae rationesque explicantur.[188]

[The first part of these deals with the science of eloquence and persuasion, the second part concerns civic and moral training, the third contains the principles of speaking, and in the fourth the secrets of nature and the causes and principles of the most recondite matters are explained.]

The first of these categories seems to have emerged under the influence of another Greek author. Diogenes Laertius' life of Aristotle had recently become available in Florence.[189] Diogenes' Aristotle has a very broad range of interests: he includes a long list of Aristotle's lost works, and he attributes several books of poetry, literary criticism and rhetoric to the philosopher. This new information allowed Bruni to set up the rhetorical books as a separate class in his own *Life of Aristotle*: most of the works he lists in this category are recorded by Diogenes but have not come down to us. It also allowed him to make another of his deductions: Aristotle cares about eloquence, or he would not have written about it; because he cares about eloquence he attempts to be eloquent; and Aristotle is the sort of man who achieves what he attempts.[190]

Another factor which modified Latin perceptions of Aristotle was a new awareness of his native language. Bruni's regard for Aristotle's eloquence could not have been sustained had he not had a higher opinion of Greeks and of the Greek language than some of his contemporaries. Shortly after Bruni's death, another Florentine, Poggio Bracciolini, made a Latin translation

---

[188] Düring has edited the *Vita Aristotelis* from a single manuscript: Düring (1957) 168–78. Baron has edited it in part (Baron (1928) 41–9). This passage is from Düring (1957) 177.

[189] Ambrogio Traversari's translation of Diogenes was dedicated to Cosimo on 30 April 1433, but it was substantially complete by 1425. Traversari ultimately made use of four Greek manuscripts for his version (Stinger (1977) 71–3). One of these belonged to Guarino and another to Filelfo. Guarino may have had his copy as early as 1419 (Mehus (1759) Epp. VI: 12, 14, 23). Filelfo owned Urb.gr.108, apparently the manuscript which he brought from Constantinople in 1427. For this manuscript, see Eleuteri (1991) 177, and Marcovich (1991) xii–xiv. Filelfo mentions a manuscript of Diogenes Laertius in his letter to Aurispa of 9 January 1431 *s.f.* (Legrand (1892) 13–17). Bruni may have been able to see the manuscripts of Guarino and Filelfo, even if his strained relationship with Traversari during the twenties denied him access to others.

[190] Düring (1957) 177.

of Xenophon's *Cyropaedia*. The liberties which Poggio takes with the original text are justified by his low regard for Greek prose in general. He wrote to a friend after he had completed the translation

Certe servata rerum gravitate effugi verbositatem qua Greci ut plurimum referti sunt, et, quoad potui, hesi rationi nostre non ut interpres verborum sed veluti historie scriptor.[191]

[I have preserved the dignity of the subject matter but avoided the verbosity with which the Greeks usually pack their works. As far as possible, I have followed my method of proceeding as a writer of history, not as a literal translator.]

He attributes verbosity to the Greek language rather than to Xenophon; that is to say, he considers it less a stylistic fault than a cultural malaise. Latin is precise, Greek spreads its matter thinly among too many words. The translator's task, as Poggio conceives it, is to eliminate this Greek element and replace it with the conciseness which is peculiarly Latin. It is possible that Poggio exaggerated the role of righteous Latin in order to disguise the fact that he sometimes did not understand his Greek original. More clearly, there is an element of cultural rivalry in his characterisation of Greek. Some Italians took a certain pride in adopting the prejudices of the ancient Romans. Poggio's views on the Greek language are related to an ancient stereotype of Greekness: of Roman fears of the devious fluency of Odysseus and Sinon, and of a defeated nation corrupting the simple virtues of its conquerors with its sophistries.[192] It is possible that Bruni originally shared something of this perspective on Greek: in 1405, in the preface to his translation of Plutarch's *Life of Antony*, Bruni, having conceded that Greek might be richer – *uberior* – than Latin, went on to cast doubt on the value of this wealth. In contrast to the 'superabundantia quaedam et luxuries' of Greek, he said, Latin is a plain but virtuous mistress.[193] Amongst those who maintained the sufficiency of the Latin language there was always the temptation to denigrate Greek.

---

[191] To Francesco Accolti (Aretinus) 1448–9, ep. IX: 32. Harth (1984–7) III: 83. For another rendering, see Loomis (1927) 498.

[192] Valerius Maximus writes that the practice of obliging Greek advocates to use Latin interpreters before Roman magistrates deprives them of their misleading *volubilitas* (*Memor.* II: 2, 2).

[193] Baron (1928) 104.

Bruni, however, could not have shared this perception of Greek verbosity, for the eloquence which he found in Aristotle must have had its basis in brevity. However the term is defined, it is probably fair to say that Aristotle's Greek is more eloquent than the medieval translator's Latin. To this extent, at least, the philosopher had been misrepresented. It is also true that the terseness of Aristotle's language sometimes gives it an epigrammatic force. In his new version, Bruni often had to disentangle and expand the philosopher's elliptical turns of phrase. Sometimes he clarified the antecedents of the clauses of the original. Consequently, Bruni's translation does have a tendency to make Aristotle neater and clearer in Latin than he is in Greek.[194] Bruni no doubt also enjoyed Aristotle's well-constructed, tightly knit arguments: if the end of eloquence is persuasion, then Aristotle sometimes compels assent. As noted above, Bruni's older contemporary, Roberto Rossi, produced a Latin version of the *Posterior Analytics* about 1406. In the preface to this translation, Rossi had pointed out that Aristotle's eloquence was due to his skilful disposition of his material.[195] This preface shows that Aristotle's eloquence had been maintained at Florence before Bruni publicised the idea; it also identifies another admirable quality in Aristotle's writing, and one that should survive any translation. Another virtue which Bruni saw in Aristotle's writing emerges from his comparison of Aristotle with Plato. Bruni's *Vita Aristotelis* of 1429 contains his cautious assessment of the value of Plato's work.[196] Bruni felt that the Socratic method of debate is destructive;[197] that many of Plato's statements are unsupported;[198] and that, for these reasons, Plato's work requires the interpretation of a well-trained and fortified mind.[199]

---

[194] See, for example, Troilo (1932) 296, on *Nic. eth.* I: iii. A short passage of Bruni's translation is discussed in chapter 2, 'The moral works of Aristotle', and see Table 1.

[195] 'pulcherrime cuncta digessit ordineque mirabili distinxit' (Manetti (1951) 55). In this preface, Rossi refers the reader to a lost work of his on Aristotle: 'Cur demus Aristoteli operam, alias diximus' (Manetti (1951) 53). Bruni probably knew this work.

[196] By 1429 Bruni had published versions of the *Gorgias, Crito, Phaedrus, Apology*, and the *Letters*. A translation of *Symposium* 215a–222a appears in a letter of Bruni's to Cosimo de'Medici, written about 1435 (Mehus (1741) VII: 1; Luiso (1980) VII: 1, 1435?).

[197] 'in disputando non tam quae ipse sentiat dicere videtur quam aliorum sententias dictaque refellere' (Düring (1957) 174).

[198] 'prolata magis hominibus quam probata' (Düring (1957) 174).

[199] 'illius libri perfectis iam robustisque disciplina hominibus aptiores sunt, teneros vero instituere non satis possunt' (Düring (1957) 174).

Aristotle's works, on the other hand, are suitable for a range of abilities:

discere qui volunt, hunc amplectantur oportet, cuius libri ita scripti sunt, ut et parvulos instituere et mediocres alere et robustos exercere ac perficere voluisse illum appareat ac omnis aetatis nostrae curam cogitationemque suscepisse.[200]

[whoever wants to learn must embrace this man, whose books are written in such a way that he appears to have wanted to instruct the young, to nourish those of middling ability, to train and perfect the strong; and he appears to have taken thought and care for our every age.]

It is significant that Bruni's contribution to a debate that was to grow increasingly heated in the middle of the century looks to the value of the philosophers as educational writers.

Bruni was particularly impressed by Aristotle's frequent quotations from, and allusions to, the poets.[201] The ability to illuminate your writing in this way also belongs to eloquence. Perhaps this explains why his admiration is more fulsome after the *Politics* translation. According to Bruni, the *Politics* is Aristotle's most rhetorical work. He says in *De interpretatione recta* that here the philosopher, moving closer to the orator's traditional territory, resorted to rhetorical devices more often:

Quod enim materia est civilis et eloquentiae capax, nullus fere locus ab eo tractatur sine rhetorico pigmento atque colore, ut interdum etiam festivitatem in verbis oratoriam persequatur.[202]

[Because the subject matter is political and can be treated eloquently, he handles almost every passage with a rhetorical colour and style, so much so that sometimes he even affects the orator's word-play in his language.]

In the list of works in his *Life of Aristotle*, Bruni cites one lost treatise which he had found in Diogenes Laertius' biography of the philosopher:

---

[200] This is from Baron (1928) 46. Düring's text is slightly different at this point.

[201] In his *De studiis*, written in the 1420s, Bruni wrote: 'Aristoteles certe Homeri, Hesiodi, Pindari, Euripidis ceterorumque poetarum versus frequentissime ponit' (ed. Kallendorf (2002) 110).

[202] Baron (1928) 90. Bruni, discussing the *Politics*, echoes these words in a letter of 8 December 1437 to Barnaba da Siena: 'Quia enim materia est civilis, et capax eloquentiae, usus michi videtur Aristoteles amplissimo quodam scribendi genere, elegantia, nitore, et incredibili exemplorum copia referto' (Mehus (1741) VII: 14; Luiso (1980) VII: 7).

hi libri in quibus sunt ab eo mores et instituta centum quinquaginta octo civitatum multa cura magnaque diligentia perscripti.[203]

[These books in which he records very carefully and with great industry the practices and constitutions of one hundred and fifty-eight city-states.]

Bruni knew that the abundance of apt illustration which he enjoyed so much in the *Politics* was the product of Aristotle's own researches into the constitutions of Greek states. Aristotle himself said as much at the end of the *Ethics*.[204] To an historian like Bruni this was a very congenial virtue.

In his discussions about the best Latin renderings, Bruni repeatedly summons the ancients themselves to judge the versions of their works. His indignation at the clumsiness of earlier translators is presented as an extension of the ancients' own horror at what has been done to their words. In the first of the *Dialogues to Pier Paolo Vergerio*, he has Niccolò Niccoli say:

hi libri, quos Aristotelis esse dicunt, tam magnam transformationem passi sunt, ut si quis eos ad Aristotelem ipsum deferat, non magis ille suos esse cognoscat quam Actaeonem illum, qui ex homine in cervum conversus est, canes suae cognoverint.[205]

[These books, which they say are Aristotle's, have undergone such a great transformation, that if someone were to show them to Aristotle himself, he would no more recognise them as his than Actaeon's dogs recognised their master after he had been changed into a stag.]

In a letter addressed to Niccoli, Bruni wrote about the differences between his version of Plato and those of his predecessors, Chalcidius the ancient translator of the *Timaeus* and Aristippus the medieval translator of the *Phaedo*:

Illi enim a Platone discedentes syllabas atque tropos secuti sunt: ego autem Platoni adhaereo, quem ego ipse michi effinxi et quidem latine scientem, ut iudicare possit, testemque eum adhibebo traductioni suae, atque ita traduco ut illi maxime placere intelligo.[206]

[For those earlier translators followed Plato's words and idioms whilst abandoning Plato himself. I, on the other hand, stay close to Plato; I imagine that he knows

---

[203] Baron (1928) 49. Diogenes V: 12.
[204] *Nic. eth.* X: 9 ix, 23.   [205] Garin (1952) 58.
[206] Mehus (1741) I: 8; Luiso (1980) I: 1, 5 September 1400. Garin cites this passage and reads 'adhibeo traductionis sue' ((1955) 361–3).

Latin, so that he can judge for himself; I will call him as a witness to his own translation; and I translate as I think would please him best.]

This passage may be compared with one from the preface to the *Ethics* translation produced many years later, where he writes of Aristotle:

si quis illi nunc sensus est rerum nostrarum, iampridem credendum est [eum] huic absurditati et inconcinnitati traductionis infensum et tantam barbariem indignatum hos suos libros esse negare, cum talis apud Latinos videri cupiat, qualem apud Graecos sese ipse exhibuit.[207]

[if Aristotle has now any awareness of our affairs, we must suppose that he has been long opposed to the absurdity and awkwardness of the [medieval] translation; and we must suppose that in his anger at their great barbarity he would deny that these are his books at all, since he wants to appear to Latin readers as he showed himself to the Greeks.]

And finally in 1429 in the *Life of Aristotle*, he writes:

Sed non sunt illi Aristotelis libri, nec si vivat ipse suos dici velit, sed merae translatorum ineptiae.[208]

[But those books are not Aristotle's, nor if he were alive would he himself want them to be called his own; rather, they are simply the absurdities of the translators.]

There is a certain degree of literary convention in this *topos*, but it does seem that Bruni subscribed to the notion that to translate well is a type of homage to the illustrious dead. If Aristotle turns in his grave at the medieval translations of his work, says Bruni, it is because he would not have said anything of the sort if he were alive and Latin. Biography, a skill Bruni had learnt at least in part from Greek writers, was an essential prerequisite for this conception of translation.

Bruni maintained that the translator must know his author intimately because he must be inspired by his work in order to translate well. In his essay on translation Bruni attempted to describe this inspiration:

Rapitur enim interpres vi ipsa in genus dicendi illius de quo transfert; nec aliter servare sensum commode poterit nisi sese insinuet ac inflectat per illius comprehensiones et ambitus cum verborum proprietate orationisque effigie.[209]

---

[207] Baron (1928) 77, who adds *eum*.   [208] Baron (1928) 46.
[209] Baron (1928) 87. For *comprehensio et ambitus*, see Cicero, *Brutus*, 162. For another translation of this passage, see Griffiths, Hankins and Thompson (1987) 221.

[The translator is carried forcibly into the style of the original. He cannot possibly preserve the sense to advantage unless he insinuates and twists himself into the word-order and periodic structure of the original with verbal propriety and stylistic faithfulness.]

Bruni does describe some specific problems for his perfect translator to overcome: the translator must understand those virtues he is to represent; he must identify the style of his author, and then adopt it when translating him; he must fully grasp the idiomatic nature of both languages; he must be thoroughly versed in the literature of his author's time so that allusions do not escape him; he must even understand when and why his author uses the rhythms of his native language so that he can reproduce their effects in his own. These considerations constitute such a demanding standard that translators must be special people. Bruni writes:

Multi enim ad intelligendum idonei, ad explicandum tamen non idonei sunt. Quemadmodum de pictura multi recte iudicant qui ipsi pingere non valent, et musicam artem multi intelligunt qui ipsi sunt ad canendum inepti.[210]

[For many are able to understand who are not able to explain. Just as there are many good judges of a painting who cannot paint, and many understand music who are not very good at singing.]

This conception of the translator as an artist is consistent with the requirements set out in the pseudo-Ciceronian *De optimo genere oratorum*. Bruni probably took the observation that those who cannot paint may still be fine judges of painting from this essay. In the ancient work, we are presented with an imaginary critic who asks why he should read these new Latin translations rather than the Greek originals. He is told that these translations are independent works of art: those who read Menander still read Terence. Versions such as these compete with the original text rather than making it redundant.

The claims of the inspired translator could be seen as a front for taking liberties with the text, and there were a number of contemporary criticisms of Bruni's *Ethics* translation. Bruni's contempt for the medieval translator was particularly provocative. About 1430, Alfonso, Bishop of Burgos, produced a short essay criticising

[210] Baron (1928) 84.

Bruni's version of the *Ethics*.[211] He pointed out that Bruni did not argue that the old version was flawed, but that it was worthless: 'quasi non vitiosa sed penitus nulla translatio fuerit'.[212] Bruni's response to this charge remained fairly consistent. In the sixteenth century Erasmus would maintain that the sanctity and learning of the Fathers did not prevent them from making mistakes; in the fifteenth Bruni argued that the good will and piety of the medieval translators did not make them fine scholars.[213] Perhaps the criticisms he encountered made Bruni think twice about his words, because at the beginning of his treatise on translation he admits that he may have over-reacted:

Ego autem fateor me paulo vehementiorem in reprehendendo fuisse, sed accidit indignatione animi.[214]

[I was, I admit, rather sharp in my rebukes, but I was deeply upset.]

From his comments in a letter of 1440 it is clear that he appreciated the restraint with which Alfonso conducted his defence of the medieval version.[215] His sharp criticisms of the earlier translator, he said, were the result of his righteous indignation at the defacement of Aristotle's prose. He describes a bad translation of a fine text as a type of vandalism. If he saw a fine ancient painting vandalised he could not but react, and Aristotle's books 'omni pictura nitidiores ornatioresque sunt'[216] [are brighter and more elaborate than any picture]. This, of course, assumes that the reader is something of a connoisseur. It was certainly an image Bruni cultivated for himself.

---

[211] Franceschini (1955) 305 n. 17. Alfonso's essay and related correspondence are edited in Birkenmajer (1922) 162–210.

[212] Birkenmajer (1922) 165. The thirteenth-century translation of Robert Grosseteste (perhaps in William of Moerbeke's revision) was the object of Bruni's scorn. He did not claim to know the identity of the medieval translator. Franceschini (1955) discusses the issue.

[213] Mehus (1741) IV: 22; Luiso (1980) IV: 29, 1424–6.   [214] Baron (1928) 83.

[215] 'ille veterem interpretationem Ethicorum suis rationibus defendebat; de me autem nichil nisi honorifice loquebatur'. Mehus (1741) VIII: 4; Luiso (1980) VIII: 11, first half of 1440.

[216] *De interpretatione recta*, in Baron (1928) 83. Bruni's language in this passage echoes his words in the earlier letter to Demetrius (Mehus (1741) IV: 22; Luiso (1980) IV: 29). For Demetrius, he used as an example an Italian painter, Giotto; for the wider audience of *De interpretatione recta* he talked of classical artists, Protogenes, Apelles and Aglaophon.

Bishop Alfonso was a more subtle critic than Demetrius. He attacked two central elements of Bruni's treatment of Aristotle: the first of these was the link made by Bruni between eloquence and philosophy. One of the reasons why Bruni repeatedly quotes Cicero in defence of Aristotle's eloquence is that he feels that the two ancient writers practised the same type of philosophy. He says in the preface to his *Ethics* translation that Cicero deals eloquently with the material he draws from Aristotle:

Ciceronem quoque in his libris in quibus haec ab Aristotele tractata perscripsit, numquam exprimendi facultas, numquam ubertas orationis defecit.[217]

[In the books in which he wrote about the things discussed by Aristotle, Cicero's power of expression and richness of speech never deserted him.]

Bruni certainly believed that all true things could be said well, and he implied that all philosophical truths could be stated in Ciceronian Latin. It was this position which involved him in controversy. Alfonso was not – unlike some of his contemporaries – hostile to Greek studies *per se*: he prefaces his criticisms of Bruni's *Ethics* translation with praise of Bruni's translations of Basil, Demosthenes and Aeschines:

Quae cum legissem, illius saeculi eloquentiam in quo illi elegantissimi oratores certarunt cum quadam admiratione conspexi, ac modernae translationis suavitas Leonardum eum ignotum carum mihi reddiderat.[218]

[When I had read them, I looked with real admiration on the eloquence of the age in which those most elegant orators competed, and the attractive modern translation made me love the unknown Leonardo.]

Alfonso says that he was ready to call him a 'novellus Cicero', an allusion to Bruni's biography of the orator, *Cicero novus*. This is a significant compliment in the context, for whilst Bruni could have asked for no higher praise, Alfonso now took the battle to Bruni by arguing that Cicero was not a good moral philosopher. Having praised Cicero's eloquence, he pointed out some of his limitations:

[217] Baron (1928) 78.   [218] Birkenmajer (1922) 164.

In scientifica autem virtutum distinctione ac documentorum moralium subtili inquisitione hanc illi praeeminentiam concessam non legimus, cum haec illum multis in locis polite, fateor, sed minus plene tradidisse cernamus.[219]

[However, in making a useful distinction between the virtues, and in the delicate inquiry into moral examples, I have not read that superiority was granted to him, since I see that on many occasions he recounts these things in a manner that is polished, certainly, but not thorough.]

Alfonso went on to attack the heart of Bruni's position: eloquence and philosophy are not the same thing, and ethical statements should not be subject to the requirements of eloquence:

Crede enim mihi: qui scientiarum districtissimas conclusiones eloquentiae regulis subdere vult, non sapit, cum verba addere ac detrahere ad persuasionis dulcedinem pertinet, quod scientiae rigor abhorret.[220]

[For believe me, those who want to subject the very precise conclusions of philosophical enquiry to the rules of eloquence are not wise, because the charm of persuasive language is maintained by adding and removing words, something which is not consistent with the inflexible method of philosophy.]

Alfonso says that even Cicero agreed that the philosopher and the orator are not one and the same. He says that although eloquence is desirable the truth is more desirable, and that it is often not compatible with eloquence. Alfonso says that the end of eloquence is persuasion, not truth.

Different conceptions of philosophical language are revealed in their attitudes to translations of Aristotle. There was more at stake than the reputation of the medieval translator. If the medieval versions were to be condemned for their language, what would become of the works of the medieval philosophers, whose Latin was also unclassical? Alfonso maintained that a philosophical work must be at liberty to define the meaning of its own terms. In this respect, the use of transliterated Greek words was convenient for the medieval translator precisely because they were alien to Latin: they brought no irrelevant semantic baggage with them; the words were empty tokens which could be filled with the philosopher's meaning. This practice was a familiar device to Latin audiences for whom Greek traditionally provided technical vocabularies. Bruni,

[219] Ibid. 173.   [220] Ibid. 175.

on the other hand, maintained that these words did mean something in the Greek, that they would have meant something to a Greek audience of the fourth century, and that Aristotle was not trying to create a new concept but to modify an existing one. Both positions are intellectually respectable. Alfonso clearly believes that immutable truth dictates the terms in which it is expressed. Bruni might have responded that profound philosophical truths are beautiful and can only be truly communicated by beautiful language; or he might have replied that the purpose of the *Nicomachean Ethics* was not simply to describe a system of moral philosophy, but to persuade his audience to adopt ethical behaviour. An attractive translation was thus consonant with Aristotle's intention in the work. To the best of my knowledge, Bruni does not specifically adopt either of these positions.

Roger Bacon, in a passage neither writer would have known, says that the translator must in fact know three things:

Nam ad hoc quod translatio fiat vera oportet quod translator sciat linguam a qua transfert, et linguam in quam transfert, et scientiam quam vult transferre.[221]

[For the translation to be accurate, the translator must know the language from which he is translating, the language into which he is translating, and the body of knowledge that he wants to translate.]

In Bruni's *De interpretatione recta* it is stated that the translator must have a deep knowledge of both languages. This may sound like a truism, but medieval translators were accused of knowing neither Greek nor Latin.[222] In the preface to the translation of the *Ethics* Bruni describes the medieval translator as 'semigraecus quidam et semilatinus', deficient in both languages, and competent in neither.[223] Bruni does raise the possibility that since the medieval translator did not know either language, his virtue must have lain in his knowledge of philosophy, but it does not seem to be a possibility

---

[221] Quoted in Franceschini (1955) 316.

[222] This rule seems more otiose in vernacular treatises on translation, where it is more reasonable to assume that the translator's grasp of his mother tongue is sound. In such works, the rule often seems to be a relic from Latin discussions of translation.

[223] 'in utraque deficiens, in neutra integer' (Baron (1928) 77). Twenty years earlier Salutati had labelled Atumano's version of Plutarch a *semigraeca translatio* (Setton (1956) 51).

he takes seriously in this confrontation.[224] Alfonso, on the other hand, because he does not know Greek, takes this alternative very seriously. Bruni may have Greek and Latin, but this does not matter because Alfonso, like the medieval translator, has Bacon's *scientia*. Reason is a third and universal language:

Ratio enim omni nationi communis est, licet diversis idiomatibus exprimatur.[225]

[For *Ratio* is common to every nation, although it is expressed in different languages.]

Alfonso believed that Aristotle spoke this language fundamentally, and Greek only incidentally. This assumption led him to formulate a remarkable principle of textual criticism:

Cum igitur Aristoteles ipse non rationem ab auctoritate, sed auctoritatem a ratione consecutus est, quicquid rationi consonat, haec Aristoteles dixisse putandus est; et Graece arbitremur scriptum fuisse quicquid Latinis verbis translatio nostra sapienter depromit.[226]

[And so, since Aristotle is thought authoritative because he is rational, and is not thought rational because he is authoritative, we must suppose that Aristotle said whatever is consistent with reason, and we should think that Aristotle wrote in Greek whatever the medieval translator judiciously renders into Latin.]

This principle gives us the right to emend Aristotle's text in accordance with universal reason rather than with reference to Greek grammar. It seems that Alfonso regarded Aristotle as a repository of true statements about real things, rather than as a man with controvertible opinions about an imperfectly known world. Perhaps there is another element to his attitude: the idea that Aristotle attempted to persuade his audience may have offended Alfonso because it suggests that he found himself unable to win assent through his formal arguments. Alfonso may have regarded persuasion as beneath the dignity of the philosopher.

Although Bruni's translation was eventually superseded by other Latin versions, the debate which he had reopened continued

---

[224] Bruni's position may have changed. In a letter to the Duke of Gloucester, produced between 1428 and 1435, he says that *interpretatio recta* requires 'recta intelligentia ipsarum rerum quae traducuntur' (Baron (1928) 140).

[225] Birkenmajer (1922) 166.

[226] Ibid. 166. This passage is discussed by Griffiths, Hankins and Thompson (1987) 204–5.

through to the sixteenth century. This was because his insistence on Aristotle's eloquence was not the product of an unfortunate misunderstanding of Cicero, but an important contribution to the ancient debate about the relationship between philosophy and rhetoric. Thus, about fifteen years after Bruni's death, Johannes Argyropoulos made his own version of the *Nicomachean Ethics* and criticised Bruni's translations of Aristotle on the grounds that they were too free and over-emphasised eloquence.[227] In the early 1480s Baptista de Finario, Bishop of Ventimiglia, took up the defence of the medieval translation against Bruni's criticisms.[228] At the end of the fifteenth century, we find that a German edition of the inelegant medieval translation of Aristotle's *Rhetoric* is prefaced with a loose (and unacknowledged) paraphrase of a passage from Bruni's *Vita Aristotelis* on Aristotle's eloquence.[229] In 1537 Philip Melanchthon took up the debate. He praised Aristotle for his *proprietas sermonis*, his *elegantia* and his *perspicuitas*, and he goes on to suggest that Cicero praised Aristotle's 'golden river' because of his frequent quotation from ancient lost works.[230] In 1558 we find that Aristotle's eloquence is still being maintained in terms which Bruni would have understood. In that year, Melanchthon's pupil Franz Burchard wrote a response to a well-known letter which Pico della Mirandola had written in 1485 to Ermolao Barbaro.[231] He recalls Cicero's verdict on Aristotle:

Aristotelis oratio, etsi brevior est, tamen et propria et pura est, et ita abundat quibusdam suis luminibus ut Cicero eam dixerit similem esse flumini aurum vehenti; et interdum adeo dulcis est, nihil ut possit cogitari dulcius.[232]

---

[227] See Seigel (1969) 245–6. Filelfo warned Argyropoulos against criticising Bruni in 1457 (Legrand (1892) 92–5). Angelo Poliziano's defence of Bruni's Aristotle against Argyropoulos is in *Miscellanea* I. Poliziano lectured on Bruni's *Nicomachean Ethics* and *Economics* at Florence in 1491–2. See Hankins (1997) nos. 698 and 551.

[228] See Grabmann (1926) 440–8.

[229] Leipzig, c.1499. An image of the preface is in the *Incunabula Short-Title Catalogue*, ia01046400. The translation is William of Moerbeke's, edited by Spengel (1867) I: 178–342. The relevant passage in Bruni's *Vita* is in Düring (1957) 174–5. Bruni's biography was first printed at Rome in 1470, among the Latin renderings of Plutarch's *Lives*.

[230] *Oratio de vita Aristotelis* (Bretschneider (1842) IX: 342–9, 348, 349).

[231] This letter, long attributed to Melanchthon, has now been restored to Burchard. See Rummel (1992) 302–5. It has been translated into English under Melanchthon's name by Breen (1952).

[232] Bretschneider (1842) IX: 689; Breen (1952) 415.

[Aristotle's discourse, although it is rather concise, is nevertheless fitting and pure; and it is so full of certain beauties of style that Cicero said it is like a gold-bearing river; and it is sometimes so charming that one can think of nothing more so.]

Like Bruni's exchange with Alfonso, Burchard's argument turned on the nature of *eloquentia*. He wrote:

Nam eloquentia non est, ut isti somniant, accersitus cultus, sed est facultas proprie ac dilucide explicandi animorum sensa ac cogitationes.[233]

[For eloquence is not – as some men dream – a straining after refinement, but rather the ability to explain accurately and clearly the opinions and thoughts of our minds.]

Like Roberto Rossi 150 years earlier, Melanchthon and Burchard admired Aristotle's lucidity in his disposition of complicated material. Bruni's regard for Aristotle's eloquence was not such an aberration that it could not find defenders a century later.

After Bruni's death, the rivalry amongst translators of Aristotle became more intense. The Greek scholars around Bessarion in the second half of the century produced many more versions.[234] Manetti produced a version which will be considered in the next chapter. Bruni's version was still a focus of criticism, partly because it remained popular, and partly because his attack on the medieval version was the most strident of any of the Renaissance translators. The debate was also stimulated by the fact that during the late fifteenth and early sixteenth centuries the versions of the medieval translator, Bruni, and Argyropoulos were all available in print. Moreover, a number of editions printed all three translations together. One of these triple versions was printed at Paris in 1510.[235] Two years later, at Basle, John Cuno may have had this edition in front of him as he embarked on another defence of the medieval version. It is worth considering his remarks in some detail because they have been overlooked by the commentators on the *Ethics* controversy, and also because he shows how a sixteenth-century scholar of the Northern Renaissance reacted to a characteristic figure of the early Florentine Renaissance.

---

[233] Bretschneider (1842) IX: 690; Breen (1952) 416.
[234] See Garin (1949–50) and chapter 2, 'The moral works of Aristotle'.
[235] Aristotle (1510), a reprint of the Paris edition of 1497.

The vehicle for Cuno's defence was the edition of his translation of Nemesius of Emesa's *De natura hominis*, printed at Strasbourg in 1512.[236] In a lengthy preface addressed to Beatus Rhenanus, Cuno talks sympathetically of the problems faced by the medieval translator.[237] He moves on to defend the medieval translator of the *Ethics* against Bruni. He goes further than Alfonso when he attacks Bruni's version of Demosthenes' *Pro Ctesiphonte*, which had by then been printed a number of times.[238] Cuno may have had a special interest in the Greek text of Aristotle, since he visited Venice some time before 1499 and managed to acquire part of the printer's copy for the Aldine *editio princeps* of 1498. We also know that he attended the lectures of Scipio Carteromachus on Demosthenes at Padua in 1504.[239] The medieval translator of the *Ethics*, says Cuno in his preface, could not have left words in their Greek form out of ignorance, since he manages to provide translations for passages of greater difficulty. Rather he followed the practice of the great writers of antiquity:

Non enim ignoravit probatissimos ante se scriptores idem crebro factitasse, qui ornatus gratia tanquam gemmas integra graeca suis scriptis inserere non dubitarunt, Ciceronem, Quintilianum, Lactantium, Hieronymum, Ambrosium.[240]

[For he knew that highly respected writers – Cicero, Quintilian, Lactantius, Jerome, Ambrose – had often done the same thing in the past. These writers did not hesitate to set Greek phrases in their writings, to adorn them as if with gemstones.]

[236] By Matthias Schurer. Cuno mistakenly attributed it to Gregory of Nyssa. See Hunt (1966) 81.
[237] Rhenanus later edited Bruni's version of Procopius for publication in 1531.
[238] 'elegantissimam illam prae ceteris Demosthenis orationem Pro Ctesiphonte fuco suo tum obliterasset, tum decreta plura, testimonia, testium nomina et leges, unde totius orationis pendet intellectus, omittens detruncasset' (Saffrey (1971) 50). There were at least five editions of Bruni's translation of *Pro Ctesiphonte* before 1500. There was some justice in Cuno's remarks. George of Trebizond had made a similar criticism of Bruni's omissions to justify his new version (Monfasani (1984) 94). Rinuccio Aretino had translated the missing *decreta* and *testimonia* some time after 24 August 1424 and dedicated them to Poggio Bracciolini. See Lockwood (1913) 52 and 84–6. Modern editors of Demosthenes mark them as later additions to the text. Cuno copied Sélestat 102, which contains Bruni's versions of *Philippicae* i–iv and *Pro Diopithe*, but not *Pro Ctesiphonte* (Hankins (1997) no. 2321).
[239] Harvard.gr.17, which has part of *Nic. eth.* on fols 39–46. See Wilson (1977) 392–3. For Cuno's visit to Venice, see Saffrey (1971) 20–4. For Cuno and Carteromachus, see Saffrey (1971) 28–33.
[240] Edited by Saffrey (1971) 45–52, 50.

This line of defence is quite different from Alfonso's, and defends the medieval translator as a stylist not as a philosopher. That he could do so is in a curious way a tribute to the revolution which Bruni had initiated. Greek words rarely appear in Bruni's letters, a clear contrast to Cicero's practice. This was partly because 'nihil Graece dictum est, quod Latine dici non possit' [nothing has been said in Greek which cannot be said in Latin] was a dictum Bruni always attempted to demonstrate, but also because most of his correspondents would not have understood even the simplest Greek words.[241] By 1512 the situation had changed. Many Latin readers with no profound Greek learning could still make out the odd Greek word or common Greek phrase they found in their Latin texts. Cuno goes on:

Non ergo integris graecis utentes semper vitio dandi sunt, cum his sanctam ecclesiam uti palam cernamus.[242]

[So using Greek phrases is not always a fault, since we may see that the Holy Church uses them in public.]

This too was a different defence of the medieval translator. Where Alfonso had cited other classical usages against Bruni, Cuno argued that the Church's use of non-classical words and phrases had made them Latin. Cuno's assertion of the validity of ecclesiastical Latin idiom was conditioned by circumstances which Bruni had not faced. Bruni, as will be seen in the next chapter, saw no need to replace the Vulgate translation of the Bible. In chapter 3 I shall describe how Erasmus confronted arguments similar to those raised here by Cuno. For the present, it is enough to note that the defence of the language of the Vulgate was under way at Basle before Erasmus published his edition of the New Testament there in 1516, and that this defence was couched in terms of a response to Bruni's position on translation.

---

[241] *De interpretatione recta*, in Baron (1928) 95.   [242] Saffrey (1971) 50.

2

GIANNOZZO MANETTI

Introduction

Bruni's younger contemporary, the Florentine scholar Giannozzo Manetti, is perhaps best known for his treatise *De dignitate et excellentia hominis*. It is less well known that he also produced Latin versions of three of the most important texts of his day: the *Nicomachean Ethics*, the New Testament and the Psalter. This fact alone would grant him an important place in the history of translation, but Manetti also produced a substantial treatise, *Apologeticus*, dealing with Scriptural translation. None of Manetti's translations have been edited, and he has not yet been assigned his proper place amongst the Latin translators of the fifteenth century. The translations have been neglected for two reasons. First, because they had a small circulation and consequently very little influence on the subsequent study of the original texts. Second, because Manetti has been studied by historians more often as a politician and as a diplomat than as a scholar.

In this chapter, I hope to place his versions in the context of contemporary scholarship in the 1440s and 1450s. I shall discuss the difficult dating of the translations. To this end, I shall first attempt to clarify what can be said about Manetti's movements in the last years of his life. Then I shall consider each of his translations in turn: the relationship between Manetti's Aristotelian versions and the many translations of Aristotle produced at Rome in the 1450s will be defined more precisely; Manetti's role in fifteenth-century debates over New Testament scholarship will be explored; and Manetti's treatise on translation will be assessed in the light of Bruni's comments on the matter and of his own experiences as a translator of the Scriptures.

Manetti's movements, 1452–1458

An examination of the circumstances in which Manetti's versions were produced makes it possible to reconstruct Manetti's participation in contemporary debates about translation. However, evidence of contact between Manetti and contemporary scholars is not abundant. His friendship with Vespasiano da Bisticci is well attested, as is that with Tommaso Parentucelli, the future Pope Nicholas V.[1] Vespasiano describes how in 1434, after Pope Eugenius had arrived to stay in Florence, Parentucelli regularly joined the daily gatherings which included Leonardo Bruni, Poggio Bracciolini, Carlo Marsuppini, Giovanni Aurispa, Gasparo da Bologna, and Manetti himself.[2] Such informal gatherings leave few direct records. Manetti's daily contact with men such as Bruni and Traversari reduced the need for correspondence between them which might have thrown some light on their relationship, and both men were dead before Manetti had cause to spend long periods away from Florence.

Manetti's relationship with Francesco Filelfo has not come to the attention of scholars and it is useful to rehearse here the available evidence. Filelfo first writes of Manetti in the preface to his translation of Lysias' *Epitaph*, published about 1429. Here, he talks of Manetti and Marsuppini as the rising stars of the Florentine literary scene.[3] In a letter written nearly thirty years later, Filelfo recalls their scholarly conversations together in Florence during his time in the city, that is, at some time between 1429 and 1434.[4] Filelfo's satire against Ambrogio Traversari, addressed to Manetti,

---

[1] For the surviving correspondence between Manetti and Vespasiano, see Cagni (1969) 121–9, 131–9. After Parentucelli's death in 1455, Manetti wrote his biography: *Vita Nicolai summi pontificis*, ed. Muratori (1734) 905–60. That part of this work which corresponds to Muratori (1734) 929–40 is edited by García (1995). For the *Vita*, see also Onofri (1979) 27–77. It was dedicated to Cardinal Antonio Cerdano of Lérida and Giovanni de'Medici. For Cerdano, see Onofri (1979) 28 and n. 3. For the date, see below, n. 75.

[2] Greco (1970–6) 42–3; George and Waters (1963) 34–5.

[3] Filelfo's preface was edited in the eighteenth century by John Taylor in the preface to his edition of Lysias. Taylor's prefatory matter is reprinted in Dobson (1828) i: 1–20, 32–60, 94–158. Filelfo's dedication to Palla Strozzi is at i: 10–12. Taylor's reading, 'Iannotium manet', must be corrected to 'Iannotium Manetum'.

[4] Filelfo was at Bologna on 4 April 1429, at Imola on 6–7 April, and at Florence on 19 April (*Epistolae* (1506)). He left Florence at the end of December 1434 (Luiso (1980) 125 n. 41).

is probably to be dated between 1433 and 1439.[5] That Filelfo chose Manetti as the recipient of this satire may be evidence that Manetti's relationship with Traversari was not always as harmonious as Vespasiano would have us believe. In addition to these notices, five letters from Filelfo to Manetti survive. The earliest shows Filelfo planning his departure from Florence in 1433. It hints that Manetti's reputation or his political position might be damaged if Filelfo should move to Milan.[6] From Milan, Filelfo wrote three letters to him in Florence. These letters are very guarded. The first is studiedly cryptic, the second ostentatiously disavows all but literary interests, while the third cautiously leaves the substance of Filelfo's communication with the bearer of the letter.[7] In 1453 Filelfo declined an opportunity to comment on Manetti's political difficulties in Florence.[8] In 1457 he wrote to Manetti, now in Naples, to congratulate him on his philosophical retreat from the storms of public life in Florence.[9]

The difficulty of establishing Manetti's contacts with his contemporaries is compounded by the difficulty of determining precisely the dates of two important movements in Manetti's life. The first is the date of his move from Florence to Rome; the second is the date of his move from Rome to his final home at Naples. Because these movements are of central importance for Manetti's relationship to Roman scholarship in the 1450s, and because they

---

[5] Satire II: 7, *Francisci Philelfi Satyrarum* (Venice, 1502): sigs c8ᵛ–d2ʳ. The satire concerns Traversari's request to Filelfo to provide translations for the verse passages in Diogenes Laertius. For Traversari's version of Diogenes, see chapter 1, '*Eloquentia* and *Interpretatio recta*', n. 189. In a letter of 2 May 1433, two days after the dedication of the translation, Filelfo is still promising to make his versions. This satire is intended to reform a living man and consequently must be dated before Traversari's death in the winter of 1439. Traversari's version of Diogenes is not listed among Manetti's Latin manuscripts (Cagni (1960)). However, Manetti made extensive use of the translation over a number of years, and it is likely that he owned a copy. Manetti did own Traversari's versions of Dionysius the Areopagite, Pal.lat.148, copied by Agnolo Manetti. See Gentile (1997) 298–300.

[6] 17 April 1433, edited in De' Rosmini (1808) I: 137: 'Aut ad Bononienses me recipiam, aut ad Senenses: nam ab utrisque honestissime accersor. Quod ni putarem a me vobis iniuriam factum iri Mediolanum libentius concederem.'

[7] These letters from Filelfo's *Epistolario* are dated 30 December 1442, 30 October 1444 and 12 November 1449.

[8] Iacopo da Camerino felt that Filelfo might know something of the matter. In a letter of 5 May 1453, Filelfo replied to his inquiry: 'De Ioannocio quod scripsisti non intelligo. Itaque nihil est quod respondeam.'

[9] The letter of 20 September 1457 is printed in Filelfo's *Epistolae* (1506): sig. b6ʳ⁻ᵛ.

are usually referred to in vague and sometimes misleading terms, I shall attempt here to clarify the matter. The first date comes from Manetti himself. In his biography of his old friend Pope Nicholas V, composed not long after Nicholas' death in March 1455, he glosses over the circumstances of his exile from Florence:

nos septimo pontificatus sui anno ab eo e Florentia apostolicis litteris in Urbem evocati . . .[10]

[in the seventh year of his pontificate, we were summoned to Rome from Florence by him in writing . . .]

Nicholas was elected on 6 March 1447, and so the seventh year of his pontificate was from March 1453 to March 1454. This seems to be Manetti's only surviving comment on the subject of his exile.

Vespasiano, in his preface to his commentary on Manetti's life, writes that he left Florence 'volontariamente'.[11] Vespasiano's words are pointed enough to suggest that another construction could have been put on Manetti's departure. His account of it makes much of the high taxes imposed on Manetti by the state, but the facts of the case remain obscure.[12] High tax assessments were often politically motivated, since outstanding tax debts to the city would usually bar the debtor from public office. It is clear that in 1452 Manetti was assessed for a large tax payment. The sum stipulated was considerably more than that required under previous assessments and Manetti was unwilling to pay. On 23 February 1453 he and Otto Niccolini were appointed Florentine ambassadors to the Pope.[13] Without waiting for his tax dispute with the authorities to be resolved, he left for Rome shortly afterwards. This sudden departure provoked a sharp response at Florence. On 16 March an order in council demanded Manetti's immediate return from Rome within ten days, on pain of exile for ten years; it also accused him of providing justification for Alfonso's war against Florence.[14] This seems to be a reference to Manetti's treatise *De dignitate*

---

[10] Muratori (1734) 927.   [11] Greco (1970–6) II: 517.

[12] Manetti's tax assessment was discussed by Gutkind (1938) 131–3. New information is available in Conti (1984) 348–53.

[13] Martines (1963) 189.

[14] See Conti (1984) 348–9 and n. 63; Greco (1970–6) II: 592–3. Otto Niccolini, Manetti's elected colleague for the mission to Rome, was present at this meeting (Conti (1984) 349).

et excellentia hominis, dedicated to the king in December 1452.[15] Having received this peremptory summons, Manetti did not set out for Florence. A letter of his to Antonio Panormita, in which he notes laconically that rumours were circulating about him in Florence, demonstrates that he was still at Rome on 25 March.[16] Before he set out for Florence, his friend Pope Nicholas made him a papal ambassador, apparently a legal shift to bestow diplomatic immunity on Manetti should he need it.[17] He then left for Florence.

Manetti's return was apparently not swift enough for the Florentine authorities: on his return journey he was intercepted at Siena and escorted back to Florence. He entered the city on 29 March, Holy Thursday.[18] Despite the grave charges implied in the order of 16 March, there seems to have been no formal trial. On 5 April another order in council pardoned Manetti for his absence.[19] He appears to have recovered his position shortly afterwards, for on 12 June he was appointed one of the Ten of War,[20] and in August a reconsideration of his tax assessment was approved.[21] On 30 September, in his capacity as one of the Ten, he delivered an oration to Sigismondo Malatesta at Vada about eighty kilometres from Florence.[22] Manetti's six-month term of office was due to expire on 11 December 1453, and Vespasiano says that he served the full term.[23] His departure from Florence must therefore be placed at the end of 1453 or early in 1454.[24] It seems likely that his political position was deteriorating throughout the second half

---

[15] According to Vespasiano, Manetti wrote *De dignitate* while he was Vicarius Mugellis, August–December 1452 (Greco (1970–6) I: 524; II: 586; George and Waters (1963) 390; Martines (1963) 184). A letter of 15 December 1452 written by Manetti at Florence to Antonio Panormita in Naples indicates that the work is finished, although the king has not yet received the copy (Graziosi (1969) 157–9).

[16] 'rumores . . . per totam fere civitatem nostram . . . hinc inde vulgati sunt . . .' (Graziosi (1969) 156–7). Graziosi's date for this letter must be corrected to 1453 (Cagni in Camporeale (1972) 461).

[17] Greco (1970–6) II: 594–5; George and Waters (1963) 391.

[18] Greco (1970–6) II: 596; George and Waters (1963) 391.

[19] Conti (1984) 349 and n. 65.   [20] De Petris (1983) xi.

[21] 18 August; Conti (1984) 350.

[22] See Vespasiano, ed. Greco (1970–6) I: 528; II: 599–600; George and Waters (1963) 393. The Italian text of this oration is edited by Fanfani (1862) 203–23. A contemporary Catalan translation of the oration is edited by Lawrance (1989) 199–228.

[23] 'Avendo finito questo uficio . . .' Greco (1970–6) I: 529.

[24] This time he obtained a licence to leave Florence from the authorities (Greco (1970–6) II: 600).

of 1453. His tax position had still not been resolved in November 1454, when he again petitioned for a reconsideration of his tax assessment. By the time a reduction in his tax assessment was finally agreed, in February 1455, he had been living in Rome for about a year.[25] A letter written at Rome by Manetti to Panormita, apparently on 27 March 1454, is the earliest confirmation that Manetti had left Florence, although his sons, Bernardo and Agnolo, were in Rome on 23 February 1454.[26]

Uncertainty also surrounds the date of Manetti's move from Rome to Naples. The sequence of events is as follows. Manetti's friend and patron Nicholas V died on 24 March 1455. His successor, Calixtus III, was elected on 8 April.[27] Calixtus promptly confirmed his predecessor's appointment of Manetti as Papal Secretary.[28] Over the following months there are few notices of his whereabouts. Calixtus was a less generous patron of letters than Nicholas had been, and Manetti may have decided to make use of his connections with Naples to find a more congenial place to spend his last days. His son Bernardo had already been granted commercial privileges in Naples by King Alfonso in 1451.[29] Manetti would probably have found a warm welcome at Naples if he had chosen to go there late in 1453 or early in 1454. He may have been hedging his bets by choosing to go to Rome instead, perhaps hoping for a change in the political landscape at Florence. The decision to move to Naples may indicate that by 1455 he had come to despair

---

[25] Manetti's petition of November 1454 was made from Naples. This visit may have been brief: Manetti wrote a letter to Vespasiano from Rome 23 November 1454 (Cagni (1969) 131–3). The petition was granted by a large majority at Florence on 12 December, but the revision was not made until 26 February the following year (Conti (1984) 351).

[26] The letter to Panormita is edited in Graziosi (1969) 159–60. In the unique manuscript, Vatican Library Vat.lat.3372, fol. 100^{r-v}, Graziosi found the month illegible. She notes that it must have been written before the Peace of Lodi, 9 April 1454. At the end of the nineteenth century Pagnotti recorded the date of this letter in this manuscript as 27 March 1454 ((1891) 436). Perhaps he was able to read what Graziosi could not. For the presence of Bernardo and Agnolo in Rome, see Cagni (1971) 299.

[27] Kelly (1986) 244–5.

[28] 'Succedette dopo papa Nicola papa Calisto, et subito lo confermò segretario, e dettegli le bolle gratis.' Greco (1970–6) I: 531.

[29] Cagni (1971) 300 and n. 6. The grant is edited in Fanfani (1862) 159–61. It coincided with the expulsion of Florentine merchants from Naples and Venice (Martinelli (1980) 36). Manetti's exemption from this act can only have inflamed tempers at Florence. Vespasiano violates his chronological framework by writing of this concession after the death of Pope Nicholas (Greco (1970–6) II: 602). Perhaps he preferred to avoid talk of foreign favours while describing his friend's departure from Florence.

of ever being able to return to his native city, for by accepting a post at Alfonso's court he closed the door to any future return to Florentine politics. Whatever his reasons, Manetti was certainly in Naples by 29 September 1455, when he attended a service at the cathedral.[30] A Neapolitan document of 30 October 1455, signed by King Alfonso, appointed Manetti president to the court of the *Sommaria*; it stipulated that its financial provisions for the Florentine were to come into effect on 1 November.[31] Manetti presented it to the authorities in Naples on 26 November 1455, and having sworn the customary oath he was admitted to the *Sommaria*.[32]

With his position at Naples now secure, Manetti returned to Rome some time between 27 November 1455 and 5 January 1456. During this stay he procured a safe-conduct from Calixtus which is dated 'anno . . . millesimo quadringentesimo quinquagesimo quinto, nonis Januarii, pontificatus nostri anno primo'.[33] The date is old style, that is, nine months after Calixtus' election, and five weeks after Manetti had been sworn in at Naples. The terms of this safe-conduct suggest that Manetti's return to Rome was in order to arrange for the transfer of his household – and probably his library – from Rome to his new home in Naples. Manetti seems to have lingered at Rome until at least 17 January 1456, when he penned a letter to Vespasiano.[34] It is unclear when he arrived back in Naples. He was nearly sixty years old at this time, rather old to be making a journey of two hundred kilometres on winter roads. Perhaps he waited for the weather to improve. He was certainly there by 5 December 1456, when he was present during the earthquake that struck the kingdom.[35] Vespasiano records that he paid a brief visit to Florence, apparently his last.[36] In the final weeks of his life he took a trip to the hot baths at Pozzuoli, but the virtues of the waters

---

[30] As appears from Urb.lat.1159, fol. 67^{r-v}. Alfonso was to have taken the crusader's cross at this service. I am preparing an edition of this document, which throws some light on Manetti's role in the negotiations between the Pope and the king.

[31] It is edited by Fanfani (1862) 155–7.

[32] This appears from a note attached to the document, edited by Fanfani (1862) 157.

[33] This document, drawn up by Giovanni Aurispa, is edited by Fanfani (1862) 153–5.

[34] This letter has been printed four times, most recently by Cagni (1969) 133–5.

[35] See Manetti's letter to Vespasiano, 8 December 1456 (Cagni (1969) 135–6). Fanfani (1862) mistakenly attributes a report of the damage done by the earthquake to Manetti (180–3). For the confusion, see Perosa (1960) 157–8.

[36] Greco (1970–6) II: 608–9.

failed him and he died at Naples on 27 October 1459, three days before the death of Poggio Bracciolini at Florence.[37]

The moral works of Aristotle

Students of Manetti are unusually fortunate in that a large part of his extensive library has been preserved intact.[38] Manetti's library seems to have followed him from Florence into exile at Rome in 1453, and then to Naples in 1456. His son Agnolo had it shipped back to Florence not long after his father's death.[39] It seems to have remained in Florence in the possession of the Manetti family until the middle of the sixteenth century, when it was sold to the German banker Ulrich Fugger.[40] As is well known, Fugger's collection was ultimately donated to Pope Gregory XV with the rest of the library of the Palatine Prince Friedrich in 1623, and it has remained the property of the Popes ever since. Consequently, we know that Manetti owned Plutarch's *Lives* in translations by Bruni and Filelfo,[41] and we know that he had copies of most of Bruni's works in his library.[42] Given Bruni's popularity and proximity, this is not in itself remarkable. It is notable, however, that he owned a copy of Bruni's treatise on translation, a relatively rare work.[43]

Vespasiano states that Manetti wrote a treatise on education, and had this work survived we might know more about Manetti's own education.[44] As it is we have few indications. While it is possible to

---

[37] Vespasiano gives the date as 26 October, 'a ore nove di notte' (Greco (1970–6) II: 621). That is, as Cagni points out, in the small hours before dawn on the 27th ((1971) 303). News of his death reached Florence on 3 November and a memorial service was held in Santo Spirito on the 8th (De' Ricci in Galletti (1847) 135).

[38] Many of Manetti's Latin manuscripts are listed by Cagni (1960). Some of his Greek manuscripts are identified in Stevenson sr (1885) 54–5, 57, 86–8, 123–4, 187. Some of his Hebrew manuscripts are detailed by Cassuto (1935) 44–7.

[39] See Cagni (1971) 303.

[40] Sold piecemeal after 1529 according to Leonard (1975) xv. For other discussions of the sale of the Manetti library, see de Petris (1981) xliv n. 4.

[41] Cagni (1960) no. 141 and n. 2. The versions of the lives of Theseus and Romulus attributed to Filelfo in this manuscript are not his. See Giustiniani (1961) 14–15 and n. 1.

[42] Cagni (1960) nos 2, 6–9, 16, 18, 20, 67, 140, 141.

[43] Now Vatican Library Pal.lat.1598, fols 109ʳ–120ᵛ, no. 2644 in Hankins (1997), no. 8 in Cagni (1960). This copy of Bruni's treatise has no significant marginalia. For the rarity of *De interpretatione recta*, see chapter 1, n. 173.

[44] In Vespasiano's life of Manetti this work is called *De liberis educandis ad Colam Gaetanum*; in the *Commentario* it is called *De liberis educandis ad Colam Ghomaritium dum Puteolis erat* (Greco (1970–6) I: 537; II: 625). Manetti's only documented visit to Pozzuoli was made in the last weeks of his life.

follow the development of Bruni's command of Greek throughout a long career and a large number of shorter translations, Manetti as a translator seems to emerge from his last years in Naples fully formed. Vespasiano says that he produced all his translations during his last years in Naples.[45] If this statement is accepted – and I hope to show later that Vespasiano's account is a simplification of a more complex situation – he produced no Latin translations until he was in his fifties. His surviving pronouncements on translation also appear to derive from this period of his full maturity as a translator. Vespasiano concedes that Manetti was a late starter: he began to study Latin when he was twenty-five, that is, about 1422. Apparently his father had not wanted him to pursue such studies.[46] These early studies are not well documented. Vespasiano records that Manetti studied Greek with Ambrogio Traversari and read Xenophon's *Cyropaedia* with him.[47] Vespasiano also states that by the time he was in Naples, that is from 1455 to 1459, Manetti had studied Latin, Greek and Hebrew 'anni ventidua o più'.[48] This would place his Greek and Hebrew studies in the first half of the 1430s. He may well have begun to learn Greek while Filelfo was at Florence. We do know that in 1433 he acquired a Hebrew manuscript.[49] Manetti's first known Latin compositions date from 1436: his *De secularibus et pontificalibus pompis*, dedicated to Agnolo Acciaiuoli, was apparently written soon after Pope Eugenius consecrated the Duomo at Florence in that year;[50] in the spring he addressed the Genoese ambassadors at Florence.[51]

[45] Greco (1970–6) II: 605–6.

[46] Greco (1970–6) I: 487; George and Waters (1963) 373.

[47] 'Chominciò con alcuni docti in greco ch'erano in Firenze, et dipoi si fece leggere a frate Ambrogio degli Agnoli alcune opere in greco, et maxime la Pedia di Ciro' (Greco (1970–6) II: 522). See also Greco (1970–6) I: 452, 487.

[48] Greco (1970–6) II: 605.

[49] On 7 August he received Vatican Library Vat.ebr.8 from Salamone di Bonaventura da Prato (Cassuto (1935) 45).

[50] This work survives in six manuscripts. Five are in the Vatican Library: Pal.lat.1603; Pal.lat.1605; Urb.lat.387; Vat.lat.2919; Barb. VIII, 120 (Pagnotti (1891) 435). Ioannis Deligiannis has told me of a sixth, Paris, BN lat.1616, fols 275ᵛ–281ᵛ. In the manuscript, this work is attributed to Guarino Veronese; in the library catalogue, it is assigned to Lapo da Castiglionchio. Luiso attributes the work to Lapo in his edition (Luiso (1904) 21–37). The consecration took place on 25 March, the first day of the Florentine new year (Hibbert (1975) 72–3).

[51] Perhaps April–May. See Balbi (1974) 6.

In his biography of Manetti, Vespasiano da Bisticci says that he translated one of the so-called *Parva naturalia* of Aristotle: *De memoria et reminiscentia*.[52] I know of no other record of this translation. Curiously, this version is not listed among Manetti's works in Vespasiano's earlier and more detailed *Commentario* on Manetti's life. The statement may simply be another of the book-seller's numerous errors. Vespasiano says, for example, that George of Trebizond translated the *Magna moralia* and the *Eudemian Ethics*. These versions have not been traced and it seems likely that Vespasiano was confusing Georgius Trapezuntius with his contemporary Gregorius Tifernas. The number of works of Aristotle actually translated by Trebizond is large enough to breed such a confusion. Tifernas, as will be seen, produced translations of both these works. In Vespasiano's defence, however, it is worth emphasising that he seems to have known Manetti's work more thoroughly than most of his contemporaries. It is odd that he should attribute the treatise so specifically to Manetti unless he had some information about its existence. It is also unlikely that he confused it with another translation: there is, in fact, no other record of a fifteenth-century version of the treatise. James of Venice translated some of the *Parva naturalia* in the twelfth century; William of Moerbeke revised these versions c.1260–70, and in this form they were widely read.[53] No new version was made until François Vatable's translation was published in 1518.[54] Manetti did own a Greek manuscript of Aristotle which contained the work, although in such a large library this is not in itself remarkable.[55] Throughout his life, Manetti took a keen interest in the medical, physical and

[52] Greco (1970–6) I: 487, 538; George and Waters (1963) 373.

[53] See Minio-Paluello (1952) 265, 284ff.

[54] At Paris by Stephanus. See Rice (1972) 406–10. Ugo Benzi wrote a commentary on *De memoria*, preserved in Vat.lat.11575, fols 12–14^v. It is not noticed in Lockwood's biography of Benzi (1951).

[55] Vatican Library Pal.gr.163, made by Johannes Scutariota. See Stevenson sr (1885) 88. Scutariota had entered Manetti's household by 1442, and he remained until at least 1447 (Cagni (1971) 296). A manuscript from Manetti's library, Pal.lat.1033, includes the medieval Latin versions of the *Parva naturalia*. Most of these treatises have been annotated by someone with a Greek text to hand. An apparently complete copy of the Greek text runs alongside the Latin version of *Physics* I–III, and much of book IV. A number of the treatises – but not *De memoria* – have marginal Latin commentaries. I do not believe that this manuscript misled Vespasiano.

mathematical sciences.[56] It is possible that he translated a brief work at Naples as preparation for his larger project. It is also possible that Vespasiano's account preserves a record of a piece of Manetti's lost *juvenilia*.

If it was ever made, Manetti's version of *De memoria et reminiscentia* may now be unknown simply because no one has thought to look for it. Manetti's other Latin translations of Aristotle are also among the least known of all his works, despite the fact that Aristotle was of central importance to Manetti. According to Vespasiano,

> usava dire avere tre libri a mente per lungo abito, l'uno era l'Epistole di sancto Pagolo, l'altro era Agostino, De civitate Dei, et de'gentili l'Etica d'Aristotele.[57]

> [He would say that he knew three books by heart: the Epistles of St Paul, Augustine's *De civitate Dei*, and from the pagans the *Ethics* of Aristotle.]

He produced versions of three major works: the *Nicomachean Ethics*, the *Eudemian Ethics* and the *Magna moralia*.[58] During the fifteenth century, translation of the *Nicomachean Ethics* seems to have been an exclusively Florentine endeavour. Despite – or perhaps because of – the controversy it aroused, Bruni's *Ethics* translation was widely available. A version was attempted with less success by Matteo di Simone Strozzi.[59] Johannes Argyropoulos made his popular version in Florence in the late 1450s.[60] Manetti's version was substantially complete but unrevised at his death in 1459, and was published posthumously by his son Agnolo about

---

[56] As appears, for example, in *De dignitate et excellentia hominis*, and in his treatise on earthquakes, *De terremotu*. For his interest in geometry, see Greco (1970–6) II: 521–2.

[57] Greco (1970–6) I: 486; George and Waters (1963) 372.

[58] Today these translations survive in five manuscripts: in the Vatican Library, Pal.lat.1021 and Urb.lat.223; in the Biblioteca Nazionale of Naples, Neapol.VIII.613; in the Biblioteca Nazionale Centrale of Florence, Magl.VIII, 1439 (de Petris (1981) xvii n. 37). A fifteenth-century manuscript at the University of North Carolina (Ms 92) contains Manetti's *Magna moralia* and *Eudemian Ethics*, with the anonymous version of *Metaphysics* XIII and XIV (*Iter Italicum*).

[59] See Garin (1957) 424 n. 14.

[60] Dedicated to Cosimo de'Medici, and perhaps made in 1457–60 (Rice (1972) 44). The exordium is edited in Brown (1992) 48–52.

1473.[61] Manetti's work must be situated within this tradition of Florentine Aristotelianism.

Florentine scholars figured prominently in the early tradition of the *Eudemian Ethics*. The Greek text of the work was not known in the West until Aurispa brought a manuscript to Italy in 1423.[62] A copy was available in Florence soon after this date thanks to Niccolò Niccoli, who traded a manuscript with Aurispa for a copy of some recently discovered texts of Cicero. Leonardo Bruni knew the *Eudemian Ethics* in the 1420s, although he did not translate it as has sometimes been claimed.[63] Another copy arrived in Italy in 1427 with Francesco Filelfo.[64] Ambrogio Traversari, Manetti's Greek tutor, did consider making a version in 1437.[65] Perhaps his death two years later forestalled his plans, or perhaps the difficulty of the task dissuaded him: he had previously had difficulties with the philosophical passages and the verse extracts in Diogenes Laertius.[66] Manetti himself owned at least two manuscripts of the *Eudemian Ethics*.[67] It is significant that an important ethical work of Aristotle was available in Greek in Italy for thirty years before it found a translator. This may indicate that many Greek scholars in the first half of the fifteenth century were more comfortable with using Greek texts to help them recast medieval Latin versions than they were with making a new translation of a difficult work.

Manetti had begun lecturing on Aristotle in Florence in the 1430s. According to Vespasiano:

---

[61] The preface to this version is in Garin (1949–50) 93–8. The version was never printed. For the date of the Urbino manuscript, see Cagni (1971) 299.

[62] Baron (1971) 66.

[63] See Garin (1949–50) 67 n. 1 for the origins of the confusion. That he knew the work appears from his *Isagogicon moralis disciplinae*, edited in Baron (1928) 20–41. For the arrival of the *Eudemian Ethics* in Florence, see Baron (1971).

[64] See his letter in Mehus (1759) XXIV: 32. In December 1432, in his prolusion to his lectures on the *Nicomachean Ethics*, Filelfo said 'inter hos [sc. libros de moribus] vero etsi Magna Moralia laudentur et Eudemia summis admodum praeconiis decantentur, Ethica tamen ad Nicomachum tantum utilitatis . . . prae se ferunt . . .' (Müllner (1899) 159).

[65] See Stinger (1977) 77; Mehus (1759) XIII: 9, 8 January 1437. He seems otherwise not to have become involved in Aristotelian scholarship.

[66] His complaints about the task are in Mehus (1759) VII: 2. See above, n. 5.

[67] Pal.gr.323 and Pal.gr.165, both made by Johannes Scutariota.

Lesse l'Etica d'Aristotile, pregato da meser Agnolo Acciaiuoli, da Mateo degli Strozi et da Antonio Barbadori, et molti uomini da bene, et litterati di quella età. Lesse parte della Pulitica a meser Jacopo da Lucca, di poi cardinale di Pavia, et lesse tutta la filosofia naturale et morale a Manuello ebreo.[68]

[At the request of Agnolo Acciaiuoli, Mateo degli Strozzi, Antonio Barbadori and many good and learned contemporaries, he lectured on the *Ethics* of Aristotle. He expounded part of the *Politics* to Jacopo da Lucca, who was afterwards Cardinal of Pavia, and he expounded all the works of natural and moral philosophy to the Jew Manuel.]

In his *Life of Matteo Strozzi*, Vespasiano adds the names of Benedetto Strozzi and Alessandro Arighi to the number of Manetti's audience;[69] in the *Life of Benedetto Strozzi* he adds the names of Palla and Marcello Strozzi.[70] A similar account in Vespasiano's *Commentario* on Manetti's life is followed by the detail that he was thirty-five years old at the time, which allows us to place these lectures in the years 1430–1.[71] It is worth observing that Bishop Alfonso produced his essay against Bruni's version at the very time when Manetti was lecturing on the *Nicomachean Ethics* in Florence.[72] Vespasiano, to illustrate Bruni's 'complessione collerica', describes how the chancellor quarrelled and was reconciled with Manetti in one of the informal, learned debates held in the Piazza at Florence in early 1437.[73] Vespasiano does not go into details, but it is tempting to speculate that Bruni's *Ethics* translation was the subject of at least some of these discussions. It is likely that Manetti's versions embody some of the notes, observations and renderings which he had made for his own use at Florence during these years. From a passing observation in Manetti's funeral oration on Bruni, we may assume that he shared Bruni's view that the medieval translations of Aristotle were inadequate.[74]

Twenty years later at Rome the situation was rather different. Manetti's versions must also be considered in the light of the many

[68] Greco (1970–6) II: 506.   [69] Ibid. 221.   [70] Ibid. 426–7.
[71] Ibid. 525–6. Greco makes this point: II: 285–6 n. 3.
[72] Franceschini puts the date of Alfonso's treatise at about 1430 ((1955) 305 n. 17).
[73] The incident is in Greco (1970–6) II: 522–3; Greco (1970–6) I: 479–81; George and Waters (1963) 367–8. Vespasiano places this quarrel shortly before Manetti's embassy to Genoa, which took place in April–May 1437.
[74] Manetti talks of 'haec Aristotelica vitio priorum interpretum corrupta' (Mehus (1741) ci).

new Aristotelian translations produced at Rome during the pontificate of Nicholas V. In his biography of Nicholas, Manetti surveys
the Aristotelian translations produced under the aegis of the Pope:

Multa Aristotelis, ut Posteriora analytica, ut tota Physica, Problemata, Magna
moralia, Metaphysica, ac plures Rhetoricorum, et XIX illos celebratos De animalibus libros tunc primum conspexerunt; quae quidem et si prius traducta fuissent,
ita tamen traducta reperiebantur, ut vix intelligi possent.[75]

[Then for the first time they set eyes upon many works of Aristotle, such as the
Posterior Analytics, the *Physics* in its entirety, the *Problems*, the *Magna moralia*,
the *Metaphysics*, several books of rhetoric, and the nineteen famous books *On
Animals*. For although they had been translated before, they had been translated
in such a way as to be hardly comprehensible.]

This, and the comments reported by Agnolo in the preface to
Manetti's Aristotelian translations, are the latter's only extant comments on the medieval translators of Aristotle. In the years after
Bruni's controversial translation of the *Ethics*, their inadequacy
seems to have become something of an orthodoxy. In this passage,
Manetti is probably thinking of Giovanni Tortelli's translation of
the *Posterior Analytics*,[76] of Bessarion's *Metaphysics*,[77] and of
George of Trebizond's versions of the *Physics*, *Problems*, *Rhetoric*
and *Libri de animalibus*.[78] Manetti discusses his own works elsewhere in the biography, and there is no indication that he had made
his own versions of Aristotle at the time of writing. The reference
to a new translation of the *Magna moralia* must therefore be to
the version made by Gregorio Tifernas. From Tifernas' dedicatory
letter to the Pope, it is clear that it was dedicated after the Peace
of Lodi, 9 April 1454, and before Nicholas' death on 24 March
1455.[79] The passage thus indicates that Manetti was aware of the

[75] Muratori (1734) 927. It was produced between Nicholas' death (24 March 1455)
and Manetti's relocation to Naples later in the year, discussed above. For the earliest manuscripts of this work, see Modigliani (1999) 63. Greco states that Vespasiano
had access to Manetti's biography when he produced his own Life of Nicholas (Greco
(1970–6) I: 35 n. 1).

[76] Complete by 7 March 1446 to judge from a letter from Valla to Tortelli (Besomi and
Regoliosi (1984) ep. 33). Valla had heard of the version but not seen it himself. Perhaps
Tortelli's close identification with Nicholas' reign led Manetti to mention it here, even
though the translation was complete before Nicholas' election.

[77] Completed in 1455 and dedicated to Alfonso of Naples (Garin (1949–50) 74–5).

[78] For George's versions see Monfasani (1984) 702, 698ff. and 705–9.

[79] Tifernas' versions are in three manuscripts in the Vatican Library: Vat.lat.2096,
Vat.lat.2010 and Vat.lat.2990. For the date, see Delaruelle (1899) 19 n. 3.

existence of this translation of Tifernas, and probably also of his version of the *Eudemian Ethics*, with which it was published.

This conclusion raises another problem. If Manetti knew of Tifernas' versions, his reasons for producing new translations of these works are harder to fathom. If he had not produced his versions before writing his *Life of Nicholas*, they must belong to his last years at Naples. Why did he then begin translations of texts which he must have known that Tifernas had just completed? Agnolo Manetti, in the preface to his edition of his father's translations, insists that the *Eudemian Ethics*, at least, was not available in Latin at the time Giannozzo made his version: 'Ethicorum ad Eudemum ea tempestate nulla apud Latinos latina traductio reperiebatur'[80] [At that time there was no Latin translation of the *Eudemian Ethics*]. And Vespasiano, in his *Life of Manetti*, made much the same claim:

tradusse l'Etica d'Aristotele Ad Nicomachum et un'altera Etica che non fu mai tradutta, ad Eudemium [*sic*], et Magni Morali d'Aristotile.[81]

[he translated the *Nicomachean Ethics* of Aristotle, and another work on ethics, *Ad Eudemium*, which had not been translated before, and Aristotle's *Magna moralia*.]

To save their statements, we might argue that Manetti's words in the *Life of Nicholas* are consistent with the contention that he knew only of Tifernas' version of the *Magna moralia*, and not of his version of the *Eudemian Ethics*; and perhaps that he had never even seen Tifernas' version, learning of its existence through a friend or from a library catalogue. This does seem rather unlikely, but it is notable that Johannes Argyropoulos, lecturing on the ethical works at Florence in February 1457, ignores the *Eudemian Ethics*.[82] In Milan, some time between 1458 and 1464, Constantine Lascaris lamented the fact that there was no Latin translation of the work

---

[80] Agnolo's preface is edited in Garin (1949–50) 93–8.
[81] Greco (1970–6) I: 534; George and Waters (1963) 395.
[82] Friday 4 February 1456, *s.f.* Argyropoulos' prefatory oration is in Müllner (1899) 3–18. He talks only of the *Nicomachean Ethics* and the 'alter liber Moralium', the *Magna moralia* (ibid. 16). The *Eudemian Ethics* was not taught as part of Aristotle's moral philosophy at Florence in Argyropoulos' day. Vespasiano writes in his Life of Donato Acciaiuoli: 'Udita ch'egli ebbe l'Etica da Messer Giovanni [Argiropulo], udì la Politica al medesimo modo, di più udì l'Economia, *che è il resto della filosofia morale*' (My italics. Cited in Cammelli (1941) 100).

available.[83] I am still inclined to believe that Manetti knew of Tifernas' version. Tifernas states in his preface that he translated the *Magna moralia* and the *Eudemian Ethics* at the request of Nicholas V, to whom he now dedicates them.[84] It seems unlikely that Nicholas, who was an old friend of Manetti, who had attended the scholarly debates in Florence in the 1430s, and who knew of Manetti's abiding interest in the moral philosophy of Aristotle, would neglect to tell him of the inception or completion of such a project.

Manetti's reasons for producing new translations of these works probably lie with the king of Naples. According to Agnolo's preface, the sequence of events was as follows: the translations were originally made at the request – *iussu* – of Alfonso of Aragon while Manetti was in Naples. When Alfonso died before they were completed in 1458, Manetti decided instead to dedicate them to Pius II. However the translator himself died before he could do so in 1459, and with the death of Pius II in 1464 the translations remained unpublished. Eventually Vespasiano stepped in and persuaded Agnolo to publish his father's work. This account identifies Alfonso as the instigator of the translations. The king's request would very likely have been one with which Manetti was happy to comply. I have already suggested that Manetti had extensive notes on the ethical works from his lectures in Florence. Perhaps he needed little encouragement to piece them together in his leisure at Naples. Earlier in his career, Manetti had enthusiastically encouraged the king's interest in moral philosophy. In the preface to the lives of Socrates and Seneca, which he rededicated to Alfonso in 1450, he writes that he would have sent him his *Life of Seneca* before, but he had not thought it worthy of the king. He goes on:

Sed cum ex litteris Franci, prestantissimi oratoris nostri, hactenus T. Livii historiis annalibusque perlectis et omnibus bellis adversus Christianos principes ac populos non immerito pretermissis, te solum ad optima Philosophie Moralis studia

[83] Lascaris made Madrid 4627 of the *Eudemian Ethics* some time after his arrival in Milan in 1458. It was seen there on 6 December 1464. See Fernández Pomar (1966) 228, 231–2. It has the colophon: 'Κωνσταντῖνος ὁ Λάσκαρις ἐκγράψας ἐν Μεδιόλανῳἐχρῆτο πάνυ δυσεύρετον τυγχάνει γε ὄν διὸ οὐ μετηνέχθη εἰς τὴν Ῥωμαίων φωνὴν ὥσπερ τὰ Νικομάχια ἠθικά'.
[84] Delaruelle (1899) 19 n. 2.

animum convertisse nuper intellexerim . . . eam transmissionem denegare atque ulterius differre non potui.[85]

[But when recently from the letters of Francus, one of our most eminent ambassadors, I understood that, having previously read Livy thoroughly, and having properly disregarded all the wars against Christian princes and nations, you had now turned your mind exclusively to the best studies of Moral Philosophy . . . I could no longer refuse or delay sending it.]

This is the first of five references to the *Philosophia moralis* in the preface, where it is presented as the complement to a prince's warlike activities against the infidel:

hoc presens et laudabile regie ac profecto regalis mentis de optimis Philosophie Moralis studiis et expugnandis barbaris gentibus propositum.[86]

[this current and praiseworthy resolution of a kingly and truly royal mind regarding the best studies of Moral Philosophy and conquering barbarian nations.]

And as the culmination of a course in political literature:

Si igitur cum oratoribus et historicis Philosophie Moralis studia coniunxeris . . . non modo ceteros nostri temporis principes longe superasse, sed antiquos etiam et celebratos reges adequasse videberis.[87]

[So if you add the study of Moral Philosophy to your knowledge of the orators and historians . . . you will appear not only to have far surpassed the other rulers of our age, but even to have equalled the famous kings of old.]

Manetti was happy to remind the Aragonese king that Seneca the moral philosopher was also a Spaniard. The death of Alfonso, who had cultivated an image as a philosopher-king, removed its most obvious patron. Manetti's death a year later cut short any search he may have begun for another recipient. Consequently, his Aristotelian versions remained unpublished until Vespasiano and Agnolo took them in hand fourteen years later. Although Manetti's translations of Aristotle are of little relevance to the evolution of Aristotelian scholarship, they are of interest when viewed as indicators of intellectual interests at the court of Naples.

---

[85] De Petris (1979) 113. This *Francus* is probably Francho Sacchetti. Antonio Beccadelli records that Sacchetti, Florentine ambassador to Naples, was present while Seneca's letters were read in the king's presence (*De dictis et factis Alfonsi regis*, ed. Duran (1990) 114).

[86] De Petris (1979) 114.   [87] Ibid. 116.

If the translations of the *Eudemian Ethics* and the *Magna moralia* grew out of King Alfonso's interests, it is clear that Manetti's version of the *Nicomachean Ethics* originally began as a reaction to Bruni's version.[88] A degree of competition between Bruni and Manetti may be seen in their other works. Bruni produced his vernacular lives of Dante and Petrarch in May 1436; Manetti completed his Latin biographies of these two writers only four years later in 1440 and went further by including Boccaccio amongst his biographies of illustrious vernacular authors.[89] In his preface to the duke of Urbino, Agnolo records his father's justification for new translations of Aristotle's moral works:

At dicet fortasse quispiam: quid opus erat novo labore, quum constet Magna moralia iam pridem traducta fuisse, Ethicorum vero ad Nicomachum non una sed plures etiam traductiones circumferrentur? Hoc ego minime inficior. Sed memoratarum interpretationum partim ruditas atque asperitas, partim vero nimia licentia, ut a patre meo saepe accepi, ad novum onus subeundum ipsum impulere.[90]

[But someone will perhaps say, 'Why was a new version needed, since the *Magna moralia*, as we know, had been translated for some time now, and the *Nicomachean Ethics* was available not in one, but in a number of translations?' I do not deny it. But, as I often heard my father say, the clumsiness and awkwardness of some versions, and the excessive freedom of others, moved him to this new undertaking.]

Clearly, *plures traductiones* refers to the medieval versions, to Bruni's popular translation, and perhaps to Argyropulos' version. Manetti's versions aimed to put the Greek text into good classical Latin without taking liberties with its strict meaning.

To illustrate Manetti's middle way between Grosseteste's *asperitas* and the *nimia licentia* of Bruni's translation, their different renderings of the same passage from the *Ethics* are reproduced in Table 2.1.[91] Bruni cites this passage in his *De interpretatione recta*, in his own translation, as an example of Aristotelian eloquence: it is thus a rendering he himself offered up for discussion. It also illustrates a number of characteristic differences between

---

[88] Manetti made an index to his manuscript of Bruni's *Ethics* translation, Pal.lat.1013 (*Iter Italicum*).

[89] The date is from Cagni (1969) 132 n. 2.   [90] Garin (1949–50) 97.

[91] *Nic. eth.* II: iv, 3. Grosseteste's translation is from Gauthier (1973) 400–1, Manetti's from Pal.lat.1021, fol. 137ᵛ, Bruni's from Aristotle (1510). I have numbered the clauses for ease of reference.

Table 2.1 *Nicomachean Ethics, book II, chapter 4*

Grosseteste	Manetti	Bruni
1. Adhuc autem neque simile est in artibus et in virtutibus.	1. Insuper nequaquam simile est in artibus ac uirtutibus.	1. Preterea nequaquam simile est in artibus et uirtutibus.
2. Que enim ab artibus fiunt, bene habent in eis; sufficit igitur hec qualiter habencia fieri;	2. Nam que ab artibus procedunt laudem in se habent. Sufficit enim eis ut bene se habeant.	2. Nam que ab arte procedunt laudem in se habeant, quare sufficit illa sic existere.
3. que autem secundum virtutes fiunt, neque si hec qualiter habeant, iuste vel temperate operata sunt,	3. Sed que a uirtutibus proficiscuntur[1] non satis est si ipsa quoddamodo se habeant, et iuste uel temperate agantur,	3. Sed que a uirtute proficiscuntur non satis est si ipsa iuste quodammodo se habeant, et modeste agantur,
4. set et si operans qualiter habens operetur; primum quidem si sciens, deinde si eligens, et eligens propter hec, tercium autem et si firme et inmobiliter habeat et operetur.	4. sed si agens quodammodo se habens agat. Primum igitur si sciens, deinde si eligens et eligens propter ipsa, tertio si firmiter ac sine mutatione se habens agat.	4. sed si agens ita egerit primo si sciens, secundo si eligens et eligens propter ipsa, tertio si certo et immobili iudicio agat.
5. Hec autem ad alias quidem artes habere non connumerant, preter ipsum scire.	5. Sed hec ad ceteras artes habendas non connumerantur preterquam scientia ipsa.	5. Ad ceteras uero artes habendas nichil horum requiritur preterquam scientia.
6. Ad virtutes autem scire quidem parum aut nichil potest,	6. At ad uirtutes acquirendas ipsum scire nihil aut parum ualet.	6. At in uirtutibus scire ipsum parum est aut nichil.
7. alia autem est non parum, set omnia possunt que ex multociens operari iusta et temperata adveniunt.	7. Alia uero non parum immo totum possunt que ex crebris operationibus iusta et temperata fiunt.	7. Vti uero atque exercere plurimum immo totum ualet, utpote que ex frequenti actione iustorum modestorumque proueniant.[2]

[1] *profici feruntur.* Pal.lat.1021.
[2] *proveniat.* Paris, 1510.

the translators. From a collation of these renderings in Table 2.1, a number of observations can be made. Bruni renders the Greek plural with the Latin singular in column 3, no. 2 (*arte*) and in no. 3 (*virtute*). The two clauses are parallel and so, having chosen to use the singular in the first, he must render it with a singular in the second. Still, it is unnecessary and Bruni may have adopted it so as not to repeat the plurals he uses in column 3, nos. 1 and 5–6. In the same passage both writers adopt *laus* for τὸ εὖ, a coincidence which seems to be a result of the influence of Bruni's version on Manetti. Next, in column 3, no. 4, Bruni's rendering of the third condition of virtuous action – 'si certo et immobili iudicio agat' – is succinct and clear, but it suggests that the action should spring from a determination to be virtuous rather than from a virtuous disposition. Manetti, perhaps unsure of Aristotle's precise meaning, translates more literally. His version at this point is certainly more likely to cause his readers to turn to a commentary than his predecessor's, something he probably considered very proper. Bruni's translation of no. 6 says less than Manetti's, who picks up the Greek article with *acquirendas*, perhaps because he does not want to repeat his earlier *habendas*. Finally, in no. 7 Manetti's *alia* correctly refers the reader back to Aristotle's second and third requirements. Bruni seems to have missed this, and replaces it with an opposition between knowing and doing. Bruni's version attempts to resolve some of the difficulties for the reader, and though such resolutions are not always successful, it does make for a more readable text. It seems unlikely that Manetti shared Bruni's conception of Aristotle's eloquence. His version is more difficult than Bruni's, but less misleading. He seems to have believed that the difficulties of his Latin version accurately reflect the difficulties of Aristotle's Greek.

The New Testament

In 1419, the same year that Bruni dedicated his *Ethics* translation to Pope Martin V, Ambrogio Traversari dedicated his new version of John Climacus' *Scala paradisi* to his prior, Matteo Guidone.[92]

---

[92] Stinger (1977) 15–16. This work of John, a seventh-century hermit and theologian, is in *PG* 89.

This is a significant but relatively unremarked event in the history of translation. A Latin version of the *Scala* had been made about a century earlier by Angelo Clareno da Cingoli.[93] This translation was highly regarded because Angelo was said to have learnt Greek through the inspiration of the Holy Spirit while he was celebrating the office of the Nativity.[94] The story illustrates the reverence which knowledge of Greek could inspire in the fourteenth century. In the preface to his new version, Traversari criticised Angelo's translation. He anticipated that he would meet criticism for remaking a version which was believed to have been the product of such inspiration:

Sanctissimum illum fuisse virum si adseverant, facile ac perlubenter consentiam. Non tamen quia sanctum fuerit, eruditum etiam fuisse sequitur atque idoneum ad transferendum. Aliud enim sanctitas est, atque aliud eruditio.[95]

[If they say that he was a very holy man, I would easily and very willingly agree. But it does not follow that because he was holy he was also learned and a good translator. For holiness is one thing, and learning another.]

Here, Traversari's words are intended to recall Jerome's often-quoted comment from his preface to the Pentateuch: 'aliud est enim vatem, aliud esse interpretem'[96] [it is one thing to be a prophet, another to be a translator]. Traversari's attempt to align himself with Jerome in defence of this minor retranslation prefigures the defensive positions taken up by his pupil Manetti and later by Erasmus, when they came to make new Latin translations of Scriptural texts. Like Bruni, Traversari found that he faced opposition not for translating, but for retranslating.

Manetti's impeccable moral credentials, as much as his scholarly abilities, fitted him for the task of translating the Bible. From the beginning of his career, Manetti seems to have been an unusually

---

93 About 1300–5 (Stinger (1977) 110).

94 This story can be traced back to the preface of the Italian version of Clareno's Latin translation: 'Et cantandosi l'ufficio et dicendosi le lectioni de' frati greci, subitamente sentendosi frate Agnolo infondere nell'animo per divino miracolo la notitia del [*sic*] lingua greca, andò al padre suo frate Liberato et dimandòli licentia di dire una lettione in quella lingua et dicendo *benedicite* . . . Et così lesse qualla lettione come se fusse nato et sempre nutricato in quella lingua greca, et da indi inançi seppe liberamente parlare in greco' (Oliger (1912) xxxv).

95 Stinger (1977) 111 and n. 84. Mehus (1759) XXIII: 7.

96 *Praefatio in Pentateuchum. PL* XXVIII: 182.

serious man. In 1430 he was responsible for the conversion of his Hebrew tutor, baptised as Giovanfrancesco Manetti;[97] as we have seen, one of his first recorded public speeches is in honour of Pope Eugenius' consecration of the cathedral at Florence in 1436; his first substantial published work was the *Dialogus consolatorius*, made at Easter time as a response to the death of his four-year-old son, Antonino.[98] He dealt with matters of theology and natural science with equal confidence. In 1439, in the preface to his *De illustribus longevis*, he discussed the reasons for mankind's shortening lifespan.[99] Vespasiano approached his friend for advice on a theological matter: in 1450 Manetti explained to him the fate of infants who die unbaptised.[100] His speech to King Alfonso at Naples early in 1451 has the air of a sermon.[101] Antonio Panormita, in a letter to Manetti, praises him for his *sanctitas*, a compliment which goes beyond the usual range of rhetorical flattery.[102] Vespasiano even makes him something of a prophet. When Manetti is called upon to arbitrate in a dispute, his condemnation of the guilty party is of Biblical proportions:

io ho examinato la vita tua et i tua portamenti, et il simile i tua figliuoli, di natura ch'io ti voglio profetezare quello che t'interverrà. Io ho voltate molte carte della Scrittura Sancta a'mia dí, tieni questo per certo, che tu hai a essere punito, tu e la tua famiglia, d'una punitione che sarà di natura, ch'ello sarà exemplo a tutta questa città, et abi pura de' giudicii di Dio, et non passerà molto tempo.[103]

[I have taken account of you, and also of your sons, as to your lives and way of living, and I wish to prophesy what will happen to you. I have read much of the Holy Scriptures in my time: you may be certain that you and your family as well will be punished in such a way so as to give an example to the city before long. Beware of God's judgement.]

[97] Cagni (1971) 294.
[98] Antonino was born on 18 January 1434; he died early in April 1438 (de Petris (1983) xii–xiii).
[99] This substantial work, dedicated to Lodovico de Guzman, has not been edited. For extant manuscripts, see Pagnotti (1891) 435. I consulted Pal.lat.1605, fols 37^r–39^r, and Urb.lat.387, fols 41^r–42^v.
[100] Written from Vacciano on 8 October 1450. It is edited in Cagni (1969) 128–9 and Fanfani (1862) 165–7.
[101] Edited by Sandeo (1611b).
[102] This letter is edited in Graziosi (1969) 157 n. 1 and Leonard (1975) xi. It is probably to be dated between 15 December 1452 and 25 March 1453.
[103] Greco (1970–6) I: 488–9; George and Waters (1963) 374.

Again, Vespasiano records how, on his way into exile, Manetti fore-told the downfall of an over-optimistic relative.[104] King Alfonso, in Vespasiano's account, also called him a prophet, this time for anticipating the perfidy of the Venetians.[105] While this was not a very remarkable suspicion for a diplomat of Manetti's experience, nor perhaps a very great surprise to the shrewd Alfonso, it does show how respect for Manetti's insight into secular affairs tended to coalesce with admiration for his theological learning. Certainly, Manetti's position as a lay theologian was an unusual one in the 1450s. He seems never to have sought or considered a clerical position: his independent wealth removed the financial motive for a career in the Church, while it allowed him the leisure to pur-sue his studies.[106] He combined the roles of active politician and profound Biblical scholar. This combination seems to have led his contemporaries to grant him a great deal of moral authority.

Manetti's New Testament translation, the first Latin version made from the Greek since Jerome's day, seems to have been even less well known to his contemporaries than his versions of Aristotle. Today only two manuscripts survive: the copy which Agnolo brought back from Naples after his father's death, which remained in the private library of the Manettis until 1529, and a beautifully produced descendant of this manuscript which entered the library of the dukes of Urbino, probably in the 1470s.[107] We do not know what Manetti's plans for the version were, nor when it was completed. We do, however, have some indication as to when it was begun. In a passage in his *Life of Nicholas V*, Manetti writes that he undertook 'duo nova ac magna coepta' [two ambitious new projects] at Rome during the life of this pontiff: his enormous trea-tise *Adversus Judaeos et gentes* planned in twenty books, and a new translation of the Bible. Unfortunately, Nicholas died before either could be brought to completion:

---

[104] Greco (1970–6) I: 529; George and Waters (1963) 393.

[105] Greco (1970–6) I: 517; George and Waters (1963) 386. The theme of Manetti's *profezia* is even more pronounced in Vespasiano's *Commentario*. Cf. Cornelius Nepos' comment that Cicero's *prudentia* was such that it was almost *divinatio* (*Atticus*, XVI: 4). For *prophetia naturalis*, see Aquinas, *Summa theologiae*, q.171, art.1.

[106] For the wealth of the Manetti family in the fifteenth century, see Martines (1963) 131–8.

[107] For Vatican Library Pal.lat.45, see Stevenson jr (1886) 8. For Vatican Library Urb.lat.6, see Stornaiolo (1902–21) I: 9–11.

nisi importuna ac maligna . . . ejus mors praevenisset, praeveniensque assiduum operationis nostrae cursum non modo non impedisset retardassetque, sed omnino etiam abstulisset, forsitan divina ope adjuti . . . utrumque opus omnibus animi et corporis viribus, quemadmodum institueramus, prosequuti, non multo post ad finem usque produxissemus.[108]

[Had his cruel and unkind death . . . not intervened (and his death not only hindered and delayed the untiring progress of our labour, but stopped it altogether), then perhaps, with God's help . . . and pursuing each task which we had undertaken with all our strength of mind and body, we would have brought it to a conclusion not long afterwards.]

There is an immediate difficulty with this statement. As noted above, Manetti was living in exile at Rome between 1453 and 1455. He had, however, already mentioned his treatise *Adversus Judaeos* to Nicholas in a letter of 4 May 1448, and there he spoke of it as a thing 'que iam pridem facere institueram'[109] [which I chose some time ago to write]. Nevertheless, this remains the earliest reference to his attempts to translate the Scriptures, and the passage suggests that he was quite far advanced in both works by the time Nicholas died. These words were written in the early months of the reign of Calixtus III, and they suggest that Manetti saw no prospect of support for these projects under that Pope.[110] He goes on:

si hic importunus dicendi locus non videretur, nimirum caussas quibus et ad traducendum et ad scribendum impellebamur paulisper commemorassemus. Quod in praefationibus praedictorum operum, si Deus (ut speramus) adjutor noster erit, absque iusta reprehensione non injuria efficere posse videbimur.[111]

[if this were not an inappropriate occasion to do so, I would certainly have briefly recounted the reasons which drove me to translating and to writing. And if God help me, as I hope, I shall do so fairly and without any just censure in the prefaces of these works.]

This passage suggests that these projects had subsequently drawn some criticism, perhaps while Manetti was engaged on them in Rome, and that he had begun to gather material for a written response to his critics. The New Testament translation never

---

[108] Muratori (1734) 927.

[109] Edited in Wittschier (1968) 44–5; Graziosi (1969) 153–4. Graziosi uses Forlì, Piancastelli 1372, fol. 130ʳ. This manuscript, apparently the only extant copy, dates the letter to 1440, but it must have been written in 1448. See Wittschier (1968) 45 n. 7; de Petris (1976) 193 n. 4; and Cagni (1971) 295 n. 7.

[110] For the date of this biography, see above, n. 75.   [111] Muratori (1734) 928.

received its preface. The dedicatory letter to the Psalter translation is not an apologetic work.[112] Some of this material in defence
of new translations of Scripture ultimately appeared in Manetti's
treatise *Apologeticus*, which is considered below. In *Apologeticus*
itself he briefly surveys the history of the Old Testament and its
translations, and promises

cum plus otii dabitur, si Deus adiutor noster erit, multo latius et uberius dissere-
mus.[113]

[when there is more time, if God help me, I shall discuss the matter in greater
depth and detail.]

This work too was never written. Manetti was certainly well aware
that translating the Scriptures was a controversial undertaking.

Although the evidence is often difficult to interpret, an attempt
should be made to establish the nature of the relationship between
Manetti and the New Testament scholarship of Lorenzo Valla.
First, it is as well to consider Manetti's possible acquaintance with
Valla's work on the New Testament before he came to Rome in
1453. Valla had probably begun his notes on the New Testament in
Lent 1442 while a member of Alfonso's court, only weeks before
Alfonso took Naples.[114] Shortly afterwards, in the early months of
1443, Manetti was sent as a Florentine envoy to Naples to witness
the king's triumphal entry into the city. A draft of the work was
certainly available by the end of 1443.[115] At the time, Valla was
probably most widely known for his treatise on the Donation of
Constantine, and may not have been sought out by a sober scholar
like Manetti.[116] Manetti was in Naples again in May 1445 for the
wedding of Alfonso's son, and for another opportunity to talk with
Valla. Vespasiano mentions parties at Manetti's house in Naples to
which learned men were invited.[117] Valla, however, had just stood
trial for heresy, and was not the most appropriate person to talk

[112] The preface to Manetti's Psalter is edited in the Appendix.
[113] De Petris (1981) 13.
[114] Perosa (1970) xlvii. Naples fell on 2 June 1442 (Bentley (1987) 13).
[115] See Valla's letter to Aurispa, 31 December 1443, in Sabbadini (1931).
[116] *De falso credita et ementita Constantini donatione*, c.1440 (Wesseling (1978) 13–14).
[117] 'In queste noze ebbe messer Giannozo grandissimo onore, perché sempre aveva la casa
piena d'uomini docti, dove o si ragionava di cose singulari o egli si conferiva, o egli si
disputava . . .' (Greco (1970–6) II: 545).

to about Biblical scholarship.[118] By late 1446 Valla had lost his only manuscript of the annotations on the New Testament, which he had lent to someone in Rome. He complains of this in a letter to Giovanni Tortelli of 1 January 1447.[119] From this letter a number of things are clear. First, the fact that he had only one manuscript of the annotations four years after their inception suggests that it was very much a work in progress, a manuscript subject to alterations and expansions over the years. Second, it tells us that Valla's lost draft was probably somewhere in Rome at this time, and potentially available for inspection. Third, the letter shows that Valla, at least before this misfortune, had been willing to lend his work to interested parties. Finally, it indicates that Valla did not believe that there was a manuscript of the annotations available in Naples at that time. In fact, Perosa believes that the two surviving copies of an earlier version of the annotations were made in the 1470s from a lost exemplar held in Naples by Antonello Petrucci.[120] Petrucci's interest in Biblical scholarship is attested by his collection of the Scriptures in Greek. All these books were in Naples during Manetti's visits.

These connections probably had little effect on Manetti's translation. I believe that he had no thoughts of making his own translation until after his move to Rome in 1453. However, Valla left Naples and moved to Rome some time after March 1447,[121] and thereafter the intellectual atmosphere of the city was also influenced by his presence. Valla's arrival in Rome coincides with one of Manetti's visits: he was one of the Florentine ambassadors sent to congratulate his old friend, Tommaso Parentucelli, on his election to the papacy in March 1447, returning to Florence towards the end of May 1447.[122] If Valla did not recover his annotations or work them up again from older notes he must have begun them again from scratch, a task he would have undertaken in Rome. A letter from

[118] Valla's trial was in spring–summer 1444. The intervention of the king removed the threat. See Wesseling (1978) 13–14.

[119] Besomi and Regoliosi (1984) 305–6. At the same time he lost the unique manuscript of his *Adnotationes in errores Antonii Raudensis*, and the latest revision of his *Elegantiae*.

[120] The two surviving manuscripts of the earlier annotations were produced in Naples in 1477 and 1478, probably from an exemplar or exemplars held in the royal library there (Perosa (1970) li–lii).

[121] Bentley (1987) 120–1.

[122] 23 March–25 May 1447. The dates are Cagni's, cited in Camporeale (1972) 460.

Theodore Gaza to Giovanni Tortelli in 1449 shows that at this time Valla was actively seeking the advice of competent Greek scholars in Rome, such as Rinuccio Aretino and Theodore Gaza, for his annotations.[123] It seems likely that if Manetti did see or use Valla's work for his own translation it was that version which he produced in Rome. Nicholas V, to whom a version of the work was dedicated, had a copy in 1449. This copy passed to Nicholas of Cusa in 1450 and on again to Marcello Capodiferro, who had it in April 1453.[124] It may even have been Valla's work which inspired the Pope to ask Manetti to retranslate the New Testament. Valla himself was unlikely to be given the commission for such a delicate task. Not only was he deeply involved in the difficulties of his Thucydides translation at this time, but he had an unfortunate reputation as a religious controversialist.[125] If Nicholas did ask Manetti to translate the New Testament in 1449, he did not show him the copy of Valla's work which he had to hand: Manetti was not in Rome in 1449, and by the time he visited it seems that Nicholas no longer had a copy. We should note that the text of the annotations seen by Nicholas was not that edited by Perosa, nor in all likelihood the late draft edited for publication by Erasmus in 1505, but some intermediate form.[126]

The relationship between Manetti and Valla is all the more intriguing because of the role the former was made to play in another Roman controversy. Valla's annotations on the New Testament are often studied to establish their influence on Erasmus' New Testament scholarship. Their place within the debate on the uses

---

[123] See Geanakoplos (1989) 86. Gaza decided to move from Ferrara to Rome in the autumn of 1449. In November he wrote to Tortelli from Grottaferrata, unwilling to enter Rome because of the plague there (Bianca (1999) 739). Rinuccio Aretino had been Poggio Bracciolini's Greek tutor in the thirties. In October 1448 Valla had looked in vain for help with his Thucydides translation: 'Dominus Nicenus [i.e. Bessarion] abest, Rinucium experiri non audeo, forsitan aut non satisfacturum mihi aut cum difficu[ltati]bus sententiarum non colluctaturum; Trapezuntium et morosum et mihi nescio quam equum consulere nolo' (Besomi and Regoliosi (1984) ep. 44).

[124] See Perosa (1970) xlix. Nicholas of Cusa was at Rome from 11 January to 31 December 1450 (ibid. xliv).

[125] In a letter of 28 October 1448, Valla writes that he has translated the first book and part of the second of Thucydides (Besomi and Regoliosi (1984) ep. 44).

[126] Perosa (1970) lii. Despite the refounding of the annotations in 1447, it is misleading to talk, as is sometimes done, of the first and second drafts of Valla's work. The annotations seem to have been expanded and revised up to Valla's death. For a survival of an intermediate stage in their development, see Fubini (1986) 179–96.

of Latin in the middle years of the fifteenth century is less often considered.[127] This debate was at its most heated at Rome, amongst the translators gathered around Pope Nicholas V. One of its most obvious manifestations is the exchange of invectives between Poggio Bracciolini and Valla in the early years of the 1450s. In these invectives, both writers attempt to claim Manetti's support for their own positions. This seems to have been done without his consent, but it can hardly have been done without his knowledge. Poggio had produced the first of his *Orationes in Laurentium Vallam* in February 1452, just a few weeks before Manetti arrived in the city for the coronation of the Emperor Frederick.[128] In this invective, Poggio writes that he has recently read Valla's *Elegantiae*.[129] He sees Valla's rejection of parts of the Vulgate translation in the context of his presumptuous rejection of many Latin usages of the ancients. He goes on to attack Valla's corrections of the Vulgate translation which he found in the *Elegantiae*.[130] Poggio has heard of Valla's annotations on the New Testament which slander the ancient translator. It is obvious, however, that he has not read them.

Valla's response, the *Antidotum primum*, was published in July 1452.[131] At the beginning of his first book, Valla puts a speech advising Poggio against attacking Valla into Manetti's mouth. In this speech, Manetti implores Poggio to hold off 'pro nostra amicicia'.[132] Valla himself then goes on to take up Poggio's complaints individually.[133] Poggio's second invective against Valla was

---

[127] Perosa's preface to his edition of the earliest extant draft of the annotations attempts primarily to establish the dating of their production. The conclusions of Morisi (1964) should be treated with caution. Bentley (1983) does not consider the Roman context of Valla's work.

[128] Manetti, as part of the Florentine delegation, joined Frederick's party on 6 February (Cagni in Camporeale (1972) 460). Frederick was crowned in Rome on 15 March (Graziosi (1969) 158 n. 3). Frederick left for Naples on 23 March (Ruysschaert (1971) 234). Manetti left Rome for Florence on 5 May (Cagni in Camporeale (1972) 460).

[129] 'Legi nuper ridendi causa, illius vacuas [*sic*] omni elegantia libros' (Fubini (1964–9) I: 194).

[130] He attacks the following places in the *Elegantiae*: I: 25 (Mt. v: 17); II: 11 (Lk XIX: 4); II: 26 (Lk X: 6; Lk XIII: 9); III: 19 (Jn XIV: 24). The other *loci* are from the Old Testament (Fubini (1964–9) I: 199).

[131] Perosa (1970) xlii.   [132] *Sic.* Wesseling (1978) 88. Book I: 24.

[133] For the speech given to Manetti, see Wesseling (1978) 86–8; for Valla's replies to each of Poggio's criticisms about Scripture versions, see ibid. 112–18.

published shortly afterwards. Here, Poggio is at pains to flatter
Manetti. He talks of him as a man *clarissimus, doctissimus, ornatis-
simus, prudentissimus*; as a man of *dignitas, autoritas, humanitas,
prudentia, sapientia*; he is *gravis, probus, maturus, veridicus*.[134]
In his *Antidotum primum*, Valla had written the speech which, he
says, Manetti would have used against Poggio, if Poggio had only
consulted him. In his reply, Poggio wrote the speech which, he
says, Manetti will give in response to Valla's claims. It is clear that
Valla's attempt to appropriate Manetti had hit a nerve. Although
Poggio's sympathies and interests lay with the Medicean faction in
Florence, Manetti was still a man of great influence and of unblem-
ished reputation. Manetti's political position was increasingly vulnerable from 1450, culminating in his arrest in March 1453. Valla
may have used Manetti as a mouthpiece simply because he was
a fellow-countryman of Poggio, because there was some political
tension between the two Florentines, and because he was sympa-
thetic to Valla's philological principles. The possible significance
of Manetti's Venetian sympathies for the Poggio–Valla exchange
has been explored by Martinelli.[135] But if Manetti was known to
be engaged in a translation of the New Testament at the Pope's
request, then Valla's use of Manetti would have had an additional
point. It seems to have been a tactic which Poggio particularly
resented.

This debate was still very much alive in February 1453, when
Manetti was appointed ambassador to the Pope, but by this time
he was no doubt far too busy with his own problems in Florence
to worry about the quarrel. The death of the Florentine Chancellor, Carlo Marsuppini, on 24 April 1453 took some of the heat
out of the situation.[136] Poggio gave up his position in the Curia
and returned to Florence to become Chancellor.[137] Late in 1453
or early in 1454, Manetti moved permanently to Rome: a contemporary letter of Poggio's to Pietro da Noceto refers to his arrival.
It speaks of him with great respect, but little intimacy. Manetti now

[134] Fubini (1964–9) I: 215–16.
[135] Martinelli (1980) 37–8.   [136] The date is from Zippel (1979) 210.
[137] He was nominated for the post on 27 April and took up his new position on 2 June
(Wesseling (1978) 37).

worked with Valla at the papal court until he moved to Naples in 1455–6.[138] We may guess that Poggio remained in contact with Manetti: when Bartolomeo Facio wrote to Poggio in April 1455 he asked him to pass on his regards to Manetti.[139] If it is true, as Bentley argues, that Valla became more conservative in the later versions of the annotations as a result of Poggio's criticism, then Manetti's translation, a product of the same intellectual atmosphere, was very likely to have been similarly affected.[140]

Throughout his confrontation with Poggio, Valla insists that he has not published his annotations on the New Testament. The controversy aroused by the few references to the Vulgate in his *Elegantiae* probably played a large part in this decision. In his first invective, Poggio writes:

Opusculum praeterea aedidit, in quo virum sanctissimum doctissimumque reprehendit multis in locis sacrae scripturae, tanquam ab eo male interpretatis.[141]

[What's more, he has published a short work in which he criticises that most holy and learned man Jerome as if he had mistranslated many parts of Holy Scripture.]

---

[138] The letter to Pietro is in Harth (1984–7) III: 167. It is undated. A reference to Manetti's office of Apostolic Secretary allows us to exclude his visit to Rome in July–August 1451, when he received that title. He visited Rome in February–May 1452 and again in February–March 1453 as Florentine ambassador. I believe that Poggio would have mentioned this honour, if Manetti had held it at the time. The letter is written from Florence. Poggio was certainly in Florence not long after 27 April 1453, when he was nominated Chancellor. This suggests that the letter refers to Manetti's exile to Rome late in 1453 or early in 1454. Poggio retained the title of Apostolic Secretary during his Chancellorship, and so this late date is not inconsistent with his calling the secretariat 'dignitas nostra' in this letter. Pietro drew up Manetti's *lettere di credenza* when Nicholas V made him papal ambassador during his difficulties in 1452 (Greco (1970–6) II: 595). As for the careers of Valla and Manetti at Rome, Valla was made *Scriptor litterarum apostolicarum* by Nicholas V on 10 November 1448; he was made *secretarius* by Calixtus III on 7 July 1455 (Perosa (1970) xxv–xxvi). Manetti had been *secretarius* since 28 July 1451 (Camporeale (1972) 375). Calixtus confirmed Manetti's appointment shortly after his accession (Greco (1970–6) I: 531). Manetti, like Poggio, retained the title of Apostolic Secretary after he left Rome. In 1458, after Alfonso's death, Pius II tried to persuade Manetti to return to Rome. Pius' letter offers him not the title – it addresses him as *secretarius noster* – but the financial settlement appropriate to the appointment: [nos, Papa Pius] 'volentes ut omnibus et singulis honoribus, oneribus, privilegiis, exemptionibus, emolumentis et participationibus, quibus ceteri secretarii nostri utuntur et gaudent . . . tu quoque plene gaudeas et uteris [*sic*]' (Fanfani (1862) 153). This detail is worth stressing because it shows that Poggio's use of his papal title while Chancellor of Florence was not necessarily a piece of vanity.

[139] Harth (1984–7) III: 335.　　[140] Bentley (1983) 48.　　[141] Fubini (1964–9) I: 200.

In his *Antidotum primum* Valla corrects him:

Aut 'edidit' accipis pro 'condidit', quod barbarum est, aut plane mentiris, cum nondum illud publicaverim nec tu unquam inspexeris, in quo tamen ais a me reprehendi Hieronymum.[142]

[Either you think that 'he published' means the same as 'he wrote', which is bad Latin, or you are simply lying. For I have not published yet the work in which – you say – I criticise Jerome, and you have never seen it.]

Poggio, however, repeats his *aedidit* in the third and again in his fifth invectives.[143] In the fifth invective he urges Valla:

Aede quoque tu epistolas et libros tuos. Aede a te opuscula contra fidem fabricata. Aede libros de beati Hieronymi erroribus, de Augustini inscitia, de Boetii ignorantia a te summa cum perfidia fabricatos.[144]

[Publish your letters and books. Publish your work written against the Faith. Publish your treacherous books on Jerome's mistakes, on Augustine's imperfect learning, on Boethius' ignorance.]

It seems that Valla had circulated his annotations amongst a select group but had not formally published them, a decision which Poggio found frustrating. Their slender manuscript tradition may indicate that they were never published. If Valla's unpublished work involved him in such controversy, Manetti may have felt that he had good reason to keep his work on the translation of the Scriptures to himself. It certainly seems that Nicholas V entrusted Manetti with the task of making a new translation of the Bible at a time when opposition to such a project was becoming increasingly strident. After Nicholas' death withdrew papal support for the project, Manetti would have been even more reluctant to publish his New Testament translation. The use of Manetti in the invectives shows that it was a debate he could easily have been drawn into. The fact that neither side was able to cite his actual words on the matter shows how carefully he avoided it.[145] He was not only too careful a politician, but also too sober a scholar. Perhaps Manetti's

---

[142] Wesseling (1978) 118.
[143] Fubini (1964–9) I: 240, 248.   [144] Ibid. 250–1.
[145] Bentley ((1983) 58) suggests that Valla and Manetti may not have got along well. If they had not got along well in the years up to 1453, I suspect that Poggio would have used the fact against his opponent in the invectives. Vespasiano comments on Manetti's restraint in such matters (Greco (1970–6) II: 611–12).

real comment on the matter lies in the fact that while this bitter and abusive academic brawl was under way he was engaged on his earnest treatise *De dignitate et excellentia hominis*.[146]

The direct influence of Valla's work on Manetti's New Testament translation seems likely, but it is not an easy thing to prove. Even if Manetti's New Testament and the latest draft of Valla's annotations had been the subjects of critical editions, it would still be difficult to establish the former's debt to the latter at any one point.[147] Many of the corrections suggested by Valla are such as might have suggested themselves to Manetti. Where Manetti does not adopt a suggestion of Valla's it may mean that he did not know it, but it may also mean that he rejected it. Clearly, the range of speculation allowed the annotator is denied the translator. Valla enjoys a licence to suggest a number of possible translations of varying boldness. That Manetti always changes less than Valla proposes may only be a product of his caution. Manetti and Valla frequently diagnose the same problem with the Vulgate's rendering, but they just as frequently disagree on the solution. A further possibility, and one which has received no attention, is that some of the results of Manetti's researches into the translation of the New Testament were subsequently incorporated into Valla's annotations. This suggestion remains difficult to prove, in part because of the uncertainties surrounding the evolution of Valla's annotations, but also because, as will be seen, it is often difficult to interpret the evidence we do have.

We find, for example, that although the two scholars were clearly relying on different manuscripts for their Greek text of the New Testament, they both seem to have accepted the readings of the late

---

[146] *De dignitate* was begun some time in 1451, and dedicated to Alfonso before 15 December 1452. Manetti's preface to Alfonso is in Leonard (1975) 1–4. Three letters are relevant to the dating of the treatise: (1) Graziosi (1969) 157–9; (2) Leonard (1975) xi; (3) Graziosi (1969) 156–7. Graziosi's dating of this last letter should be corrected to 1453 (Cagni in Camporeale (1972) 461).

[147] A comprehensive analysis of Manetti's debt to and influence upon fifteenth-century Biblical scholarship requires an edition of his translation. According to de Petris in the introduction to his 1981 edition of the *Apologeticus*, Eugenio Massa is preparing an edition of Manetti's New Testament. It has not yet appeared. Because of the difficulty of reading Erasmus' closely printed edition of 1505, Valla's annotations are usually consulted in a facsimile of the sixteenth-century Basle edition of Valla's Works: Valla (1962).

Byzantine textual tradition represented by manuscripts at Rome and in Naples.[148] Where the two scholars are in agreement, it could simply be that their Greek manuscripts coincided. In his annotations on Matthew's Gospel, Valla complains that the Latin text of the Lord's Prayer is faulty because it does not include the Greek doxology.[149] Manetti also accepted the doxology: it appears in his translation of the prayer, and he wrote the Greek in the margin of his own Latin Bible.[150] Both took a similar approach in Mark VI, where their Greek manuscripts had a verse which was absent from the Vulgate. Valla had noted it and compared its omission from the Latin text to the omission of the doxology.[151] Manetti translated it in his version. Both scholars seem to have had a high opinion of the readings of the Greek text, and this results in a tendency to conflate the text of the New Testament at the expense of the Latin tradition.[152] In these circumstances, it is hard to imagine that any reading in Manetti's New Testament translation could constitute conclusive proof that he had consulted Valla's work. Valla, it is true, often suggests a striking or unusual rendering, and one which we might hope to find echoed in a contemporary translation; but it seems that it is just such turns of phrase that Manetti most studiously avoids.

The difficulties of establishing links between Valla's annotations and Manetti's translation are further complicated by the possibility that they used the same Greek–Latin lexica in the production of their work. In 1441 Valla was at work on a prose translation of the *Iliad*. He evidently complained to Alfonso about the lack of proper lexica, and the king wrote to Spain in March 1441 to ask for a Greek lexicon to be brought over to Naples.[153] It is likely that many of

---

[148] For Valla's Greek New Testament manuscripts, see Celenza (1994) 41 n. 27. Three Greek New Testament manuscripts owned by Manetti are in the Vatican Library: Pal.gr.171, Pal.gr.189 (Gospels only), and Pal.gr.229 (Gospels only). See Stevenson sr (1885) 90, 96, 123–4.

[149] Perosa (1970) 34; Valla (1962) I: 810.

[150] Vatican Library Pal.lat.18, fol. 321ᵛ.   [151] Valla (1962) I: 825.

[152] Erasmus, more critical of the Greek tradition, rejected the former and suggested that the latter might have been added from Matthew.

[153] Ruiz-Calonja (1950) 114. This lexicon has not been traced. Valla had translated – but perhaps not revised – the first ten books when he made this request. He had translated books I–XVI by December 1443 (Besomi and Regoliosi (1984) ep. 23, to Aurispa). The remaining books were translated by his pupil, Francesco Aretino (Griffolini), after Valla's death.

the lexica used by Valla remained in Naples when he left, and Manetti may well have used them in any work on his translation undertaken during his last years at Alfonso's court.[154] Similarly, the two scholars are likely to have consulted a number of the same lexica at Rome in Pope Nicholas' new library. Finally, a more subtle contamination of their mutual resources is worth noting. Many scholars learnt Greek through the Vulgate, and compiled their elementary Greek–Latin lexica from a collation of the Vulgate Bible with its Greek equivalents. Consequently, the equations of the Vulgate often formed the basis of the lexica, which, in their turn, were used to retranslate the Vulgate. Perhaps for this reason, attacks on the Vulgate translation often focussed on its internal inconsistencies. Many of Valla's comments take this form, and many of Manetti's changes were made for this reason. It should nevertheless be noted that although both writers believed in the importance of the consistent use of terms, Manetti consistently uses terms of which Valla disapproves.

It is possible to get a glimpse of what a version of the New Testament made by Valla might have looked like. At certain points in his annotations, Valla pieces together his corrections of the Vulgate into a translation of the passage under discussion. One of the longest of these translations can be extracted from his comments on Mark VII: 32–7, the cure of the deaf-mute. Consequently, at this point we can compare the Vulgate text with Manetti's and Valla's renderings. These three versions are reproduced in Table 2.2.[155] The precision of Valla's version is striking. He makes full use of the range of Latin pronouns so that it is always clear who is doing what to whom. In fact, not all the clarity of Valla's version is present in the original: he does tidy up some of the implausible but possible

---

[154] There are two manuscripts in the Vatican which may throw some light on Manetti's use of Valla's work: an incomplete Greek–Latin lexicon in Manetti's hand, and a Bible which was once owned by Manetti and is annotated in his hand with Greek and Hebrew. The lexicon is Pal.gr.194. See Cagni (1960) 6–7. The Bible, Pal.lat.18, is no. 28 in Cagni (1960). Cagni also includes a photograph of a page of the Old Testament (25). In his edition of Vespasiano's correspondence, Cagni suggests that this Bible is the one accepted by Manetti in a letter of 23 November 1454 (Cagni (1969) 132 n. 1).

[155] The Vulgate translation is from Hetzenauer (1922) 993, Manetti's from Urb.lat.6, fol. 41^r, Valla's from Perosa (1970) 81. Alternative renderings suggested by Valla in this passage are recorded in the footnotes.

Table 2.2 *Mark's Gospel, chapter VII, verses 32–7*

Vulgate	Manetti	Valla
32. Et adducunt ei surdum et mutum, et deprecantur eum ut inponat illi manum.	32. Et adducunt ei surdum et mutum ut imponat ei manum.	32. Et ferunt ei surdum mutum, et obsecrarunt eum ut illi imponeret manum.
33. Et adprehendens eum de turba seorsum misit digitos suos in auriculas; et expuens tetigit linguam eius.	33. Et apprehendens eum a turba seorsum misit digitos suos in aures eius; et cum expuisset tetigit linguam suam.	33. Et cum subduxisset eundem a turba seorsum immisit digitos in aures illius; et cum sputasset tetigit eiusdem linguam.
34. Et suspiciens in celum, ingemuit et ait illi: *Eppheta*, quod est adaperire.	34. Et cum respexisset in celum, ingemuit et dicit: *Effata*, quod est aperire.	34. Et cum suspexisset in celum ingemuit,[1] et dicit illi: *Ephphetha*, quod est aperiare.
35. Et statim aperte sunt aures eius, et solutum est vinculum lingue eius, et loquebatur recte.	35. Et confestim aperte sunt aures eius, et solutum est vinculum lingue sue, et loquebatur recte.	35. Statimque aperti sunt auditus eius, et solutum est vinculum lingue ipsius, locutusque est recte.
36. Et precepit illis ne cui dicerent. Quanto autem eis precipiebat, tanto magis plus predicabant,	36. Et precepit eis ne cui dicerent. Quanto autem eis precipiebat, magis abundantius predicabant,	36. Et imperavit illis ut necui dicerent. Quanto autem ipse illis imperabat, magis[2] vehementius predicabant,
37. et eo amplius admirabantur dicentes: Bene omnia fecit, et surdos facit audire et mutos loqui.	37. et abunde admirabantur dicentes: Bene omnia fecit, et surdos fecit audire et mutos loqui.	37. et plusquam vehementer admirabantur dicentes: Bene omnia fecit, et surdos fecit audire et mutos[3] loqui.

[1] Or *suspiravit*.
[2] Or *quantum autem ipse illis imperabat*.
[3] Or *elingues*.

ambiguities of Mark's Greek. Still, it is easy to regret that a version along these lines was not commissioned by Pope Nicholas.

Where Manetti did make a distinct contribution was in his application of his knowledge of Hebrew to the Greek New Testament. In Mark's Gospel, Jairus' daughter is raised with the words *talitha cumi*. The unfamiliar word seems to have been corrupted by a superficial similarity to Acts IX: 40: some Greek manuscripts, including at least one consulted by Manetti, read *tabitha cumi*, and Manetti's own manuscript of the Vulgate read *thabita cumi*. Manetti seems to have reasoned that *talitha* was a corruption of the interpolation, *tabitha*, and that the original text had been lost. Consequently, in his own version of the passage he translated Mark's Greek translation of the phrase into classical Hebrew. This attempt to reconstruct Jesus' actual words produces a unique reading in Manetti's Gospel version at this point: *Iaalda cumi*. Here, *iaalda* is Manetti's transliteration of the Hebrew יַלְדָּה, 'girl'. This new reading is noted in the margin of Manetti's Vulgate manuscript.[156] It is noticed in his *Adversus Judaeos*.[157] It appears in *Apologeticus*.[158] A similar piece of reconstruction can be seen in Manetti's handling of Jesus' words from the cross in the Gospels of Matthew and Mark.[159] This time, instead of translating the versions of the Evangelists, he returns *ad fontem* and his version reads 'eli eli lamma azavtani', a transliteration of the Hebrew text of the first words of the twenty-second Psalm.[160] In fact, although his methods were sound, Manetti goes too far in his reconstructions: *talitha* seems to represent the Aramaic מְלִתָא and the words from the cross seem also to represent an Aramaic version of the Psalm.[161] It does appear that Manetti believed that Jesus' spoken language was very like the Hebrew of the Old Testament.

[156] 'non thabita cumi, sed Iaalda cumi, i.e. puella surge in hebreo'. Pal.lat.18, fol. 331ʳ.
[157] 'Laalda cumi, non thabita, ceu in Evangelio corrupte ac mendose legitur' (Vatican Library Urb.lat.154, fol. 44ᵛ), cited in Fioravanti (1983) 21. Manetti would not have written *Laalda*. Presumably the scribe of the Urbino manuscript misread the unfamiliar word from the lost archetype.
[158] De Petris (1981) 123.   [159] Mt XXVII: 46; Mk XV: 34.
[160] Here, Manetti may have taken his cue from Jerome, *De optimo genere interpretandi* (*PL* 22: 577).
[161] See Grimm and Thayer (1898) 565, 614. Elio Antonio Nebrija took up the discussion of this first passage with Reuchlin and Erasmus in an essay of 1522. The essay is edited by Gilly (1986) 204–14.

The Psalter and *Apologeticus*

Manetti's Greek tutor, Ambrogio Traversari, used the Greek version of the Psalter in his lessons.[162] According to Vespasiano, Traversari also taught Manetti Hebrew, although there is no evidence that the friar himself got very far with that language. It is likely then that Manetti's earliest experience of the different translations of the Psalms dates back to his early years as a student of the Biblical languages. The pattern of Hebrew marginalia in Manetti's Vulgate Latin Bible may preserve some clues to his earliest Hebrew studies. In this manuscript, the marginalia, unpointed, and in a hand that is presumably Manetti's, are confined to the books of the Pentateuch and the Psalms. The Hebrew text is only transcribed at length alongside the first chapters of Exodus, and beside Psalms 1–9 and Psalm 14. These transcribed passages are exactly the sort of text which a student of the language might have used in their first lessons. Manetti would certainly have been aware that the translation of the Psalter had been a matter of debate since the Patristic period. Three Latin versions had circulated since late antiquity: St Jerome had made a Latin translation of the Greek Septuagint version, which came to be known as the Roman Psalter; later, he produced another translation, this time from the Hebrew text; finally, a third rendering, the so-called Gallican Psalter, was in popular use.[163] The existence of three ancient and respected Latin versions meant that the problem of differences between the Greek and Hebrew texts often confronted the Latin reader of the Psalms. When Manetti undertook a new translation of the Psalter, he was aware that his version would supplement an already complex western tradition.

The dating of this translation of Manetti's is as problematic as that of his New Testament translation. Vespasiano says that Manetti translated the Psalter in Naples, that is between 1455 and 1458.[164] We have already seen that Manetti began work on a new translation of the Bible at Rome under Nicholas V, and that Vespasiano's claims must be regarded with some caution. It is clear, however, that

---

[162] See Bertalot (1975a) 263. The letter is undated.
[163] Manetti refuses to speculate on the origins of this version. See de Petris (1981) 55–6.
[164] Greco (1970–6) II: 605.

the final touches at least were placed on the version while he was at Naples. The dedication manuscript which he presented to King Alfonso survives.[165] This seems to be the only one of Manetti's translations which he considered ready for publication. The fact that this dedication copy was part of the Manetti library after his death is explained by the fact that in June 1460 the hard-pressed Aragonese court pawned a manuscript of Manetti's Psalter for 15 ducats.[166] This must have been the large and valuable dedication manuscript, and it was presumably retrieved by Agnolo Manetti. It is not easy to be precise about when Manetti began the version. In the dedicatory preface to the Psalter, he writes

laborem nove amborum testamentorum traductionis non injuria nuper assumpsi.[167]

[I have recently and properly undertaken the task of a new translation of both Testaments.]

Nuper is of course a difficult word to pin down, and Manetti's vagueness may be deliberate. As indicated above, Manetti said that he had begun a version of both Testaments under Pope Nicholas V. It seems likely that Manetti simply revised for the king while he was at Naples a version of the Psalms he had already begun, and perhaps one he had already completed. It is also clear from this preface that Manetti regarded this version of the Psalter as the first instalment of a larger work of translation:

Sed cum huiusmodi opus . . . partim ob magnam eius longitudinem, partim etiam ob nimiam difficultatem diuturnum fore videatur et sit, ut parvulam interea reliquorum omnium degustationem tibi absque longa dilatione preberem, accuratam quandam ac integram solius Psalterii interpretationem nuper edere atque ad te mittere constitui.

[But since a work of this sort, because it is so long and because it is so difficult, seems to be – and in fact is – a lengthy task, I have now decided to publish and

---

[165] For the manuscripts of Manetti's Psalter, see the Appendix. Manetti's versions of Psalms 1, 2, 8, 19, 40, 130 and 150 have been edited by Dröge (1987) 146–66. Psalms 2, 110, 130 and 139 have been edited by Garofalo (1946) 373–5. He has also edited Psalms 73–83 (Garofalo (1953) 232–41). All these editions have been taken from the dedication manuscript, Pal.lat.41. A Hebrew Psalter now in the Vatican Library, Vat.ebr.28, belonged to Manetti (Cassuto (1935) 45).

[166] See Garofalo (1946) 360.

[167] Manetti's preface to the Psalter translation is edited in the Appendix.

send you an accurate and complete translation of the Psalter alone, so as to provide you in the meantime and without further delay with a brief foretaste of all the rest.]

Perhaps Manetti's New Testament translation, complete but not dedicated, was intended as the second instalment. Besides the Psalter, nothing survives of Manetti's work on the Old Testament.

This dedication manuscript of the Psalter translation seems to have been put together under Manetti's supervision: here, his own version is set alongside the two earlier versions of Jerome. Vespasiano, in his commentary on Manetti's life, writes that

messer Giannozo per sua giustificazione come integerrimo cristiano, fece iscrivere il Saltero de' Settantadua uno verso, di poi uno verso di quegli di Santo Girolamo De Hebraica veritate, dipoi uno verso di messer Giannozzo della sua traductione.[168]

[Giannozzo, to vindicate himself as a most upright Christian, arranged his Psalter so that one verse from the Latin translation of the Septuagint was followed by one verse of St Jerome's translation from the Hebrew, and then by one verse from his own translation.]

Vespasiano was writing after Manetti's death and had the dedication manuscript to hand, so his observations need not have come from Manetti himself. Still, there is an element of *giustificazione* in the construction of the dedication manuscript. It includes Manetti's critical essay on Biblical translations, *Apologeticus*. The rationale behind this new rendering of the Psalter, at least as it is represented in the dedication manuscript, is not to replace the ancient versions but to allow Latin readers to compare variant readings. This purpose is sustained by the substantial critical apparatus included in the third and fourth books of *Apologeticus*. Here, additions, omissions, alternative renderings and variations in the titles of the Psalms are catalogued in detail. This arrangement recognises that new translations of sacred texts do not have the same status as new translations of profane texts. It suggests that the reader might learn more about the original text from a collation of different renderings than from any single translation, however well made. It implies that all the versions are valuable because none is a perfect equivalent. But,

---

[168] Greco (1970–6) II: 605.

of course, this arrangement of the versions also drew the reader's attention to the points at which Manetti differed from Jerome.

Manetti, aware of the criticism his new translation might face, appended to it the essay *Apologeticus* to defend and explain his practice. Bruni's essay on translation *De interpretatione recta* has been considered in the previous chapter. The fifth and final book of Manetti's treatise draws upon Bruni's work, and Manetti himself seems to have considered this to be the title of this fifth book.[169] In the list of works which accompanies Vespasiano's *Commentario* on Manetti's life, *Apologeticus* in its entirety is called *De interpretatione recta*. Bruni's treatise did not circulate widely, but Manetti owned a copy.[170] *Apologeticus* probably found even fewer readers than Bruni's treatise.[171] Discussions about translation had a very limited audience: most fifteenth-century readers did not need to make their own translations themselves, and were not equipped to assess those of others. Manetti's discussion in *Apologeticus* differs from Bruni's in that it focusses specifically upon Scriptural translations. While the Vulgate translation was the revered text of the Latin West, its relationship with the Hebrew text and the Septuagint Greek version had not been clarified since Augustine and Jerome had debated the issue in the fifth century.[172] Manetti had clear ideas about this relationship. Before examining these ideas, it is as well to look at contemporary attitudes to the Hebrew Scriptures.

At Florence in the fifteenth century Hebrew studies were often regarded with suspicion. In 1442, near the end of his life, Bruni had written to a younger friend, Giovanni Cirignani, to discourage him from learning Hebrew.[173] He advised his friend against undertaking, 'rem . . . quasi minus utilem, ac ut ita dixerim, super-vacaneam operam' [a rather useless task and, to my mind, a super-fluous labour]. The friend's letter does not survive, but it would

---

[169] 'reliquum est ut hoc quinto et ultimo de interpretatione recta non nulla memoratu digna in medium afferamus' (de Petris (1981) 111).

[170] See above, p. 70 and n. 43.

[171] It survives in three Vatican manuscripts: Pal.lat.40, Pal.lat.41 and Urb.lat.5. See de Petris (1981) xliii–li.

[172] For Augustine's attitudes to the Greek language and the Septuagint, see Courcelle (1969) 149–65.

[173] Bruni's words in this paragraph are from Mehus (1741) IX: 12; Luiso (1980) IX: 13, 12 September. This letter is translated in Griffiths, Hankins and Thompson (1987) 333–6. It is discussed in Trinkaus (1970) II: 578–81.

seem that he had made some reference to the desirability of a
return *ad fontes*:

At enim, inquis, fundamenta rectae fidei a Judaeorum libris existunt, qui etsi sint
translati, melius tamen est fontes consectari quam rivos.

[But, you say, the foundations of the true faith are derived from the books of the
Jews, and even if these have been translated it is still better to seek out the sources
than the stream below.]

But *ad fontes*, after all, is only an image; it is not an argument.
Bruni responds with his own image for the consequences of an
over-zealous search for origins. He writes:

Dare igitur te operam hebraicis litteris, voluptatem fortassis animi afferre tibi
aliquam potest, utilitatem vero nullam. Ceu si quis vinum ex praelo haurire malit
quam ex dolio, quoniam in praelo ante quam in dolio fuit.

[And so although the study of Hebrew may give you some intellectual pleasure
it will be of no use to you. You would be like someone who prefers to take his
wine from the press rather than from the bottle simply because it was in the press
before it was in the bottle.]

That Hebrew is old is no guarantee that it is good. All worthwhile
Hebrew texts, he maintained, were available in satisfactory Latin
translations. In this instance, at least, Bruni seems to have believed
that a translation could provide a substitute for the original text.

Litterae enim illae quicquid habuerunt boni iampridem in latino translatum est,
nec leves quidem auctores sed gravissimi ac doctissimi transtulerunt. Hic tu quid
iam amplius requiras non equidem intelligo, nisi forte illis interpretibus diffidis, ac
eos in disquisitionem et judicium vocare contendis; quod si feceris, crede michi,
ineptus sis.

[For whatever was good in that language has already been translated into Latin,
and no superficial scholars but the most eminent and learned men have translated
it. I do not understand what more you need, unless perhaps you do not trust these
translators and are eager to summon them to an investigation and judgement.
Believe me, if you were to do that you would be foolish.]

Bruni was satisfied with the equations of the Vulgate. Poggio Bracciolini, whose views on the Greek language and the Vulgate translation have been noticed above, studied Hebrew in Constance, and
he did so with the encouragement of Niccolò Niccoli. In 1416,
Poggio says cautiously of his Hebrew studies:

etsi nullius usus esse conspiciam ad sapientie facultatem, confert tamen aliquid ad studia nostra humanitatis, vel ex hoc maxime, quia tamen morem Hieronymi in transferendo cognovi.[174]

[although I can see that it adds nothing to the stock of wisdom, it is still of some use to our *studia humanitatis*, particularly since I now understand Jerome's manner of translating.]

The careful modesty of Poggio's claims for Hebrew learning may be due to his awareness of the sort of criticisms which Bruni would later put into his letter of 1442. As Poggio understands it, the *sapientia* sufficient for salvation is available in Latin translations; methods of translation – even methods of Scriptural translation – clearly belong to the *studia humanitatis*.

Manetti maintained an older and clearer idea of the uses of Hebrew learning, and one which did not need to be located within the *studia humanitatis*. He learnt Hebrew, according to Vespasiano, 'per confusione degli Ebrei'[175] [for the confounding of the Jews]. One of the advantages of an accurate translation of the Old Testament is that it enables Latin Christians to refute Jewish interpretations. The embarrassment of Christian theologians when faced with acute Hebrew scholarship is a theme that goes back to the Fathers. Whereas knowledge of Greek can be justified by appeals to the utility of a wide range of Greek texts, knowledge of Hebrew is more often identified as a weapon to use against the Jews. In Vespasiano's account, Manetti's Psalter translation was produced because the Jews would often criticise interpretations based on the Greek Septuagint translation. Vespasiano writes of Manetti:

Era veementissimo disputatore, et volentieri disputava co'Giudei, co'quali non si può disputare chi non ha peritia della lingua loro, per la forza de'vocaboli. Aveva questa conditione, quando egli disputava cor un Giodeo, ch'egli diceva loro: 'mettevi in punto et trovate l'arme vostre, ch'io non vi voglio ofendere, se non con l'arme vostre medesime'.[176]

[He was an ardent controversialist and eagerly debated with the Jews, with whom no one can debate who does not know their language because the words are so

---

[174] Harth (1984–7) I: 128, 18 May.
[175] Greco (1970–6) I: 486; George and Waters (1963) 372.
[176] Greco (1970–6) I: 486; George and Waters (1963) 372. Cf. Vespasiano's comment: 'non era ebreo che none avesse paura di lui per la peritia della lingua ebrea et per la prestantia de lo ingegnio' (Greco (1970–6) II: 525).

important. When he debated with a Jew he would say to him: 'Put yourself on guard and get your weapons ready because I want to attack you with those very weapons of yours.']

And, of course, Manetti always won these battles. Although some of the triumphalism in this passage attributed to Manetti may actually belong to Vespasiano, we do know that Manetti was responsible for the conversion of his Hebrew teacher, and that he helped Cardinal Cesarini convert a Spanish physician resident at Florence, Giovanni Agnolo.[177] To understand Manetti's attitude to Biblical translations, we must look at the relationship, set out in *Apologeticus*, between the ancient Greek translators and the Hebrew Scriptures.

In the second book of *Apologeticus*, Manetti traces the history of Scriptural translations. In order to provide some context for the following discussion of Patristic attitudes to Scriptural translations, I shall summarise here the story of the production of the Greek version of the Old Testament, given in the so-called 'Letter of Aristeas'. The story was probably forged at some time in the second century before Christ by a Hellenised Jew. It claims that in the third century before Christ, Ptolemy Philadelphus, king of Egypt, wrote to the high priest at Jerusalem to request that seventy-two learned men – six from each of the twelve tribes – be sent to translate the Jewish Law into Greek. Gifts and civilities were exchanged and the translators soon arrived in Alexandria. For several days the translators were brought to banquets: each had a question put to him by the king, and each answered to the king's satisfaction. Having thus demonstrated their wisdom, they withdrew to seventy-two separate cells on the island of Pharos and began work on the translation. This was completed in seventy-two days. It was read to the assembled Jews on the island and unanimously approved. A curse was pronounced upon anyone who dared to alter the translation. Although the letter makes it clear that the translation was of the Pentateuch only, the term came to be applied more generally to the Greek translation of Hebrew Scripture.

---

[177] For Manetti's Hebrew teacher, Emmanuel Judaeus, see Cagni (1971) 294. *Iter Italicum* records that Emmanuel's autograph manuscript *Super libros psalmorum* is now at Venice, Marc.gr.67 (2061). For Giovanni Agnolo, see Trinkaus (1970) II: 582.

Jerome alone amongst the Fathers seems to have been aware of this distinction.[178]

This story was retold many times, and different writers displayed different attitudes to the role of the translators. The seventy cells and the role of Ptolemy in the creation of the translation were justified in a number of ways. An account of the production of the Septuagint appears in Philo Judaeus' *De vita Moysis*. Manetti's interest in Philo dates back to at least 1448, when he wrote in a letter that he was using his worn Greek manuscript of Philo in his work on his treatise *Adversus Judaeos et gentes*.[179] However, he is likely to have encountered Philo's account even earlier. Francesco Filelfo brought a Greek manuscript of Philo to Italy in 1427.[180] A translation of Philo's *De vita Moysis* was begun by Filelfo in 1428, one year before he arrived in Florence.[181] In 1431 Traversari acquired a large Greek manuscript of Philo from Filelfo,[182] probably the same one which he had brought to Italy four years earlier. According to Philo, the translators chose the island of Pharos for its cleanliness and isolation. Josephus has a version of the story in his *Jewish Antiquities*.[183] He wrote that the translators are led to the island by Demetrius Phalereus, the king's librarian, because he thought its isolation appropriate for such a serious undertaking. Christian accounts are more hostile. According to the account of the second-century author Irenaeus, quoted in Eusebius' *Ecclesiastical History*, Ptolemy does not invite the translators as honoured guests,

---

[178] 'tota scola Judaeorum quinque tantum libros Moysis a LXX translatos asserunt.' *In Ezech.* 5, cited in Swete (1902) 23.

[179] The letter is in Graziosi (1969) 153–4 and Wittschier (1968) 44–5. The correct date is supplied by Wittschier (1968) 45 n. 7, de Petris (1976) 193 n. 4 and Cagni (1971) 295 n. 7. Manetti's substantial treatise has not been edited, although de Petris has described its contents (1976). It survives in a unique manuscript, Urb.lat.154. Manetti's manuscript of Philo, Vatican Library Pal.gr.183, contains *De vita Moysis*. See Stevenson sr (1885) 94–5.

[180] Sabbadini (1905–14) 48.

[181] Filelfo's incomplete version is now in Laur.69.11 (Stinger (1977) 145 and n.). This manuscript is no. 1179 in the catalogue of the Florentine Library made about 1500: 'Philonis Hebrei de vita Moysi, et alia opera ad divinam legem pertinentia, in membranis' (Ullman and Stadter (1972) 261). Philo's description of the production of the Septuagint is at *De vita Moysis* II: v–vii.

[182] Stinger (1977) 145.

[183] *Ant. iud.* VII: 103. Manetti's manuscript of this work, Pal.lat.815, has the colophon: 'completus per me Thomam Jacobi Tani Jannoçio mihi legente anno M.cccc⁰. xxxviiii⁰. Die xxviiii Februarij' (fol. 243ᵛ). That is, 1440 n.s. See Cagni (1960) 32 n. 6.

but summons them as subjects of his fellow Greek, the Hellenistic king of Macedonia.[184] Irenaeus says that the seventy cells are constructed to prevent the translators conspiring to conceal the divine wisdom of the Scriptures. Augustine, with his great respect for the Greek Scriptures, will say only that Ptolemy made them translate separately 'to try their faith', but Jerome states that the seventy translators concealed from King Ptolemy the meaning of all the passages in which Christ's coming was promised.[185] Eusebius' version in the *Praeparatio evangelica*, quoted in *Apologeticus*, is consistent with the anti-Jewish stance of Irenaeus and Jerome: the Old Testament was put into Greek, the *lingua franca* of the ancient world, so that the Jews could not hide it or corrupt it. The Greek version was divinely ordained to remove the Old Testament from the control of the Jews and give it to the Christian world; and to this end Ptolemy was inspired by God to order this inspired translation. Manetti gives another reason for the king's decision. The seventy-two interpreters, he says, were put into their separate cells by the order of Ptolemy in order to secure the *reputation* of the Greek translation:

Quod a Ptholemeo de industria factum fuisse legimus, ut singuli seorsum interpretarentur, ne qua forte inter interpretandum future traductionis suspitio oriretur.[186]

[We read that this was done deliberately by Ptolemy, so that each could translate separately, and so that no suspicion of the resulting translation could possibly arise during the process of translating.]

For not only must the translation be good, but it must be seen to be good. He goes on to suggest a justification for their isolation which befits a textual scholar. He says that the translators produced seventy-two separate versions so that if any one of them had made

---

[184] *Hist. eccl.* V: 8, 11–15. Irenaeus III: 24, 1. The *Ecclesiastical History* had been available to the West since late antiquity in a translation probably to be attributed to Rufinus. Niccolò Niccoli, Ambrogio Traversari and Tommaso Parentucelli all had access to Irenaeus' *Adversus haereses* in its Latin translation. See Reimherr, asst. Cranz (1992) 21.

[185] Augustine said 'ita enim eorum fidem Ptolomaeo placuit explorare'. *De civitate Dei* XVIII:xlii. Manetti reproduces the next two chapters, lxiii and xliv, in *Apologeticus* (de Petris (1981) 40–2). Jerome's words on the translators are in the preface to his *Hebraicae quaestiones in Genesim*. See Schwarz (1955) 31.

[186] De Petris (1981) 31.

a scribal error it could be corrected by collating it with the other copies. But this is merely an ingenious aside. Manetti is in full agreement with the Patristic suspicion of Jewish motives, which he quotes at great length.

This suspicion informs Manetti's description of Jerome's Biblical scholarship. He gives three reasons why Jerome learnt Hebrew. They are far more comprehensive than the apologetic stance of Poggio, quoted earlier. First of all, Jerome learnt the language for

quedam troporum ac metaphorarum copia, quibus ea lingua vel maxime abundabat, ubi non nulla ingentia divinarum rerum mysteria interdum abstrusa latere videbantur, que quidem in alienam linguam cum tanta ac tam propria illarum sententiarum expressione transferri non poterant.[187]

[that abundance of tropes and metaphors, which the language had in plenty, in which a number of great mysteries regarding divine matters sometimes seemed to lurk unseen, and which could not be translated into a foreign language in words as weighty and appropriate as the original.]

That is to say, the primary reason for learning Hebrew is that some qualities of the text are simply untranslatable. The second reason was that there were a number of Greek translations of the Old Testament available in the fourth century, and their differences were numerous and significant. Manetti writes that Jerome believed that a new translation from the Hebrew was needed in order to eliminate all the ambiguities which arose from the variety of translations.[188] The third reason which made Jerome learn Hebrew was to silence the complaints and calumnies of the Jews. Yet this, Manetti continues, is a function which Jerome's translation had not fulfilled:

Hebrei nanque post hanc ultimam, de qua loquimur, divinorum librorum interpretationem de falsitate Scripturarum nostrarum adversus Christianos quotidie insultare ac latrare non desinunt.[189]

[For the Jews, after this last translation of the divine books which we discussed, still scoff at and rage against Christians every day over the deceitfulness of our Scriptures.]

It is here that Manetti reveals his justification for a new translation. He did not retranslate the Psalter because he felt that the

---

[187] Ibid. 48.   [188] Ibid. 49.   [189] Ibid. 49.

inaccuracies of current versions threatened the salvation of Latin Christendom. Rather, he felt that the Latin translation which had completed the conversion of the Western Empire in late antiquity was now, because of its inaccuracies, a barrier to the conversion of the Jews.

Manetti develops in *Apologeticus* an idea taken from Augustine about the appropriation of the Old Testament by Christians. The Jews resent this:

Nobis deinde in sacris litteris vel maxime invident, quoniam nos eam sacrarum scripturarum copiam, quibus soli ipsi vel maxime gloriari solebant cum cetere gentes illas apprime contemnerent, tum grecis interpretationibus tum etiam hac presertim lingua latina ab illis arripuimus ac nobismet ipsis vendicavimus.[190]

[They heartily resent us over the Scriptures, since by means of the Greek versions and especially by the Latin language, we have taken from them and claimed for ourselves the *copia* of the Holy Scriptures. The Jews alone used to take great pride in the Scriptures, in the days when those writings were utterly despised by other nations.]

Manetti maintains that he may know Hebrew better than the Jews themselves because he knows Latin and Greek as well. He repeats a traditional accusation that Jewish culture was introspective, narrow and self-regarding, 'suis ergo duntaxat contenti nec aliena querentes'. In fact, he says, this attitude has weakened their hold on the Scriptures. Very few Jews after Philo and Josephus, says Manetti, knew Greek or Latin. Consequently, they cannot judge the corruptions or mistranslations of the Latin versions. However, Manetti goes further. It was a standard defence of Greek studies in the fifteenth century that one could not have a profound knowledge of Latin without at least some knowledge of Greek. Manetti develops this idea and applies it to the Jews:

Fieri enim non potest ut una lingua, presertim regulis canonibusque et normis instituta, sine aliquali vel modica saltem alienorum excellentium idiomatum cognitione ad unguem percipi perfecteque cognosci possit et valeat, ceu in latina lingua manifestissime apparet, quam grecarum litterarum penitus expertes probe nancisci ac sibi ipsis omnino vendicare non possunt.[191]

[For no language, especially one constructed according to *regulae*, *canones* and *normae*, can be thoroughly learnt and perfectly known without at least some

[190] Ibid. 49–50.   [191] Ibid. 50.

knowledge, however small, of other learned languages. This is very clear from the Latin language: those who are completely ignorant of Greek cannot master it properly and claim it as their own.]

If they do not know other languages, then they cannot perfectly know their own. Lorenzo Valla famously maintained that he could know Latin better than the ancient Romans themselves. Manetti maintained that he could know Hebrew better than the Jews, because he knows Latin and Greek as well. All monoglot cultures, according to Manetti, are necessarily limited.

Perhaps the most surprising of Manetti's positions in *Apologeticus* is that he insists that *interpretatio recta* can only be made from and into one of the learned languages. This follows from the definition which he gives the term at the beginning of book five:

Est ergo interpretatio recta idonea quedam et commoda de quacunque celebrata ac preceptis et regulis instituta lingua in aliam pariter vel pene similem, iuxta subiectam de qua tractatur materiam, conversio.

[*Interpretatio recta* is an appropriate and fitting transformation of the subject matter from one language organised according to principles and rules into another language organised in the same, or in a very similar, way.]

Since the vernaculars are not constructed according to *precepta* and *regulae*, they cannot adequately represent a language which is. He lists Hebrew, 'Chaldaic', Greek and Latin as the most important – but not the only – languages which are structured in this way.[192] He continues:

si de aliquo predictorum [idiomatum] in maternum sermonem forte transferretur, quanquam cuncta alia convenirent que ad rectam interpretationem requiruntur, non tamen proprie recta interpretatio diceretur; recta quippe conversio certam quandam eloquii illius lingue, in quam traducitur, dignitatem exigere et postulare videtur.[193]

[If a translation were to be made from one of the learned languages into the vernacular, it would not properly be called *interpretatio recta*, even if all the other requirements of *interpretatio recta* are fulfilled, for this *conversio recta* seems to demand a certain dignity of expression from the language into which it is made.]

---

[192] Cf. Dante, *De vulgari eloquentia*: 'Est et inde alia locutio secundaria nobis, quam Romani gramaticam vocaverunt. Hanc quidem secundariam Greci habent et alii, sed non omnes . . .' (Mengaldo (1968) 3). Manetti lists *De vulgari eloquentia* among Dante's works in his life of the poet, but he may have known no more than the title.

[193] De Petris (1981) 111.

Manetti believes that because of their structure these languages have a *dignitas* which the vernaculars lack. This observation is important because it precludes the accurate translation of the Scriptures into the vernaculars. It is also important because it states something which many more scholars took for granted. Whatever other virtues were granted it – 'et habet vulgaris sermo commendationem suam', wrote Bruni – the vernacular was not regarded as a tool for philosophers.[194]

Manetti then proceeds to develop the idea that different genres require different methods of translation. In this he may be taking his lead from Jerome.[195] Philosophy and theology require a different type of translation from poetry, oratory and history:

Caeterum de philosophis ac theologis, quanquam recte, ut diximus, in quibusvis interpretationibus ad verbum interpretari nequeamus, non ita tamen lata ac vaga et ampla cum verborum tum sententiarum quoque luminibus ornamentisque expolita, sed aliquando pressior ac gravior et exactior in predictis duobus quam in tribus superioribus esse debet.[196]

[As for philosophers and theologians, although, as we have said, we cannot produce *interpretatio recta* in some translations if we translate word for word, yet neither should the translation be too loose and free and magnificently embellished with the beauties and decorations of words and phrases; instead, it should where necessary be closer, more serious, and more precise for these two sorts of writer than for the three previous ones.]

Although he does not recommend an *ad verbum* translation for the former category, he does say that the translator's freedom is more limited. Manetti also argues that Cicero felt the same way, and that he translated Demosthenes' *De corona* rather differently than he translated Plato's *Protagoras* and Xenophon's *Oeconomicus*.[197]

---

[194] Bruni's Letter to Biondo. Mehus (1741) VI: 10; Luiso (1980) VI: 15. In his *Life of Dante* he says that 'ciascuna lingua ha sua perfezione e suo suono e suo parlare limato e scientifico' (Baron (1928) 61).

[195] In *De optimo genere interpretandi*: 'Ego enim non solum fateor, sed libera voce profiteor, me in interpretatione Graecorum, *absque Scripturis sanctis, ubi et verborum ordo mysterium est*, non verbum e verbo, sed sensum exprimere de sensu' (Ep. 57 ad Pammachium, *PL* XXX: 571. My italics).

[196] De Petris (1981) 120–1.

[197] Cicero may never have made the translation from Demosthenes: see Dihle (1955). The other two translations have been lost. Both are mentioned by Jerome in his *Praefatio in Pentateuchum* (*PL* XXVIII: 182). A few fragments of the *Protagoras* translation survive in Priscian. *Cat. maj.* 59 is a paraphrase of *Oeconomicus* 4: 20ff. See Jones (1959)

None of these versions is extant, but Manetti cites Cicero's words from *De finibus* as evidence. Cicero says:

si plane sic verterem Platonem aut Aristotelem ut verterunt nostri poetae fabulas, male, credo, mererer de meis civibus.[198]

[If I were to translate Plato or Aristotle as our poets translated plays, I would not deserve well of my fellow citizens.]

In *Apologeticus*, Manetti says that although the translators of poets, orators and historians are at liberty to trim the dull and explain the obscure, the translators of philosophy and theology are more restricted. He says that:

Fidi vero philosophorum theologorumque interpretes non ita pro suo arbitrio vagi ac liberi, quasi per latos et apertos campos hinc inde discurrere et pervagari debent, sed arctioribus quibusdam interpretandi legibus pressi et quasi certis cancellis astricti, modestius graviusque iuxta severam quandam professionis sue normam incedere progredique coguntur.[199]

[Faithful translators of the philosophers and theologians ought not to roam and stray so wilfully as over a wide open space. Rather they should be bound by the strict laws of translation and restrained as if by bars. They are obliged to proceed more discreetly and advance more seriously in accordance with the austere rule of their profession.]

Such translations must pursue a mean between the obscurity of a translation *ad verbum* and the misrepresentations of freer renderings. He continues that they should proceed

nec ab incepto convertendi proposito longius evagantes, nec primis etiam auctoribus omnino ac penitus ad verbum adherentes, sed medium et tutum, ut dicitur, iter tenentes, inter interpretandum ita se mediocriter habere decet ut neutram in partem declinare ac propendere videantur.

23, 25. Cicero's partial translation of Plato's *Timaeus* is listed by Bruni among Cicero's translations in *Cicero novus* in 1415 (Baron (1928) 116). Bessarion is known to have used this translation at Mistra 1431–6 to learn Latin. See Saffrey (1976) 374–9; Bernardinello (1973) 405. Humphrey of Gloucester was expecting a copy of the *Timaeus* translation from P. C. Decembrio in July 1441 (Weiss (1967) 59).

[198] De Petris (1981) 121. *De fin.* I: iii, 7.

[199] De Petris (1981) 128. This metaphor was a favourite of Manetti's. It occurs in his funeral oration for Bruni of 1444 (Mehus (1741) xc). It occurs in three of his speeches to Alfonso: of May 1445 (Sandeo (1611a) 170); of early 1451 (Sandeo (1611b) 178); and of April 1452 (Pal.lat.1604, fol. 10ʳ). The conceit is from Cicero, *Acad. prior.* 35.

[neither straying far from their undertaking to translate, nor sticking too closely to the very words of the original works, but keeping to the safe middle way, as it is called, they should translate so moderately as to seem to favour neither side.]

Manetti believed that the translator should look for the *via media* between the poles of rendering *ad verbum* and *ad sensum*. The moral earnestness of Manetti's tone, and the seriousness of the responsibility he imposes on the translator, distinguish his remarks from Bruni's. Manetti only ever attempted translations which required this sort of restraint and balance from the translator. From Agnolo Manetti's preface to his father's translations of Aristotle, it appears that Giannozzo saw his own version as moving between the literal rendering of the medieval version and the freedom of Bruni's version. In much the same way, Manetti's version of the New Testament avoids the controversial renderings which frequently appear in the annotations of Lorenzo Valla, and steers a path between the solecisms of the Vulgate and Valla's precise classicism. There is in fact an implicit criticism of Bruni's method of translation in this part of Manetti's theory of translation, a criticism shared by Bruni's critic, Alfonso of Burgos. Bruni's contribution to the debate was to suggest that translation must begin with the biography of the author to be translated. Consequently, he tended to apply the same method to the translation of all the different literary genres. One of Manetti's contributions was to demonstrate that the form of the text to be translated was as important to the translator as the character of its author.

Manetti also deserves credit for the way in which he justified his new versions of the Scriptures. Valla has been congratulated by modern scholars because he was the first to deny Jerome's authorship of the entire Vulgate translation.[200] In fact, Valla seems to have stumbled across this important truth while searching for defences against his critics: after all, it is easier to correct the Vulgate if you can deny that it was the work of the Church Father. Manetti is bolder because his perspective on the history of translation as a discipline is broader. He makes no attempt to deny Jerome's authorship of the Vulgate translation. Rather, he accepts and recapitulates Jerome's

---

[200] See annotations on Luke XVI, 2; I Cor. II: 9; II Cor. II: 9 and Preface 6, 10 (Perosa (1970)).

opinions about translation in order to justify his own method of translation and the replacement of Jerome's text. Similarly, Manetti does not attempt to discredit the Septuagint translation in order to replace it. Instead, he places it in a historical context which makes it of less importance to the fifteenth century. Although he did not draw out all the implications of the accounts which he quotes, he did more than any of his contemporaries to show just how complex an undertaking the translation of Scriptural texts could be. Erasmus made it his business to know of earlier versions of the Scriptures in order to justify his own, but he did not know of Manetti's translations.[201] He would certainly have sympathised with Manetti's efforts to show that new translations of the Scriptures can be justified because they are created to serve new purposes.

[201] He would certainly have mentioned it in his letter to Henry Bullock if he had (Ep. 456, *EE* II: 324).

3

ERASMUS AND THE NEW TESTAMENT

Introduction

Between 1516 and 1535, Erasmus saw five editions of the New Testament through the presses at Basle. Each of these editions was made up of three elements: the Greek text, his own Latin translation of that text, and his annotations discussing or defending both the Greek and the Latin. Of these, the Greek text was perhaps the least remarkable. This is not to dismiss Erasmus' efforts as an editor, nor to underestimate the enormous influence of his final Greek text on New Testament scholarship until the nineteenth century. Even if it was not the first edition of the Greek text – that title belongs to the Complutensian edition of 1514 – it was still the most often reproduced, and the most widely used. Yet if Erasmus had not put his efforts into producing an edition of the Greek New Testament in 1516, someone else would certainly have done so very soon after. Perhaps the most remarkable thing about this Greek text of the New Testament is not that it was printed in 1516, but that it had not been printed earlier.

This Greek text was largely inspired by Erasmus' decision to publish his own Latin translation of the New Testament. He realised that a new Latin translation of the New Testament required an edition of the Greek text on which it was based. This itself was a significant contribution because, as indicated in the previous chapter, neither Valla nor Manetti seems to have done very much to question the readings of the Greek text which they used in their revisions of the Vulgate. Erasmus' translation was the most controversial part of his edition, and it is perhaps the most controversial translation ever made. I know of no other version which has been so comprehensively defended by its author. The techniques employed by Erasmus in the construction of his Greek text, and the principles of textual criticism which he expounded in his annotations, clearly challenged the traditional translation at many points. But it was his new translation which demonstrated how the consistent application of these principles might revolutionise the reading of the New Testament.

The third element of Erasmus' edition, his annotations, forms the basis of many of the following observations. He did more to diagnose the faults of the Vulgate than either Manetti or Valla, and he did so largely because he found himself obliged to defend his new versions on so many fronts. The quantity of apologetic literature produced by Erasmus in defence of his editions of the New Testament dwarfs the output of Bruni, Manetti and Valla. Consequently, Erasmus' solutions to many of the familiar problems of translation are very well documented. These solutions are the subject of this chapter.

Reading the Vulgate

In the previous chapter I showed that Manetti seems to have believed that Jesus' spoken language was Hebrew. Erasmus was no Hebrew scholar, but he did recognise the diversity of the languages which had been spoken in Roman Judaea. In his annotations on the New Testament he discussed the Apostles' language in a controversial note, and he added a comment on Jesus' own language:

ipse Christus . . . vulgatissimo maximeque populari sermone est usus, Syriace loquens et fortassis aliquando Chaldaice, et haud scio an Graece nonnunquam.[1]

[Christ himself . . . used the commonest vernacular, speaking in Syriac, perhaps sometimes in Chaldaic, and maybe occasionally in Greek.]

This perception of the foreignness of Jesus' very words informed Erasmus' writing on the New Testament, but it was a perception which many of his contemporaries did not share. In the years after the publication of his Latin translation of the New Testament in 1516, Erasmus was obliged to defend himself against the charge that he had dared to alter Scripture. In one of the many defences he produced against his critics he wrote

---

[1] Acts x. A. Reeve (1990) 299. Added 1519.

Sunt enim qui cum sibi pulchre docti videantur, vix norint Joannem aliter scripsisse quam Latine.[2]

[There are some who, whilst they think themselves very learned men, are hardly aware that John did not write in Latin.]

This is an exaggeration but it confronts a real problem. Those who objected to new versions of the works of Aristotle could point out that a great deal of thought and interpretation had accumulated around the terminology of the medieval translators. The translator of the Scriptures had to contend with a further problem: not only had a complex written tradition evolved about the language of the Vulgate translation, but through repeated recitation and quotation something like an oral tradition also existed. Many of its readers had large parts of it by memory. So, while there were a number of reasons for Erasmus' critics to maintain the excellence of the Vulgate translation, the objections to his new version were the more vehement because of a deep emotional attachment to the words in which their earliest observances had been conducted and which had attended the first stirrings of piety. Erasmus believed that a new version could eliminate some of the barriers between the Latin reader and the true meaning of the original Greek text, but he had first to persuade these readers that such barriers existed. In short, he had to tell them that they did not know the New Testament as well as they thought they did. The first step in the process of challenging the renderings of the Vulgate was to insist on its status as a translation.

Erasmus' version of the New Testament was one of the most controversial translations ever produced because the problems created by the Vulgate translation ran so deep. A reader certain that a flawed translation is meaningful is likely to develop some unusual reading habits. The very strangeness of some of the Vulgate's phrases made it memorable. Erasmus observes that some passages of the Vulgate only communicate because the reader has already decided what they mean on the basis of other information. Sometimes the meaning of a passage had to be deduced from its context. In the first edition of the *Annotations* he notes:

---

[2] *Apologia pro 'In principio erat sermo'*, LB IX: 1136.

sermonis usus in hoc adhibetur, ut per eum cognoscant discantque rem ii quibus antea fuerat incognita, non ut agnoscamus ac divinemus quod prius noveramus.[3]

[language is used so that by it they might understand and learn something which they had not known before; not so that we might recognise and guess what we already knew.]

Countless previous readings enabled the construction of plausible hypotheses to fill in the gaps left by the obscurity of the translation. Since it was widely regarded as the product of the greatest trilingual scholar of the great age of the Church, a reader might reasonably assume that the translation was good. After all, Jerome was a Doctor of the Church – a title which augmented his authority in mysterious and undefined ways.[4] How could he not have had divine assistance in a task so vital for the world's salvation? And if Jerome's translation had been inspired how could it possibly be faulty? The reader's confidence in the translation was part of the problem. Since the text translated might reasonably be supposed to contain many difficult and mysterious sayings, many difficult and mysterious Latin renderings might come to be treated with veneration rather than suspicion. At best, corrupt texts might obscure the true import of Holy Writ. At worst, incomprehensible passages might be misread as aspects of the inscrutable divine, and careless translations might be misinterpreted as revealed truth.

Consequently, when Erasmus noted bluntly in his Annotations that '*Post dies* Latine nihil significat', he was only half right.[5] Because it was so familiar, the Vulgate was able to communicate in a rather privileged way. It was possible to read it in ways unlike any other text, using the words as an *aide-mémoire* to a narrative which was actually constructed from a number of sources – religious iconography, the paraphrases and interpretations of preachers, and liturgical variations on its themes. In the *Annotations* on John's Gospel, Erasmus writes of a certain passage:

---

[3] Mt I. A. Reeve (1986) 2. From 1516.

[4] 'The requisite conditions are enumerated as three: *eminens doctrina, insignis vitae sanctitas, Ecclesiae declaratio* . . . Though general councils have acclaimed the writings of certain Doctors, no council has actually conferred the title of Doctor of the Church' (Herbermann *et al.* (1907–14) V: 75).

[5] Mk II. A. Reeve (1986) 118. From 1516. Manetti and Valla agree on *per dies*, which is suggested but not preferred by Erasmus. All references to Manetti's New Testament translation are taken from Pal.lat.45.

Intelligebamus non quod Latine sciremus, sed quod huiusmodi soloecismis esse-
mus assueti. At quanto simplicius ita reddere sententiam Evangelistae ut non
sit opus hac gratia novam discere balbutiem, sed quisquis Latine norit protinus
intelligat.[6]

[I did not understand it because I knew Latin, but because I was used to this sort
of solecism. But it is so much simpler to translate the Evangelist's meaning in
such a way that there is no need to learn a new kind of babbling to understand it;
and instead whoever knows Latin can understand it immediately.]

Erasmus' marginal note beside this comment reads:

Facilius semel discitur latina lingua, quam multae balbutiendi species.[7]

[It is easier to learn the Latin language once, than to learn all the dialects of this
nonsense.]

The understanding of every part of the Scriptures must begin with
a command of the language into which it is translated. It should
not be left to the chance associations of the preacher or the painter.
The Vulgate translation was such that its reader had to rely on the
interpretation of others in order to understand a passage which was
perfectly clear in the original. A good grasp of classical Latin and
a good translation of the Greek text into the same language could
free the reader from this sort of dependence.

One example of this *balbutiendi species* occurs near the beginning of Matthew's Gospel. When John the Baptist initially refuses
to baptise Jesus, Christ replies, according to the Vulgate, '*Sine
modo*'. Erasmus' note demonstrates his impatience with such
renderings:

Rogo quis est hic lusus in litteris divinis? Aut dicendum erat, *Omitte nunc*, ut
intelligas id quod est consentaneum, Ioannem, injecta manu, conatum vetare
Jesum.[8]

[What is this doing in Holy Writ? He should have said 'Let it be now' so that you
might understand – as it is reasonable to suppose – that John had put out his arm
to try to stop Jesus.]

---

[6] Jn i. A. Reeve (1986) 228. Added 1519. Cited by Rummel (1986) 105.
[7] Jn i. A. Reeve (1986) 228. From 1519.
[8] Mt iii. A. Reeve (1986) 22. From 1516. Manetti retains *Sine modo*, and Valla does not
   comment on the phrase in the annotations which Erasmus edited in 1505. Valla did pick
   it up in his earlier draft (Perosa (1970) 23).

The Vulgate requires the intervention of scholarship to help its reader out of his difficulty, but the Greek original at this point is unambiguous. Erasmus believed that the original Gospel narrative was essentially and intentionally clear. The Evangelists themselves frequently interject translations or clarifications of unfamiliar terms. For this reason, the best translation should require no gloss; a competent translator should not require further translation. In this instance, it is likely that Erasmus was particularly aggrieved because the translator's fudge occurs at a moment of high drama in the Biblical story as the Baptist yields to Christ. The Baptist seems to have been a vivid image for Erasmus. Annotating Mark's Gospel, he observes that the Vulgate rendering which has John *vestitus pilis cameli* has fostered a false image of the Baptist:

Pictores onerant Joannem exuvio cameli, quemadmodum Graeci vestiunt Herculem exuvio leonis. Imo vestis erat contexta non e lana Britannica aut Serum velleribus aut lino Hollandico, sed e pilis camelorum.[9]

[Painters weigh John down with a camel skin much as the Greeks dress Hercules in a lion skin. In fact his clothes were not woven from British wool, nor from Chinese fleeces or from Dutch linen, but from camel hair.]

As a translator, Erasmus wished to resolve the obscurities of the Vulgate text by rendering the original Greek as accurately as possible. As a Christian responding to a Scriptural image, he wished to correct a more pervasive misreading of the Scriptures. Here, he is less concerned with what exactly John was wearing than with contemporary classicising tendencies which set Biblical heroes within another tradition. Classical cultural iconography had become ubiquitous, and Erasmus felt himself justified in seeing the failures of the Vulgate and their cure in the context of a wider malaise.[10]

Erasmus' comment quoted above, that it was possible to become familiar with the characteristic errors of the Vulgate, shows that he was aware that the Latin of the Vulgate had its own grammar. In fact, the Vulgate translation had for centuries tended to remake Latinists in its own image. Many learnt a good portion of their Latin from it and reproduced its language in their own writings. Some

---

[9] Mk I. A. Reeve (1986) 115. Added 1535.
[10] In the National Gallery, Parmigianino's John the Baptist, painted in the 1520s with a pelt draped across his knee, is just such a Herculean figure.

of the Vulgate's un-Roman turns of phrase had become enshrined in the liturgy and in the idiom of ecclesiastical Latin. Erasmus' project in retranslating the New Testament was primarily intended to enable the reader to get closer to the meaning of the Greek text, but it is important to note that Erasmus also wanted to demolish the idea that the type of Latin that the Vulgate represented had any ecclesiastical sanction. He suggested that the Latin of the Vulgate represented the common speech of late antiquity. Since the Vulgate translator clearly needs to be excused, he writes,

Mea sententia non potest melius excusari interpres, quam si dicamus tum temporis vulgus ad imitationem Graecorum ita solere loqui, cui navabat hanc operam potius quam eruditis.[11]

[In my opinion the translator's best excuse is that in his time the common people were accustomed to imitate the Greeks in their way of speaking, and that he aimed this translation at them, not at the learned.]

This note was added in the final edition of 1535. By then, the possibility that the Greek language had influenced contemporary vernaculars was beginning to be discussed. In 1529, two years after Erasmus' fourth edition, Guillaume Budé's *Commentarii linguae graecae* came off the presses at Paris. Budé pointed out a number of parallels between the French and Greek languages.[12] Erasmus' suggestion that the popular Latin of the late Empire had been substantially altered under the influence of Greek does not appear to have been noticed by modern critics.[13] If this was so, his argument runs, then the Grecisms of the Vulgate do not indicate where the translator has been defeated by his original, but where he has accommodated his language to that of his audience. This is an effective defence because it has a respectable motive, but is also another nail in the coffin of the Vulgate translation: if it had originally been intended for the masses it was now obsolete, because the masses no longer spoke Latin. Latin was now the medium of the educated class and this audience required a new translation: if we adopt the motives of the ancient translator we must reject his translation as a tool for the lettered elite. As indicated in the

---

[11] Rom. II. A. Reeve (1986) 355.   [12] See Trapp (1990) 8–21.
[13] Rabil mentions this passage only as a retreat by Erasmus from a more uncompromising position on the inspiration of the Vulgate translation (Rabil (1972) 122).

previous chapter, Manetti had argued sixty years earlier that philosophical texts require a different type of translation from works of poetry or rhetoric, and that a new version of the Psalter was needed to convert the Jews. Manetti came close to formulating the position that every translation was made to serve a specific purpose. Now Erasmus was looking to the purposes which the Vulgate had been constructed to serve. He believed that there were better ways of attaining these ends.

Parallel texts

Erasmus' solution to the flaws of the Vulgate version was carefully constructed. Before considering his edition it is instructive to look at a contemporary response to the same problem. Between 1514 and 1517 the first printed polyglot Bible came off the presses at Alcalá – *Complutum* in Latin – in Spain.[14] The Complutensian Polyglot Bible attempted to maintain the primacy of the Vulgate translation whilst embracing trilingual scholarship. The prologue of the Polyglot described the relationship between its texts:

Mediam autem inter has [interpretationes] latinam beati Hieronymi translationem velut inter Synagogam et Orientalem Ecclesiam posuimus, tanquam duos hinc et inde latrones, medium autem Iesum hoc est Romanam sive Latinam Ecclesiam collocantes.[15]

[We have put the Latin translation of St Jerome between these versions, as though between the synagogue and the Eastern Church, placing them on each side like the two thieves, with Jesus, that is the Roman or Latin Church, in the middle.]

The 'Chaldaic' versions of the books of the Pentateuch, which were clearly subordinate to these three texts, were placed in smaller

---

[14] The history of the Polyglot is as follows: the colophon was placed on the first volume printed, the New Testament, in January 1514. The last volume received its colophon in July 1517. At least one copy of the New Testament seems to have found an owner in 1514, for which see Lyell (1917) 100. The first volume of the Old Testament acquired a papal letter of commendation dated 22 March 1520, and the bulk of the edition circulated after this date. Screech has established that some pages from the Complutensian New Testament were reprinted to take account of Erasmus' edition. See A. Reeve (1990) xvi–xxiii.

[15] *Ad lectorem*, vol. I, sig. +3ᵛ.

Hebrew characters beneath them. The rationale behind this conception of the authority of the Vulgate might be stated as follows: the Vulgate translation was made by an accomplished trilingual scholar from the best manuscripts of the Scriptures in the original tongues. Because these manuscripts have perished, and because the Hebrew and Greek texts extant today are pale shadows of their pristine excellence, only the Vulgate translation preserves all the perfections of the original texts. As a translation from a lost original the Vulgate is effectively an original text, and those who are equipped to assess the effectiveness of a translation from Greek or Hebrew must make their assessments in the light of the established authority of the Latin translation. This is what might be called the philological argument for the pre-eminence of the Vulgate. Its most obvious weakness is the necessary competence of the ancient translator. The theological arguments for the primacy of the ancient Latin version confront this problem: they assert that the Latin translation was divinely inspired, and maintain that the divine sanction was similarly granted to the subsequent interpretations of the Church. Nevertheless, although the prologue suggests that the doctrinal purity of the Roman Church is reflected in and founded upon the excellence of its version of the Scriptures, the arrangement on the printed page hints that the Vulgate is only *primus inter pares*. The Complutensian Bible reflected a growing interest in the Biblical languages whilst attempting to indicate the poles within which the new criticism could operate. It did, however, encourage new ways of reading the Scriptural texts because it showed its readers that although the Vulgate was the most reliable witness to the truth, it was only one of a number of witnesses.

Erasmus' own New Testament brings four different texts together for the reader: the Greek text, Erasmus' Latin translation, the Vulgate translation, and Erasmus' annotations on the Greek and Latin texts. The Greek is printed in Froben's clear typeface. Alongside it is set Erasmus' Latin translation from the Greek, which will be considered later. In the fourth edition of 1527 the Latin Vulgate, which the translation recalled and challenged and to which the annotations referred, appeared for the first time beside the Greek text and Erasmus' translation. The title page of this edition states

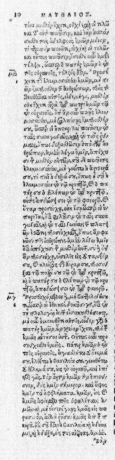

Fig. 1 The *Pater noster* and the Greek Doxology in the fourth edition of Erasmus' *Novum testamentum* (Basle: Froben, 1527). By permission of the Syndics of Cambridge University Library.

that it had been added 'quo protinus ipsis oculis conferre possis, quid conveniat quid dissideat'[16] [So that you can see with your own eyes where it agrees and where it differs]. The arrangement of the printed text serves to emphasise that the Vulgate has been made available for reference purposes only. Erasmus' translation occupies a column in the centre of the page, the Greek text is on the left in a slightly narrower column and a smaller typeface, whilst the Vulgate is set to the right in the narrowest column and the smallest typeface.[17] Its inclusion has been seen as a sop to Erasmus' critics, but its presence on the page actually sharpens the attack on the traditional text.[18] The presence of the Vulgate provides another commentary on Erasmus' translation and allows the reader to make his own comparisons to supplement those which the *Annotations* bring to his attention. I have seen no work on this printed text of the Vulgate. It is likely that it is a close reproduction of a reputable printed text, although it did not print the text of the rival Complutensian Polyglot Bible. The fourth edition of 1527 was the first for which Erasmus had access to the Polyglot,[19] and it is mentioned in the prefatory matter of the edition.[20] Erasmus can hardly have avoided reflecting upon the relationships between the texts in the different editions; nor could those readers who had been able to look at the expensive and relatively rare Polyglot Bible.[21] In 1535, in the fifth edition of the *Novum testamentum*, the Vulgate translation disappeared. No explanation was offered. Perhaps the reason

---

[16] Erasmus (1527).   [17] See Fig. 1.

[18] Bouyer, for example, feels that it was a retreat ((1963–70) 498).

[19] It did not reach Erasmus in time for the third edition of 1523. The Polyglot is cited thirteen times in the *Annotations* on the Gospels and each citation was added in the fourth edition. See A. Reeve (1986) 26, 43, 72, 121, 139–40, 144, 145–7, 164, 165, 175.

[20] EE VI: 467.

[21] According to the letter of Ximenes' executors printed beneath the papal letter, the cost of the Polyglot was to be six-and-a-half gold ducats a set: 'Taxavimus totum opus ducalium aureorum numerorum precio sex cum dimidio aut aliquanto pluris, prout distrahendorum librorum ratio exegerit, habita pro vectura impensarum aestimatione' (vol. I, sig. +8ᵛ). However, on 4 November 1523, Ferdinand Columbus bought a copy at Alcalá for only three gold ducats (Bataillon (1937) 46 n. 3). Perhaps the bulky and expensive sets were not selling quickly: cheaper alternatives were available by 1523. As for their rarity, Pope Leo's prefatory letter states that about 600 copies were printed: '. . . usque ad sexcenta volumina vel amplius' (vol. I, sig. +8ᵛ). Since more than 100 sets survive, *volumina* must refer to complete sets of six volumes. This number may have been reduced significantly when a ship carrying copies for sale in Italy sank: 'perdido en la mar un gran multitud dellas llevándolas á Italia . . .' (from a letter of Philip II, sent to the duc d'Albe by Arias Montanus in 1568, edited in Carvajal (1832) 144).

was more commercial than scholarly: the addition of the Vulgate increased the costs of the edition, and prospective customers no doubt already owned a copy of *this* text.

Some months before the publication of the *Novum instrumentum* Erasmus rejected Nicholas Gerbel's call that the Greek text and his Latin version be printed separately within the same volume.[22] In September 1515, Gerbel criticised the arrangement of the text

ut columna columnae respondeat, sintque intermixta omnia, Greca Latinis et rursum Latina Graecis.[23]

[so that one column corresponds to another and everything is mixed together, Greek with Latin and Latin with Greek.]

He argued that those whose Greek was good would find the Latin a distraction; that those whose Greek was poor would not exercise it when they could fall back on the Latin; and that after all it would not be so very inconvenient for the reader to turn over a few pages to compare the two versions. He suggests that Erasmus' New Testament should be printed like the Aldine edition of the poetry of Gregory Nazianzenus, so that the reader could remove the Latin text if he wished.[24] Gerbel concludes,

Quid autem erit illo magnificentius quam quod eruditi non offendantur ineruditorum ... adminiculo, et ineruditi gaudeant, si adminiculo olim non sit opus?[25]

[What then could be more wonderful than that the learned should not be inconvenienced by the apparatus intended for beginners, and that beginners might be happy when they no longer need the apparatus?]

Erasmus disagreed and Gerbel went on to publish the Greek text from the second edition separately with another printer and publisher.[26] There are a number of possible reasons for Erasmus' preference. It may be that he did not want his careful translation treated with that disdain which Aldus usually reserved for his parallel versions. It is also likely that he hoped that those with little or no

---

[22] For Gerbel, see *EE* II: 120 and Bietenholz (1985–7) II: 90–1.

[23] Ep. 352. *EE* II: 141. *CWE* III: 172. See *CWE*'s note on Gerbel's statement.

[24] Erasmus owned a copy of this volume. In 1518 he sent it to Marten Lips. See Ep. 807. *EE* III: 261–2. For Aldine parallel texts, see Botley (2002) 207–11.

[25] Ep. 352. *EE* II: 141. *CWE* III: 173.

[26] This, the first separate edition of the Greek New Testament, was published at Hagenau in 1521. It was based on Erasmus' edition and the Aldine Greek Bible of 1518.

Greek might be drawn into the language if it was printed on the same page as the Latin. A diligent reader could pick up many points of Greek grammar from the *Annotations*. A more important reason was his reluctance to present either text without distractions. He wanted the correspondence of the Latin with the Greek to be easily challenged and verified. The reader with no Greek at all should be unable to forget that he was reading a translation, and the accomplished Greek scholar must be constantly reminded that western Christendom communicates in Latin. Gerbel saw the publication of a Greek text of the New Testament as the principal end of Erasmus' efforts. Erasmus, despite his championing of Greek studies, envisaged a different and broader readership. He knew that the Greek text could not replace a Latin translation as the primary text of educated Christians. His version occupied a great deal of his time and was not to be compared with the parallel versions of the Aldine Press. He did not regard his Latin translation as simply an *adminiculum*.

The last text, the *Annotations*, is placed at the end of the volume in the first edition; in subsequent editions it had grown to the point that a separate volume was needed to accommodate it.[27] It seems that Erasmus had originally planned to publish only notes on the Vulgate.[28] In 1529, Frans Titelmans wrote that Erasmus' Greek text and his Latin version did not always correspond to the observations in the annotations. Erasmus replied that he had written the annotations before he had settled on the final text of his translation.[29] It was no doubt partly as a consequence of this development that the *Annotations* referred not to Erasmus' translation but to the Vulgate text, but there were other reasons. First, the arrangement allowed the Greek text and Erasmus' version to appear unencumbered by such an extensive apparatus: some of the more substantial of Erasmus' notes would have buried the text they were intended to support. Second, and an important practical consideration, was that this arrangement meant that Erasmus could

---

[27] In 1516 the pages of the New Testament and the annotations were numbered consecutively.

[28] See Allen's discussion and references, *EE* II: 181–2.

[29] See Rummel (1989b) II: 18–19. *Responsio ad collationes cuiusdam gerontodidascali* (Antwerp, 1529). LB IX: 987a, 1011a.

revise the text of his own translation without having to revise the *Annotations* and vice versa. This was not always an advantage: several months after the publication of the first edition of the *Novum instrumentum*, Wolfgang Köpfel warned Erasmus that the discrepancies between the annotations and the Greek and Latin texts might attract criticism, as of course they did.[30] Third, the decision also recognised that the Vulgate text was firmly established in the liturgy of the Church and was unlikely to be replaced. As he described the *Annotations* in the essay *Contra morosos*, which he prefaced to the second edition:

Nos quid nobis videretur et quamobrem videretur separatim ostendimus, nequaquam admoventes manum receptae versioni.[31]

[I have indicated separately what I think correct and why I think it correct, making no attempt to change the version in common use.]

They are a critical tool for assessing the Vulgate translation of the New Testament, and as such they may usefully outlive the translation which they are ostensibly prepared to defend. This arrangement corroborates Erasmus' insistence that he does not intend his version to replace the Vulgate. To Pope Leo X in August 1516 he wrote:

Nec enim hoc labore veterem ac vulgo receptam aeditionem convellimus, sed alicubi depravatam emendamus, aliquot locis obscuram illustramus.[32]

[For I have not overthrown the ancient and commonly accepted text by this labour of mine; but at some parts I correct what is corrupt, in some places I explain what is obscure.]

Here, he presents his text of 1516 to the Pope as a service to the Vulgate text. This, it must be said, is not an attitude which is sustained in the *Annotations* themselves, although the translation published in 1516 certainly retained more of the Vulgate text than later editions.[33]

The practical considerations which made two volumes of the *Novum testamentum* also ensured that the *Annotations* could

---

[30] *EE* II: 334–5.   [31] *Contra morosos*. LB VI: sig.∗∗∗.

[32] Ep. 446. *EE* II: 290. *CWE* IV: 5. Erasmus uses very similar language in his letter to Pucci of August 1518: Ep. 860. *EE* III: 381.

[33] The genesis of Erasmus' translation, and its relationship to the Vulgate, have until recently been obscured. See Brown (1984) 351–80.

circulate separately. Erasmus had resisted this tendency too. The *Annotations* are present to defend the particular renderings and broader principles which the translation exemplifies. A Latin translation had seldom required such a formidable defence. Where he changes a cherished reading in the Vulgate translation he fortifies it with a substantial entry: the length of individual notes tends to be proportional to the resistance Erasmus anticipated, or had already encountered. Although he did allow his Latin translation to be printed separately on a number of occasions, and even provided a preface, he seems to have done so reluctantly, protesting that his version 'nudum et inerme Zoilorum dentibus obiiceretur'[34] [had been thrown naked and defenceless to the teeth of critics]. Perhaps his previous experiences at the hands of unscrupulous printers had persuaded him that if he did not authorise an edition, an unauthorised one would appear. These prefaces at least allowed him to say a few words in his own defence and to urge his readers to read cautiously.[35] His misgivings seem to have been based on the possibility that some readers might read his translation as a summary of the opinions expressed in the *Annotations*. That is, that it represented Erasmus' final opinion as to the best rendering of the Greek, when often it represented only one of a number of possible interpretations. He urges any reader offended by his version to look to his *Annotations*. These *Annotations* sometimes refer directly to Erasmus' own translation, but more often they use a rendering of the Vulgate as a starting point for a discussion of a number of possible translations. They also allowed Erasmus to retreat from some of the positions adopted in the translation. As a translator Erasmus must make hard decisions; as an annotator he can place at least some of these decisions in the hands of his readers. He would prefer his reader to agree with him, but if they could not agree, they might at least be able to understand his methods, sympathise with his motives, and agree to differ.

The arrangement of these three texts in Erasmus' edition made possible new ways of reading the New Testament. In 1505, in the preface to his edition of Valla's annotations, he had written that

---

[34] Ep. 1010. *EE* IV: 58. *CWE* VII: 64.   [35] See Allen's notes to Ep. 1010. *EE* IV: 58.

si quibus non vacat totam Graecorum linguam perdiscere, ii tamen Vallae studio non mediocriter adiuvabuntur.[36]

[those who do not have time to learn the whole Greek language thoroughly will be greatly helped by Valla's work.]

Erasmus' New Testament was another, more comprehensive, aid to such readers. Its readers did not need to have mastered the Greek language in order to be able to extend the semantic possibilities of the Latin translation. While the principal aim of the work was to furnish the Christian reader with an accurate Latin translation of the New Testament, with the revised translation printed in the second edition of 1519 this end had been largely attained. Thereafter, Erasmus' attention increasingly turned to the *Annotations* in the controversy that followed their publication. These were addressed not only to the textual scholar and the potential critic, but also to the Christian reader. They put a form upon some of the speculations that the juxtaposition of the Greek and Latin stimulates. John Fisher wrote gratefully to Erasmus shortly after the publication of the *Novum instrumentum*

Tibi et istud debeo, Erasme, quod coniicere aliquousque possum, ubi non omnino Latinis Graeca respondeant.[37]

[I also owe you this, Erasmus, that up to a point I can draw conclusions about places where the Greek and the Latin do not entirely correspond.]

This must have gratified Erasmus, for it is precisely the attitude to the New Testament that he wanted to encourage in his readers, and one which the Greek text was included to facilitate. The interventions in the *Annotations* allow Erasmus to modify the Greek–Latin equation set up in the first half of his edition. He intervenes to indicate the limitations of his own version, but also because he felt that translation could be more than simply a shortcut for the Greekless: the procedure can provide its own revelations. The *Annotations* allow the reader to participate in the process of constructing a Latin text from the Greek. They draw attention to the processes of translation in order to show that the translator has been conscientious, but also because he feels that the ways in which the Greek

---

[36] Ep. 182. *EE* I: 412. *CWE* II: 96.
[37] Ep. 592. *EE* II: 598. *CWE* IV: 397. Allen dates this letter to c.June 1517.

becomes Latin throw further light on the Greek. By describing how he translated he may enable the reader to do otherwise. As Fisher discovered, and as Erasmus showed by his continued expansion of the *Annotations* in subsequent editions, the possibilities inherent in this procedure were vast. Erasmus' Latin translation attempts to communicate what it is like to read the Greek New Testament. It is not entirely fanciful to suggest that the *Annotations* attempt to show what it is like to translate it.

Elegantiae

In May 1518, in a letter addressed to Marten Lips, Erasmus gave a detailed reply to the criticisms of his work on the New Testament made by an anonymous critic.[38] Discussing his critic's views on the Latinity of the Vulgate translation, Erasmus complains that:

tota hac disputatione commiscet elegantiam sermonis, quae grammaticorum est, cum eloquentia cumque poetica, quasi nihil intersit.[39]

[throughout this debate he confuses elegance of language, which is a matter for grammarians, with eloquence and with poetry, as though there were no difference.]

Erasmus' opponent does not use, and may not have understood, his distinction between *elegantia* and *eloquentia*. Erasmus insists on it because it is a concept of some importance for his work on the New Testament. In the essay *Methodus* prefaced to the first edition of the New Testament, Erasmus emphasises the value of the Biblical languages for the Christian scholar. However, he goes on, only a basic competence is required:

Nec flagitamus ut in his [linguis] usque ad eloquentiae miraculum proveharis; satis est si ad mundiciam et elegantiam, hoc est mediocritatem aliquam, progrediare, quod sufficiat ad iudicandum.[40]

[I do not ask you to become prodigiously eloquent in these languages. It is enough if you make tolerable progress, and acquire just so much neatness and elegance with the language as will enable you to make up your own mind.]

---

[38] Allen identifies this critic with Edward Lee (*EE* III: 312). Rummel refutes this proposal ((1989b) I: 115ff.).
[39] Ep. 843. *EE* III: 315. *CWE* VI: 8.   [40] Delègue (1990) 100.

Erasmus regards elegance as a valuable acquisition, but clearly it is a lesser attainment than eloquence. He seems to have drawn this specific meaning of the word, as he drew so much else, from the work of Lorenzo Valla.[41] Erasmus had met Valla's *Elegantiae* long before he came across Valla's work on the New Testament in the monastic library near Louvain in 1505. Although Erasmus' epitome of the *Elegantiae* was not published until 1529, it was a product of his youth.[42] Valla's *Elegantiae* were at least in part the product of his long experience as a translator of Greek texts.[43] Consequently, it is not surprising that this carefully limited use of the word *elegantia* should have given the later translator another tool with which to analyse his own translation. For example, in the *Annotations* Erasmus notes as *elegantiae* those distinctions which are language-dependent:

Latinius erat, *neque binas tunicas*. Nam Graeci nesciunt hanc elegantiam, quae tamen non erat negligenda Latino interpreti.[44]

['Neque binas tunicas' would have been better Latin. The Greek language does not make this distinction, but the Latin translator should not have passed over it.]

Nor was Valla the only one to write *elegantiae*. Jerome, says Erasmus, commented on the difference between *agnoscere* and *cognoscere*: 'indicat hanc elegantiam duorum verborum et divus Hieronymus'[45] [St Jerome points out this distinction between the two words]. Erasmus himself in his *Annotations* remarks upon more *elegantiae* than he found in Valla's work. He goes even further when he comments on some of the elegances of the Greek language. In a note on John's Gospel, he explains the meanings

---

[41] For a discussion of Valla's use of the word *elegantia*, see Marsh (1979) 100–3. Pseudo-Cicero seems to distinguish the two words in *De optimo genere oratorum* 2.

[42] Erasmus made two paraphrases for private use. The first was perhaps made about 1488; the second some years later, probably before 1500. An unauthorised edition of his first paraphrase was printed in 1529. Erasmus published his own revised version in 1531. See *EE* I: 108 n.106, and Heesakkers and Waszink (1983) 187–351.

[43] Besides the well-known and often-printed versions of Herodotus and Thucydides, Valla also produced versions of Aesop (33 fables), Basil (the nineteenth homily), Demosthenes (*De corona*), Homer (*Iliad* I–XVI) and Xenophon (*Cyropaedia* I: 1–4).

[44] Mt x. A. Reeve (1986) 47. From 1516. Valla does not comment on this rendering. Manetti retains *duas tunicas* from the Vulgate text.

[45] Lk *prologue*. A. Reeve (1986) 152. From 1516. Valla does not comment on this word. Manetti uses *cognoscere*.

of four Greek verbs which can all be rendered by the Latin verb *mittere*.[46] Clearly Erasmus took Valla's sense of elegance to heart.

Erasmus insists on the distinction between eloquence and elegance because it is consistent with a more fundamental and more ancient distinction. Eloquence is the capacity to persuade, and it is the province of the *rhetor*. Elegance is the careful use of language to distinguish between fine shades of meaning, and it belongs to the *grammaticus*. Quintilian discusses the different fields of the grammarian and rhetorician: 'Nos suum cuique professioni modum demus'[47] [Let us grant each profession its own competence]. A certain type of commentary was also the realm of the *grammaticus*: the commentaries of Servius on Vergil and of Donatus on Terence were representatives of the tradition. The Fathers too, says Erasmus, were grammarians. In a letter to Henry Bullock of August 1516, he wrote:

Neque negari potest Hieronymum, Ambrosium, Augustinum, quorum autoritate potissimum res theologica nititur, ex hoc grammaticorum ordine fuisse.[48]

[And it cannot be denied that Jerome, Ambrose and Augustine, whose authority above all sustains our theology, were all grammarians.]

Erasmus' adoption of the role with regard to the New Testament was stimulated by Valla. In 1505, in his preface to his edition of Valla's *Annotations*, he called him a *homo grammaticus*, and went on to define the translator's task as that of a grammarian:

totum hoc, divinas vertere scripturas, grammatici videlicet partes sunt.[49]

[this whole task of translating the Holy Scriptures is plainly the role of the grammarian.]

He continued in the same letter:

Ac ne ipsa quidem, opinor, disciplinarum omnium regina theologia ducet indignum admoveri sibi manus, ac debitum exhiberi obsequium, a pedissequa grammatica.[50]

[And indeed I believe that theology herself, the queen of all sciences, will not think it beneath her dignity to be attended – and shown due deference – by her handmaid grammar.]

---

[46] A. Reeve (1986) 223. From 1522. [47] *Inst. orat.* II: i, 4.
[48] Ep. 456. *EE* II: 325. *CWE* IV: 49. [49] Ep. 182. *EE* I: 409, 410. *CWE* II: 94.
[50] *EE* I: 410.

Erasmus, who had in his early years styled himself *poeta*, who had laboriously acquired the degree which entitled him to write as *theologus*, insisted in 1516 that his role with regard to the Latin translation of the New Testament was that of *grammaticus*. One very practical reason for this was that it allowed him clearly to delimit the extent of the *Annotations*. Many critics have commented upon the polemics which Erasmus attaches to a number of the *Annotations*, but it should be noted that the majority deal with purely linguistic matters in restrained, even curt, prose. Another less obvious reason for this stance was that he did not want to translate the New Testament *oratorio more*, as some earlier scholars had done with pagan Greek authors. The grammarian undertakes one type of translation, the rhetorician another.[51] Erasmus would not strive to make his Latin version eloquent: eloquence is a property of the original text and the translator must attempt to convey it where it is present and avoid it where it is not. But any accurate translation must be elegant at every point.

Erasmus' early enthusiasm for Valla's work and his adoption of his position with regard to the Scriptures are often noted. Less obvious are Erasmus' growing reservations about the application of Valla's methods to Scriptural texts. About 1497 Erasmus composed a brief educational tract, *De ratione studii*. After an unauthorised edition of this was published in 1511, Erasmus revised his original work and it was printed in 1514.[52] Amongst a number of important changes, it is significant that although Valla is still recommended, the young student is now also cautioned:

Neque enim te velim per omnia velut addictum Laurentianis servire preceptis.[53]

[But I would not have you give yourself over entirely to Valla's rules.]

Erasmus' *Annotations* are his most substantial and subtle commentary on Valla's New Testament commentary. They provide ample evidence for Erasmus' qualifications of Valla's method. Many of Erasmus' references in the *Annotations* to Valla's work are criticisms of his fastidiousness. Erasmus believed that an important function of accurate translation is to forestall irrelevant exegesis.

---

[51] Cf. pseudo-Cicero, *De opt. gen. orat.* 5: 'nec converti ut interpres, sed ut orator . . .'
[52] Hyma (1932) 106–7. He edits both versions, 129–34.   [53] Hyma (1932) 132.

Valla's trivial or strained grammatical notes are potentially as much of an obstacle to good translating – and hence to good reading – as the sophistries of the theologians. A number of examples from the *Annotations* will demonstrate that Erasmus repeatedly questions the value of Valla's elegances in the context of the New Testament. From Matthew's Gospel:

quae Valla cavillatur hoc loco de *Maria* et *Mariam*, minutiora judicavi quam ut his lectorem voluerim onerari.[54]

[Valla's quibbles at this point about 'Maria' and 'Mariam' are more trivial, I have decided, than I would want to burden the reader with.]

Or again:

Porro quod taxat Valla, πόλιν non *urbem* sed *civitatem* esse versum, non solum minutius est, verum etiam iniquius.[55]

[In fact, Valla's criticism that 'πόλις' was not rendered by 'urbs' but by 'civitas' is not only rather trivial, but actually quite misleading.]

From Mark:

quod Valla mavult *exstitit* pro *fuit*, et cavillatur nescio quid de *fuit Joannes baptizans*, haud multum ad rem theologicam pertinet.[56]

[that Valla prefers 'exstitit' over 'fuit', and argues something or other about 'fuit Joannes baptizans', is not really theologically relevant.]

And from Luke:

Laurentius videtur suspicari scriptum fuisse, *vel* et *ut*. Caeterum quod de mutata conjunctione cavillatur, leviculum est, et ad elegantiam sermonis attinens magis quam ad rem theologicam.[57]

[Lorenzo seems to suspect that 'vel' and 'ut' were originally written. His other objections about the change of conjunction are of little importance, and are more concerned with the elegance of the statement than with its theological significance.]

---

[54] Mt I. A. Reeve (1986) 3. Valla's first note in the edition of 1505, and a lengthy one. Manetti retains the Vulgate: *Ioseph virum Mariae*.

[55] Mt v. A. Reeve (1986) 26. Valla's note is among his notes on Mt v, but seems to refer to Mt IV: 13 (Valla (1962) I: 809).

[56] Mk I. This is the reading of the second edition of the *Annotations*. The punctuation of the fifth edition is rather confusing (A. Reeve (1986) 114). By 1535 Erasmus has substituted the rare verb *argutatur* for *cavillatur*. Manetti's version retains *fuit* from the Vulgate.

[57] Lk XVIII. A. Reeve (1986) 203. Valla (1962) I: 837.

All these notes appear from the first edition of 1516. They draw attention to the sins of too much elegance. It is not so much that some matters which fall within the sphere of the grammarian are beneath the notice of the Scriptural commentator, more that it is possible to vindicate unimportant truths at the expense of important ones. Speculations which do more to demonstrate the author's ingenuity than to advance the reader's understanding have no place in a grammatical commentary on Scripture:

Ut est elegans in huiusmodi minutiis apte philosophari in arcanis litteris, ita foedum extra rem nugari.[58]

[Although it is elegant to philosophise appropriately about *minutiae* of this sort among Scriptural mysteries, it is detestable to talk irrelevant nonsense.]

Erasmus seems to have recognised a negative quality in Valla's criticisms. Erasmus' annotations explore the connotations of the Greek at greater length than those of Valla. Whereas Valla tends to eliminate false readings, Erasmus' notes more often attempt to enumerate those which are possibly true. He also takes very deliberate steps to distance himself from some of the more ostentatious elegances of Valla's commentary:

Neque vero libet hic commemorare ridiculam differentiam inter *aperire* et *adaperire*, quam Laurentius argutius irridet quam gravem deceat virum, etiamsi merito id facit.[59]

[Nor indeed can we recount here the absurd distinction between 'aperire' and 'adaperire' which Lorenzo mocks with more cleverness than becomes a serious man, even though he is right.]

Erasmus certainly had a point about the way Valla chose to conduct the debate. It is also true that Erasmus had enough real battles to fight in the *Annotations* without entering the lists over every minor distinction. But Erasmus' note here, like many of his criticisms of Valla, serves other purposes. It allows him to draw attention to Valla's grammatical distinction. At the same time, he is able to emphasise the decorum of his own commentary by highlighting Valla's lapse. Valla's philology may be sound, says Erasmus, but

[58] Lk I. A. Reeve (1986) 155. Added 1519.
[59] Mk VII. A. Reeve (1986) 132. From 1516. Valla (1932) I: 826. Manetti also changes the Vulgate *adaperire* to *aperire*.

he is in danger of neglecting the end it was created to serve. In fact, Erasmus repeatedly holds up Valla as an example of the sort of pedantry for which Erasmus himself was often attacked. Yet if Erasmus often attempts to make Valla carry some of the opprobrium directed at the *Novum instrumentum*, his numerous sharp or satirical entries in the *Annotations* show that Erasmus was not always the *gravis vir* that he would have us believe.

Despite these defensive manoeuvrings around Valla's work, Erasmus did believe that the Scriptural commentator was vulnerable to a dangerous loss of perspective. The grammarian is liable to fall into his own brand of exegetical excess as he plies his craft among the Scriptures. *Elegantiae* are a necessary resource for the translator, but must be used cautiously. Erasmus would have known the discussion of the word *elegans* in Aulus Gellius.[60] Gellius notes that in early Latin authors it had a pejorative sense, denoting a style of life – not a quality of mind – characterised by an unnecessary fastidiousness or niceness. Even when the pejorative sense receded, it remained a quality which it was desirable to have in moderation rather than abundance. Valla's *Elegantiae* showed just how precise an instrument Latin could be, but Erasmus believed that such precision was not always relevant. It was certainly dangerous to construct doctrine upon such points, although they might be used to buttress practices with a clearer Scriptural foundation elsewhere. Erasmus uses the notion of the extent of the grammarian's competence to exclude certain types of discussion from the *Annotations*, and whenever the grammarian can leave well alone he likes to do so. When Matthew and Mark disagree with Luke his note draws the reader's attention to the discrepancy:

Hoc admonui ne quis temere scripturam mutet: difficultatem quaestionum explicant doctores.[61]

[I make this point in case any one should rashly change what is written: the theologians explain the problems it raises.]

The grammarian establishes the best text of Scripture with all its problems, but does not undertake its interpretation. Further difficulties belong to the theologians.

---

[60] *Noctes atticae* XI: 2.   [61] Mk IX. A. Reeve (1986) 135. Added 1527.

Erasmus saw that the distinction he was making was of central importance for the substance of the *Annotations*. Of course, it was not always clear where grammar ended and the *res theologica* began. An example will illustrate the sort of problems the grammarian might face. Erasmus notes that sometimes scribes wilfully corrupt passages where the meaning offends them. In Matthew's Gospel, Erasmus' text translates 'Whoever is angry with his brother without a cause shall be in danger of the judgement.'[62] Erasmus suspects 'without a cause', εἰκῆ, to be an interpolation. He translates the word in his Latin because it appears in some Greek manuscripts and is an accepted Vulgate reading; but, as his note makes clear, he does so under protest and with St Jerome's support for his scepticism:

Additum videtur ab audaculo quopiam, qui ceu mitigare voluerit quod alioqui durius dictum videbatur.[63]

[It seems to have been added by some bold scribbler as if he wanted to soften what seemed otherwise a rather harsh statement.]

This putative scribe presumably felt that Christ could not have said what the words say that he said; Erasmus thinks that he could and did, and so emends back. Both alterations involve judgements as to Christ's style and purpose: to restore the text is thus to reinstate a particular conception of Christ. Erasmus saw that perceived theological difficulties can corrupt the text, and that corrupt texts create problems which can generate unusual theological solutions. Ideally, the determinable letter constitutes the realm of the grammarian, whilst the interpretation of the Spirit belongs to the theologian. Practically, the grammarian must always read the text with a keen eye for its theological implications if interpolations are to be discovered and excluded. Problems of demarcation had led to a tension between the two:

Rideat qui volet has grammaticarum annotationes, modo fateatur terque quaterque Theologos in his labi. Tolerabile, si tantum laberentur, nisi lapsui jungerent impudentiam calumniandi.[64]

---

[62] Mt v: 22. This is the reading of the King James Version. Manetti too retained *sine causa*; Valla prefers the manuscripts which have it (Valla (1962) 1: 809); Theodore Beza retained it (Beza (1642) 16). The editors of the Sixtine and Clementine recensions of the Vulgate, and modern scholarship, side with Erasmus.

[63] Mt v. A. Reeve (1986) 27. From 1516. [64] Lk 1. A. Reeve (1986) 157. Added 1527.

[If anyone wants to laugh at these grammatical notes, let him; but let him confess again and again that theologians have made mistakes over them. We might have tolerated their mistakes, if they had not added impudent abuse to their error.]

This sort of language was not likely to promote harmony between the self-styled representatives of each class. I suspect that Erasmus was less concerned with drawing the difficult line between the two disciplines than with making the point that they were two disciplines. Historical philology was still so young a science that he might well go on the offensive in order to establish its value as an aid to so august a discipline as theology.

Consistency

Lorenzo Valla never wrote a treatise on translation, but a number of principles can be extracted from his comments in his annotations on the New Testament. Valla should be given some of the credit for making explicit some of the assumptions that most readers and translators bring to any translation. Such assumptions are part of the data of reading as well as translating. If the translator and the reader share certain beliefs about what it is to translate, the reader may be able to form a clearer idea of the relationship between the original and the translation, and may be able to use the translation to evaluate some of the internal relationships of the original text. I have already noticed Erasmus' concern to eliminate irrelevant exegesis. He saw that some false interpretations had evolved because exegetes assumed that the Vulgate translator was following such a system when in fact he was not – or at least was not following it consistently. Erasmus frequently drew attention to the variations in the quality of the Vulgate translation. For example, in Matthew's Gospel:

Latine vertit interpres, et eleganter magis quam suo more: ut hic quoque admonendus sit lector, ne fallatur.[65]

[The translator writes in good Latin, and more elegantly than he usually does. The reader should be warned of this here, so that he does not stumble.]

[65] Mt XXVIII. A. Reeve (1986) 107. From 1516.

In Mark:

proprie quidem et eleganter vertit interpres . . . haud scio an lector tantum expectet.[66]

[The translator renders accurately and elegantly . . . I do not know whether the reader expected as much.]

And in Luke:

Interpres eleganter reddidit magis quam ad verbum, aut suo more.[67]

[The translator has translated elegantly, rather than literally, and contrary to his usual practice.]

Of course, Erasmus' surprise is an ironic stance, as his marginal note indicates:

Interpres amore Latinitatis recedit a verbis.[68]

[the translator departs from a literal version from his love of Latinity.]

The notion that unexpected moments of competence from the ancient translator might unsettle the reader is not meant to be plausible. The point is that the reader might reasonably demand a consistent tone and a carefully considered set of principles from his translator. The first and most easily adopted principle is set out by Valla: different words in Greek should be rendered with different words in Latin, and the same Latin word should be used for any one Greek word.[69] Once a translator has declared an equivalence he must stand by it. Valla also declared that the construction of Greek sentences should be imitated in Latin as far as the rules of Latin grammar and syntax allow.[70] This rule raises the question of synonymous constructions but suggests that there will be an inevitable conflict between the structures of the two languages. The translator might make a virtue of this necessity: two words might not be truly synonymous, but two sentences might be more nearly so.

---

[66] Mk xiv. A. Reeve (1986) 145. From 1516.
[67] Lk xxii. A. Reeve (1986) 214. From 1516.
[68] Mt xxvii. A. Reeve (1986) 107. Added 1535.
[69] See for example Valla on Mt vii: 24; I Cor. iv: 3–4; and Schwarz (1955) 133.
[70] See for example Valla on Mt xviii: 24; I Cor. xv: 1; and Schwarz (1955) 133.

Yet these simple principles were problematic. In what sense might any Latin word claim to be synonymous with a Greek one? Valla knew as surely as Erasmus that for a translator such rules could only be guidelines. Allegiance to their spirit might well involve compromising their letter. Erasmus certainly advocated consistency in *ad verbum* translations:

Debebat sibi constare interpres postea quam coeperat nomina vertere in verba.[71]

[The translator must be consistent with himself once he has begun to turn nouns into verbs.]

But he knew that not all translations could be made *ad verbum*. In his translations of classical works, Erasmus' willingness to set aside the Letter of the original is an indication of his confidence that he is in touch with its Spirit. Such confidence is misplaced in a Biblical translator: if it be granted that Scripture contains more mysteries than a man can understand, translating *ad verbum* is safest. As Jerome noted, one who translates according to the sense can only translate what he understands;[72] one who translates according to the word may succeed in transmitting mysteries he himself does not understand and of which he may not even be aware. Erasmus is not sceptical of the existence of such mysteries, but he does doubt their relevance to the pressing matter of the reader's salvation. For this reason he was often prepared to move away from the most literal rendering. In his translation of the New Testament, he seems never to use two complementary nouns to cover the range of meaning present in a single Greek word, although it is a common enough strategy in his classical translations.[73] This might be taken as indicating a further principle which he adopted for his Scriptural translations: that one word in the Greek should be translated by one word in the Latin. That is, the translator should translate *ad verbum* where this does not violate the sense. Erasmus reserves for his annotations words and phrases which might communicate those aspects of the original which he had sacrificed to a close

---

[71] Mk XXII. A. Reeve (1986) 140. From 1516.
[72] For example in the *Praefatio ad Pentateuchum*: 'Aliud est enim vatem, aliud esse interpretem. Ibi Spiritus ventura praedicit: hic eruditio et verborum copia, ea quae intelligit, transfert' (*PL* XXVIII: 182).
[73] See Rummel (1985) 25, 96–7.

verbal rendering. That the best Latin synonym for a Greek word may exclude some of the connotations of the original word, or that it may introduce meanings not present in the original text, is to be accepted as one of the fundamental limitations of the art.

In different contexts the same Greek word may require different translations. Valla's principle can be saved by ensuring that these different translations are consistently employed in each context. The failure of the Vulgate to observe this begins to seem like carelessness because the ancient translator obviously understood the principle involved:

Hoc loco interpres recte omisit ὅτι: quod, cum alicubi faciat, mirandum cur non idem perpetuo faciat quoties sermonis exigit ratio.[74]

[In this place the translator correctly omits ὅτι, and since he does it in some places it is remarkable that he does not do it all the time, whenever the nature of the statement requires it.]

In fact, such inconsistencies occur so frequently that we might suspect the translator of introducing his own rhetorical variety into the text. 'Amat variare interpres' [the translator delights in variety], Erasmus complains. 'Quorsum obsecro conducit ista varietatis affectatio?'[75] [What, I ask, is the point of this affectation of variety?] Nor is his inconsistency the result of a frustrated talent, for he is not very good at it. Erasmus remarks with heavy irony:

Latrones nunc vertit quod modo verterat *Nequam*, homo nimirum copiosus.[76]

[This man's store of words is so extensive that now he translates as 'latrones' the word he translated as 'nequam' just before.]

The Vulgate translator, he says, 'mire lascivit sua copia' [is so very free with his store of words]. He is 'immodicus copiae affectator'[77] [affects the abundant style without restraint]. This, an unwarranted liberty for a translator to take with any text, is a particularly dangerous indulgence for a translator of Scripture. The translation may introduce a subtlety, foreign to the original, about which idle speculation may gather. In John's Gospel, for example, the Vulgate

[74] Mk I. A. Reeve (1986) 117. From 1516.
[75] Lk xvi. A. Reeve (1986) 200. From 1516. III Jn. A. Reeve (1986) 773. Added 1527.
[76] Lk xxiii. A. Reeve (1986) 215. From 1516.
[77] Mk v. A. Reeve (1986) 125. Lk xiii. A. Reeve (1986) 196. Both from 1516.

translates φῶς as *lux* and as *lumen*. Erasmus consistently translates *lux*,

ne quis Graecanici sermonis ignarus in commutata voce Latina somniet subesse mysterium.[78]

[In case anyone who does not know the Greek language dreams that some mystery lies behind the change in the Latin word.]

It is not unnatural to assume that distinctions in the Latin text correspond to distinctions in the Greek. That they often do not, says Erasmus, is due to the Vulgate translator's wanton inconsistency.

Even with more reliable translations to hand, careful theologians still ought to consult the Greek text before embarking upon a detailed exposition of a passage. When poor theologians set to work upon a poor translation the result would be absurd were it not for the dangers that attend their errors:

Recentiores aliquot theologi ingens mysterium subesse volunt in hisce praepositionibus *ex* et *de*, cum apud Graecos eadem sit praepositio, apud nos diversa, tantum quia libuit interpreti, qui frequenter affectat varietatem ubi nihil opus.[79]

[Some more modern theologians feel that a great mystery lies beneath these prepositions 'ex' and 'de'. In Greek it is one preposition; in Latin it is several, at the discretion of the translator, who often varies his words when there is no need.]

This is an example of theological *elegantiae*, although here it is groundless. In this case Valla has already exposed their error, as Erasmus indicates.[80] He saw that centuries of speculation had been founded upon subtleties created by the translation and not present in the Greek text. Some of these subtleties had come to play an important part in contemporary theology. Erasmus provoked a storm of protest when he changed 'Ave gratia plena' of the Vulgate text to 'Ave gratiosa' because he was felt to be threatening the concept of Grace. When he translated 'poenitemini' [do penance] as 'resipiscite' [come to your senses] some saw it as an assault on the sacrament of penance. While Erasmus struggled conscientiously to

---

[78] Jn 1. A. Reeve (1986) 223. From 1516. Valla remarked on the ancient translator's practice (Valla (1962) 1: 809). Manetti retained *lux* and *lumen* from the Vulgate.
[79] Mt 1. A. Reeve (1986) 9. From 1516.
[80] A. Reeve (1986) 3. From 1516. Valla (1962) 1: 804.

produce the most accurate translation he could, the Vulgate translator's apparently casual attitude to the text was defended by its
antiquity. In 1523, in his preface to his edition of St Hilary, he
complained

Nunc erga veteres pene superstitiose candidi, in horum libris qui nostra scri-
bunt aetate quaedam etiam recte scripta depravamus, omnia incommode
interpretamur.[81]

[Now we are almost too scrupulously fair toward the ancients, we distort even
what is well said in the books of our modern writers, and we interpret everything
in a bad sense.]

Erasmus the 'laudator temporis acti' had come a long way from the
optimism of 1516. To defend his own translation he had to show that
his predecessor's failure was just that, and invective was the tool of
his age. Still, Erasmus' dismay was more than a rhetorical stance,
and after a thorough acquaintance with the Vulgate translator's
freewheeling equations, this dismay often became irritation. When
the Vulgate translates χάσμα by *chaos* he writes

Mirum quid venerit in mentem interpreti ut Graecam vocem alia Graeca redderet,
nec ea sane idem significante.[82]

[What was the translator thinking of, to translate one Greek word by another
Greek word which has a different meaning?]

Mirum recurs so frequently throughout the *Annotations* that it even
begins to seem a little understated. It does not represent Erasmus'
surprise, but his exasperation with the Vulgate translator.

Resolving ambiguities

The problem of the degree to which a translator should unravel the
ambiguities of the original text is particularly acute for the Biblical
translator. Dorp had claimed in a letter to Erasmus that the meaning
of the Scriptures is clear. Thomas More replied on behalf of his
friend:

---

[81] Prefaced to his edition of St Hilary: Ep. 1334. *EE* v: 175. *CWE* ix: 249.
[82] Lk xvi: 26. A. Reeve (1986) 201. From 1516. Manetti renders *chaos*. Valla comments
on the passage (Valla (1962) i: 837).

Neque quisquam est antiquorum omnium qui se fateri est ausus intelligere, ut cuius intellectum putant altissimo dei consilio, vel ob id ipsum profundius obstrusum esse, ut curiosos oculos provocaret et semotis ac labore eruendis opibus segnia excitaret ingenia, quae alioquin ad obvios expositosque thesauros ipsa securitate torpescerent.[83]

[Not one of all the ancients dared to claim that he understood it, for they thought that its meaning was the more deeply buried according to God's great plan so as to stimulate inquiring eyes and rouse sluggish minds with the prospect of distant and buried treasures; otherwise the assurance of easy access to exposed treasures might allow such minds to grow dull.]

The difficulty of reaching this treasure sustains the right attitude towards it: we are inclined to value what we have to work for. On the other hand, it is the task of the translator to ease our entrance to the text. If God deliberately veils his wisdom, how accessible can or should the translator make it? If the translator attempts to make explicit what is recondite in the original he may destroy delicate shades of meaning. In fact, what Dorp probably meant was that Scripture is clear enough. The translator must proceed on the assumption that if the Greek is ambiguous, it cannot be so upon a subject necessary for salvation. In Matthew's Gospel, for example, just how insulting is *racha*, and how necessary is it that we know? Could Erasmus have translated it? He suggests some possibilities:

Nonnulli sic distinguunt inter *racha* et *fatuum*, ut differentia peccati non sit in dictis sed in animo dicentis. Nam Dominus suo more doctrinam suam attemperans ad captum simplicium . . .[84]

[Some distinguish between 'racha' and 'fatuus' in this way: the difference between the sins is not in the words but in the mind of the speaker. For the Lord, accommodating his teaching to the capacity of the uneducated as is his way . . .]

Swearing is something that we tend to do in our native language. The word seems to be a fragment of Christ's very speech, an example *suo more* of his down-to-earth directness. Some might feel that this is sufficient reason for leaving it as Matthew found it. Besides, translating Hebrew – or Aramaic for that matter – was not Erasmus' speciality. What is more important is that if the Evangelist left it in,

[83] Letter to Dorp, in Kinney (1986) 59.
[84] Mt v. A. Reeve (1986) 28. Added 1527. Manetti follows the Vulgate.

he presumably had very good reasons for doing so. That we may not understand those reasons is beside the point. The translation must not stand in the way of another being able to do so. Even those difficulties of Scripture which seem to be purely linguistic may harbour divine mysteries.

In fact, Erasmus had several subtle strategies at his disposal. Some of his reservations are embedded in the printed text. Unlike Valla and Manetti, Erasmus doubted the authenticity of the Greek Doxology at the end of the Lord's Prayer, and this doubt, registered in the Annotations, is reflected in the text of his own version: he caused the clause to be set in a slightly smaller type.[85] Erasmus seems to have been able to influence even the smallest elements of the printing process.[86] More fundamentally, he could also make use of certain translations to preserve the text they embody. Erasmus saw his edition of the New Testament as a device to halt the progressive decay of the Scriptures. He attempted to correct the corruptions which had crept into the text down the centuries, and to provide a foundation upon which future scholarship could build, much as he built on it during his own lifetime by expanding successive editions. When Erasmus wrote that

hic meus labor non solum amolitur mendas sacrorum voluminum, verumetiam obstat ne posthac queant depravari.[87]

[This labour of mine not only removes blemishes from the Scriptures, but it also provides an obstacle to corruption in the future.]

he was probably thinking principally of the ways in which the *Annotations* defend his Latin translation. However, he does make a particular translation specifically to forestall a scribal error. He finds *reconciliari* in his Latin manuscripts, and suggests that it has been corrupted from the imperative *reconciliare*:

---

[85] See Fig. 1. The Doxology is in Erasmus' Greek text, but not in his edition of the Vulgate.

[86] Did Erasmus dictate or influence the punctuation or capitalisation of his works? Both varied considerably between different editions of his New Testament. He was aware of its importance: in his late treatise on the pronunciation of Greek and Latin he wrote: 'Recta distinctio credi vix potest quantum adferat lucis ad intelligendam sententiam, ut non inscite dixerit eruditus quidam, aptam distinctionem, commentarii genus esse' (Cytowska (1973) 38; LB I: 927b). According to *CWE*, several classical authors write about punctuation; none of them call it a 'commentarii genus' (XXVI: 596 n. 127).

[87] Ep. 860. *EE* III: 381. *CWE* VI: 97.

Unde nos vertimus *Reconcilieris*, ne perinde facilis esset depravatio.[88]

[And so we have translated 'reconcilieris', so that it might not be so easily corrupted.]

This is not a consideration which would influence a modern translator of the New Testament, and it suggests that Erasmus was still thinking of the written transmission of the Word. The reputation of Erasmus as a man of the printed book should not be allowed to obscure the fact that most of the sources he consulted were manuscripts. Of course, the fact that he makes a note about the possibility of corruption also forestalls that corruption. An explanation of a related strategy occurs in his note on one reading of the Vugate, *venimus*:

Venimus prima acutum pronunciandum est, utpote praeteriti temporis, ἤλθομεν. Quod ego minutius esse ducerem quam ut admoneretur, nisi passim audirem multos in hoc et ambigere et errare. Proinde nos vertimus *accessimus*.[89]

['Venimus' is to be pronounced with the accent on the first syllable, since it is in the past tense, 'ἤλθομεν'. I would have considered this point too trivial to mention were it not that everywhere I hear people in doubt and making mistakes. Accordingly, we have translated 'accessimus'.]

Here, all the clarity of the Latin text could not avoid the possibility of ambiguity. The Greek text incontrovertibly clears up a potential problem. It is significant that in this note Erasmus has identified another transitional stage during which the text might be corrupted: in the translation from written to spoken word.

Faulty translation is often easily remedied. Where the Vulgate is ambiguous and the Greek is not, Erasmus retranslates. For example, in the Letter of Jude the Vulgate has 'fluctus feri maris'. Erasmus comments simply: '*Feri* epitheton est fluctus, non maris' [*Feri* describes the waves, not the sea]. And he translates 'undae efferae maris'.[90] Where the Greek word is ambiguous an assessment of the sense of the passage can be made. At Mark 1: 7 the Greek verb ἔρχεται may indicate a present or a future coming. Erasmus retains the Vulgate translation, which eliminates one of

---

[88] Mt v. A. Reeve (1986) 28–9. From 1516.
[89] Mt ii. A. Reeve (1986) 13. From 1516. This point is raised by Jodocus Gallus in a letter to Reuchlin, 21 January 1500 (Geiger (1875) Ep. 70).
[90] Jude. A. Reeve (1993) 775. From 1516.

the possibilities of the Greek, because he can offer nothing better.[91] When manuscript evidence is indifferent or inconclusive and the Greek ambiguous he finds another reason to change the Vulgate. In the first chapter of Luke's Gospel the Vulgate has Elizabeth say to Mary 'beata quae credidisti' whilst Erasmus translates 'beata quae credidit'. He comments,

Nos itaque vertimus per tertiam personam, non quod damnemus id quod vertit interpres sed quod hic sermo videatur habere quiddam propheticum. Certe utraque persona eumdem reddit sensum.[92]

[And so we have translated in the third person, not because we reject the ancient translator's rendering, but because here the statement seems to have something prophetic about it. Certainly, either person of the verb gives the same sense.]

Erasmus means that Mary is the subject of either Latin verb. Most frequently, however, it is the principle of clarity which licenses minor expansions of the Greek text:

Jesus non erat in aureo codice. Quanquam arbitror et apud Graecos haec nonnunquam addi, ob sermonis consequentiam, praesertim si quando decerpta recitantur e codicibus Evangelicis.[93]

['Jesus' was not found in the *Codex Aureus*. Although I think that the Greeks sometimes add it to clarify the narrative of the passage, especially when extracts are read aloud from the Gospel manuscripts.]

Erasmus' familiarity with the Vulgate as a spoken document has enabled him to identify another source for minor corruptions of the text. The reading of the Vulgate and the evidence of some manuscripts are here used to sustain a reading for which the principal support is utility and clarity. In the next chapter of Matthew's Gospel the word *Jesus* makes the passage no clearer and so he removes it from the Vulgate translation on the basis of manuscript evidence ('nec in Graecis, nec in vetustis Latinorum codicibus').[94] In Mark's Gospel he inserts the word and makes it clear in the accompanying note that he knows what he is doing:

---

[91] Mk I. A. Reeve (1986) 115. From 1516. Later, Theodore Beza also preferred the present tense, *venit*, but for a reason: 'praesentis significatio magis convenit: ut Christum intelligamus jam fuisse in via' (Beza (1642) 100). Erasmus would probably not have sympathised with this literalism. For Erasmus' response to another ambiguous Greek word, see Mt I. A. Reeve (1986) 8.

[92] Lk I. A. Reeve (1986) 156. Added 1522.   [93] Mt IV. A. Reeve (1986) 24. Added 1522.

[94] Mt V. A. Reeve (1986) 25. From 1516.

Ex graecis verbis apparet de mundato dictum. Proinde ne quid hic haereret lector, pro αὐτὸν subjecimus *Jesus*, hoc est nomen pro pronomine. Ne quis hoc ut temere factum statim corrigat.[95]

[From the Greek words it seems to have been said of the man who had been healed. So that the reader is not at a loss here, we have substituted 'Jesus' for 'αὐτός', that is, a noun for a pronoun. I say this to prevent anyone from correcting it, under the impression that it is an accident.]

When he finds *fratrem Simonis* in Mark's Greek he suggests that it is the pious clarification of a Greek scribe:

opinor additum a quopiam qui voluerit effugere ἀμφιβολογίαν, ne intellegeremus fratrem ipsius Christi.[96]

[I believe that it was added by some scribe who wished to avoid ambiguity, so that we shall not think that it means Christ's own brother.]

Erasmus obviously does not feel that there is much danger of this confusion here and so retains *fratrem eius* from the Vulgate. In the previous chapter, I showed that in these circumstances Valla made use of the resources of Latin pronouns to resolve such ambiguities. Varying noun phrases is one of the devices of the copious style, and *nomen pro pronomine*, its simplest form, here provides a solution to a strictly grammatical ambiguity. Pronouns constitute an aspect of ambiguity in the Greek text which Erasmus, like Valla, feels that the translator can safely resolve for his reader's convenience.

An application of the principle of clarity often means sacrificing some of the more subtle connotations of a Greek word. Clarity is not, of course, valued more highly than accuracy, but when strictest accuracy is found to be unattainable it is at least a compensating virtue. Some aspects of the Greek original exploit the peculiarities of that language. Obviously, this is a resource to which the translator does not have access. Erasmus always describes these features in his annotations:

---

[95] Mk I. A. Reeve (1986) 117. Added 1519. 'Jesus' *sic* 1519, 1535.
[96] Mk I. A. Reeve (1986) 116. From 1516. cf. Donatus, *Ars grammatica*: 'Amphibolia est ambiguitas dictionis' (Keil (1855–80) IV: 395). For More's use of *amphibologia*, see below, 162.

Pestilentia et fames) Jocundam vocum affinitatem Latinus interpres non potuit reddere in λιμοì et λοιμòι, quae scriptura magis quam pronunciatione discerni possunt.[97]

[*Pestilentia et fames*) The Latin translator cannot render the fortunate similarity of these two words 'λιμοì' et 'λοιμοì', which can be distinguished more by their written form than by their pronunciation.]

Or again:

Et mutos loqui, ἀλάλους λαλεῖν. Gratiam annominationis non potuit interpres reddere, quasi dicas *elingues linguaces* aut *infantes fari*.[98]

[*Et mutos loqui*, ἀλάλους λαλεῖν. The translator cannot convey the charm of this phrase. It is as if you were to say that 'the tongueless give tongue' or 'the speechless speak'.]

Such annotations qualify the translator's defeat. It is not so much that some aspects of the Greek are irreproducible, as that some of its qualities can only be communicated at the expense of others. The *ad verbum* translation in the notes communicates to the Latin reader the form of the Greek construction. It is the sort of literalism for which he elsewhere upbraids the Vulgate translator. Erasmus would never have allowed it to leave the *Annotations*, which provide a half-way house for translations which convey some but not enough, or not the most important aspects, of the original. In his note on the first chapter of Matthew, *in transmigratione Babylonis*, Erasmus gives seven alternative translations and prejudices none of them to the reader. In his own translation he does, however, choose the shortest and simplest – and one moreover which takes a slight liberty with the letter of the Greek. He then goes on to suggest that:

Evangelista rei acerbitatem verbi lenitate temperavit, captivitatem et exsilium, demigrationem appellans μετοικεσίαν, quod convenit et in eos qui sua sponte sedes et domicilia mutant.[99]

[The Evangelist has moderated the harshness of the matter through the mildness of his chosen word, calling their captivity and exile an 'emigration', μετοικεσία, which is appropriate to those who change their hearths and homes of their own free will.]

---

[97] Mt xxiv. A. Reeve (1986) 95. From 1516.
[98] Mk vii. A. Reeve (1986) 132. From 1516.   [99] Mt i. A. Reeve (1986) 3. From 1516.

This of course raises a very interesting question: why did Matthew want to 'moderate the harshness of the matter'? It is not a question Erasmus attempts to answer. He assumes that the Evangelist wanted not only to refer to the Babylonian captivity, but also to colour his reader's view of it. The entry leaves the reader speculating upon Matthew's motives and wondering about their relationship with the inspiration of the Holy Ghost. Many subtle readings can be based entirely upon Erasmus' reconstruction of the connotations of the Greek word, but it would be difficult to be dogmatic about any of them. In this respect it is a good example of a quality of Scriptural language which Erasmus wished to stress: it can be endlessly suggestive without being at all definitive. Structurally, the development of this note is typical of many entries in the *Annotations*. It shows Erasmus opening up a range of meanings within a single Greek word. It shows that when, as a translator, he must select only one of the alternatives, he puts clarity and brevity before a translation *ad verbum*. The note moves on to consider the original Greek word as the product of a comprehensible and hence reconstructable authorial process. It even has a typically Erasmian postscript. By 1527 Erasmus had realised – or someone had pointed out to him – that the word *transmigrare* occurs in Suetonius. In the fourth edition he acknowledges this but maintains 'tametsi *demigrare* Latinius est' [nevertheless *demigrare* is better Latin].[100] Which, if it seems to beg the question, perhaps does so deliberately: although he has granted that there are several possible translations, he must ultimately rely on his own sense of *Latinitas* when choosing the best.

Latinitas and the limitations of translation

Erasmus might have drawn another principle from Valla regarding the nature of the language the translator is to use: guidance in respect of all linguistic questions is to be found in the works

---

[100] Erasmus had edited Suetonius for the Froben edition of the *Historiae augustae scriptores*, published in June 1518. See Ep. 586. *EE* ii: 578–86 and Ep. 648. *EE* iii: 69–71. In his *Epistola apologetica adversus Stunicam* of June 1529, Erasmus said that those 'qui exactius requirunt Romanae Linguae castimonium, rejecturi sunt Suetonium ex albo judicum' (LB ix: 395b, noticed in Rummel (1989b) i: 174).

of pagan authors.[101] This rule defines the Latin language and the authorities by which *Latinitas* is to be judged. The classical corpus had substantial advantages as a linguistic standard: it was well defined and readily available, and something very like it was already spoken amongst lettered Europeans. The classical authors were certainly the best place to learn classical Latin. In 1528, in his treatise on the pronunciation of the classical languages, Erasmus wrote that:

Sacratior quidem est liber psalmorum quam Odarum Horatii; sed ex his quam ex illis, rectius discitur sermo Latinus.[102]

[The Book of Psalms is certainly more holy than the Odes of Horace, but it is better to learn Latin from Horace than from the Psalms.]

The Latin language was no longer a vernacular language but an international medium for Christian scholars. This in itself was another of its advantages: the language was immune to the shifts which worked ultimately to render writings in the vernacular languages incomprehensible. Latin had over the centuries been removed from the influence of the inconstant masses and offered unique possibilities for consistency and permanence. In his dialogue on the pronunciation of Greek and Latin, Ursus seems to sum up Erasmus' thoughts on the value of the vernaculars:

Nec expedit quidem vulgo committere quod sincerum ac perpetuum velis . . . Praestat igitur has linguas quibus maxima ex parte commissae sunt disciplinae tantum ab eruditis servari, quarum integritas non a populo (pessimo rerum bonarum custode) sed e libris eloquentum scriptorum petatur.[103]

[So it is not a good idea to entrust to the vernaculars what you wish to remain uncorrupted and permanent . . . It is better, then, to use only those languages which have been used almost exclusively by learned men in their writing, for the purity of these languages does not depend on the people (the worst guardian of good things) but on the books of eloquent writers.]

Latin must be made to serve the needs of its new audience. Yet there were problems inherent in using old words for new things. On the

---

[101] See Valla on Mt IV: 10 (Valla (1962) I: 808) and Schwarz (1955) 133.

[102] *De recta latini graecique sermonis pronuntiatione dialogus* (Basle, 1528). Cytowska (1973) 30; LB I: 922b; CWE XXVI: 386. This appears to be an allusion to Jerome's Ep. 22, *Ad Eustochium*: 'Quid facit cum Psalterio Horatius?'

[103] *De recta pronuntiatione*. LB I: 924c. CWE XXVI: 390.

one hand, since Christianity was outside the range of experience of the classical authors, their language might not say enough. Why should the Christian Vulgate Bible be corrected with reference to authors who knew nothing of the Christian revelation? On the other hand, the words might retain meanings from their original, pagan, contexts and they might say too much.

In the same year, in his *Ciceronianus*, Erasmus presents a mock-translation of a passage of Scriptural language, parodying the extreme classicising tendencies of those who would use no word not to be found in Cicero. He offers a passage of Latin filled with the Christian idiom which had developed over the centuries:

Jesus Christus, verbum et filius aeterni Patris, juxta prophetias venit in mundum, ac factus homo, sponte se in mortem tradidit, ac redemit Ecclesiam suam, offensique Patris iram avertit a nobis, eique nos reconciliavit, ut per gratiam fidei justificati . . .[104]

The Ciceronian, he says, would render it in the following way:

Optimi Maximique Jovis interpres ac filius, servator, Rex, juxta vatum responsa, ex Olympo devolavit in terras, et hominis assumpta figura, sese pro salute Reipublicae sponte devovit Diis Manibus, atque ita concionem sive civitatem, sive rempublicam suam asseruit in libertatem, ac Jovis Optimi Maximi vibratum in nostra capita fulmen restinxit, nosque cum illo redegit in gratiam, ut persuasionis munificentia ad innocentiam reparati . . .[105]

This is Erasmus' attempt to make a return to the more ancient idiom sound like a piece of outlandish modernism. Clearly, it is not an *ad verbum* translation but a translation into a different cultural context. Erasmus saw that there are close links between such contexts and their language. The translator of an ancient text cannot begin until he understands the differences between his own context and that of the original text:

Quocunque me verto, video mutata omnia, in alio sto proscenio, aliud conspicio theatrum, imo mundum alium. Quid faciam? Christiano mihi dicendum est apud Christianos de religione Christiana: num ut apte dicam imaginabor me vivere aetate Ciceronis, et in frequenti Senatu apud Patres Conscriptos in arce Tarpeja dicere?[106]

---

[104] Gambaro (1965) 142.   [105] Ibid.   [106] Ibid. 126–8. *CWE* XXVIII: 383.

[Wherever I turn I see everything changed, I stand on a different stage, I see a different theatre, or rather a different world. What am I to do? As a Christian, I must speak among Christians about the Christian religion. In order to speak appropriately, must I imagine that I am living in the age of Cicero, and speaking in the crowded Senate to the conscript fathers on the Tarpeian height?]

The Ciceronian's language is long-winded and fails with all its words to attain the power of the first passage. Christian Latin has imported words such as *prophetia* and *ecclesia* from the Greek language and has endowed Latin words such as *gratia* and *fides* with a complex set of meanings which they did not have in Cicero's day. These words have accumulated associations during centuries of usage by Christians. In the *Annotations* Erasmus wrote:

mihi sane nimium morosi videntur qui nusquam concedunt evangelicis literis sua peculiaria vocabula.[107]

[certainly, those who do not allow the Gospels to use their own words in any circumstance seem to me to be very difficult to please.]

This licence extends only to Christian terminology, not to grammar proper, which was to remain classical although not necessarily Ciceronian. In practice, this distinction had few consequences, for despite the efforts of Nosoponus in the *Ciceronianus* to imitate Cicero's *clausulae*, the debate over Ciceronian usage tended to turn on the provenances of particular words. Earlier we saw that Manetti attempted to place his version of the *Nicomachean Ethics* between Bruni's freedom and Grosseteste's *asperitas*. Here, Erasmus searches for another middle way, between strict Ciceronianism and the popular Latin of late antiquity. He attempted to avoid linguistic antiquarianism whilst remaining faithful to the common standard set up by the classical texts. He insisted that the non-classical connotations of some Latin words were an essential part of sixteenth-century Latin.

The translator's desire to respect the polyglot roots of his original texts may involve him in difficulties. Luke may have known Latin; Matthew probably knew Aramaic and Hebrew. Erasmus is sceptical of – though he does not deny – the tradition that Matthew wrote his Gospel in Hebrew.[108] This tradition raises the possibility that

[107] Mt x. A. Reeve (1986) 50. Added 1527.
[108] See Mt i. A. Reeve (1986) 1–2. From 1516.

there is another inspired and lost text exerting its influence on the anonymous Greek translator of Matthew's Gospel. It is impossible to identify all the Evangelists' and Apostles' Hebraisms, and even if it were possible, it is unlikely that any Latin translation would be up to the task of communicating such subtleties to the reader. Erasmus, for example, identifies a particular turn of phrase in Luke's Gospel as a Hebraism. He says that the translator translates 'haud male' when he renders the Greek ἐν as *cum*. Nevertheless:

castius erat prorsus omittere, quod apud nos nec ullum habeat usum, et orationem reddat inelegantem.[109]

[It would have been more correct to have left it out entirely, because in our Latin language it serves no purpose and it makes the passage inelegant.]

The Vulgate translation is approved because it moved away from the literal rendering of the Hebraism and the Greek, and that approval is qualified because it did not move far enough. In his own translation Erasmus retains the Vulgate reading, perhaps because it satisfies a higher principle which this note does not mention: in *apud nos* the preposition may be redundant and even inelegant, but it makes the sense of the words it governs a little clearer. It is consistent with Erasmus' frequent use of prepositional constructions to narrow the range of meaning possible to an inflected noun. The reader who has no Hebrew or Greek has probably learnt as much about the Evangelist's style as he is able when he has read Erasmus' translation and annotation together. If the translator attempts the impossible task of preserving Luke's idiom in every detail, then he may sacrifice one of the attainable virtues of the Latin translation.

The Vulgate and Erasmus' translation often leave words in Hebrew, Aramaic and Greek. At such points the texts draw attention to their historical and linguistic evolution. If the original text was determinedly polyglot, a translation should reflect this. Neologism may be used to overcome the deficiencies of pagan Latin just as the authors of the New Testament enriched Christian Greek with their borrowings, but it is a potentially disruptive force. Improperly used it may debase the currency of other words. Its expressive possibilities must be weighed against the fact that it may fail to mean

[109] Lk xiv. A. Reeve (1986) 198. Added 1519.

anything at all. Erasmus' manoeuvrings about the best word for
baptise suggest that he feels that they are sometimes more trouble
than they are worth. Granted, there is a certain propriety in using
a new word for a new thing:

verbo baptizandi, tametsi Graeco, tamen quoniam res ipsa nova eo ad nos
permanavit, placuit constanter uti.[110]

[Although the word 'baptise' is Greek, nevertheless since a new thing itself has
come down to us by it, I am content to use it throughout.]

But it was not a new word for the Greeks. Certainly, Erasmus
uses the word consistently in his translation, and in the *Ciceronianus* he says that only a Ciceronian pedant would use *tinctura* for
baptismus.[111] On the other hand, in the same note he cites Cyprian
using *tingere* to show that a Father of the Church did not baulk at
translating the term, and in a later note he uses *tingere* to mean
baptise.[112] Later still, in his defence of *In principio erat sermo*,
he suggests that *baptizare* should be retained in the liturgy because
it is not worth upsetting the sensibilities of the ignorant with the
subtleties of the learned. And besides, God does not really care
about such subtleties anyway:

Receptum est ut tingentes semigraece loquamur *baptizo te*. Nolim apud idiotas
dicere *tingo te*, quum tamen apud Deum nihil referat.[113]

[It is customary that when we are wetting we say, half in Greek, 'I baptise you'.
I do not want to say amongst the uneducated 'I wet you' even though it does not
matter to God.]

Had he wanted to change the word in his translation he might have
argued that *tingere* as an ordinary Latin word communicates the
ordinariness of the action it describes. Baptism is no more and
no less a sacrament because there is a special word for it, but
once words come into use meanings tend to gather about them.
'Sacramental' feelings had accumulated around a word which
had a less specialised meaning in the original Greek. It may be
that Erasmus felt that the spiritual significance of the act depends

---

[110] Mt III. A. Reeve (1986) 21. Added 1519.
[111] Gambaro (1965) 142. *CWE* XXVIII: 388.
[112] Mt III. A. Reeve (1986) 21–2. Added 1519.
[113] Jn I. A. Reeve (1986) 219. Added 1527.

entirely on the attitude of those who participate in it. If so, it was not a battle he wished to fight.[114]

Earlier in their very different careers, Thomas More and Erasmus had worked together upon a number of versions from Lucian. After the publication of the *Novum instrumentum*, More entered the debate to defend his friend's conception of translation. In his *Letter to a Monk*, he defends Erasmus' decision to dispense with a trivial Grecism.[115] In the Vulgate, Matthew's text reads 'simile est regnum caelorum sagenae missae in mare' [The kingdom of heaven is like a net cast into the sea]. Erasmus' translation reads 'verriculo jacto in mare' on the grounds that *sagena* is strictly a Greek word.[116] The Monk's argument is that to change the Vulgate at this point is unnecessary since either word is good Latin and neither makes a doctrinal distinction. Later I shall describe More's case for changing what may be changed within the limits of the archetype.[117] Here he chooses to argue the distinction between the Greek and Latin languages:

Si Latinus quispiam vocabulum graecum mediis latinis interserat, neque desinit tamen esse graecum, neque protinus efficitur latinum. Neque enim cuiquam in manu est omnia vocabula Romana ciuitate donare, nihilo magis hercule quam omnes homines.[118]

[If some Latin writer were to use a Greek word in his Latin, it does not stop being a Greek word and it is not immediately made into a Latin one. For it is not in anyone's power to grant Roman citizenship to every word, any more than to grant it to all people.]

The last sentence echoes Suetonius' *De grammaticis*.[119] In a passage in the *De copia*, Erasmus talks about mixing Greek forms with Latin. It is possible that More had his friend's words in mind when he wrote these words. Erasmus had written:

[114] For a discussion of Erasmus' sympathies with anabaptism, see Bainton (1969) 313–14.

[115] Kinney (1986) 198ff. In the introduction to this volume Kinney states that 'the identity of More's correspondent has at last been established quite firmly by Dom David Knowles, who points out that in letters of this period Erasmus complains about only one young monkish critic from England, the London Carthusian John Batmanson.' ibid. xli.

[116] Mt XIII: 47. A. Reeve (1986) 62. From 1516. Manetti agrees with Valla and Erasmus here. Beza retains *sagenae* from the Vulgate (Beza (1642) 49).

[117] 'Archetypus' – More's word.   [118] Letter to a Monk. Kinney (1986) 233.

[119] See Kinney (1986) 577 n. 22. 'Tu enim Caesar civitatem dare potes hominibus, verbis non potes' (Suetonius, *De grammaticis*, 22).

Sunt non paucae Graecorum voces quas antiquitas Latinitate donavit. Iis perinde atque Latinis uti licebit.[120]

[There are quite a number of Greek words which were given Latin citizenship in the classical period, and these may be used just like native Latin ones.]

In Suetonius, the observation shows that there are limits to even an Emperor's powers. More enjoys it because it shows that there are very clear practical limits to what an individual can do to common property. He feels that the consensual nature of language is one of its strengths. Clearly, some Greek words have in the course of time become naturalised to the Latin language. The Monk might take issue with More's *protinus* and argue that a thousand years in the Vulgate has naturalised the word to the sixteenth-century Bible whatever its status in the fourth. This raises the question whether the Latin Vulgate should be granted a prescriptive authority in matters of grammar and vocabulary, that is, to make it what the works of Cicero were to some Latinists. In a letter to Marten Lips, noticed earlier, Erasmus quotes a statement from his anonymous critic:

Sola integritas sermonis, ornatus, elegantia seu eloquentia est in sacra Scriptura.[121]

[The sole source for purity of language, for ornament, for elegance or eloquence, lies in Holy Scripture.]

More and Erasmus faced similar opponents. If the classical standard was an arbitrary one, selected because shared standards made communication possible, then why not select the Latin of the Vulgate as a different standard? And if the standard was not arbitrary, but based on the excellence of the classical language, on what grounds did it surpass the language of the first centuries of the Church?

Neither More nor Erasmus was willing to accept the Latin of the Vulgate as a grammatical standard. The classical writers provided a flexible basis for sixteenth-century Latinists, a common resource which admitted variations and expansions. The Latin of the Vulgate and of the Church Fathers was not always consistent and so could not be used as a standard. More importantly, the Fathers themselves

---

[120] Knott (1983) 52. LB I: 12 ff. *CWE* XXIV: 318.   [121] Ep. 843. *EE* III: 316. *CWE* VI: 9.

had conceded linguistic authority to the classical authors. In the debate on the use of Latin as a religious language the usage of the Latin Fathers was carefully examined. For Erasmus' purposes, the best Fathers to cite are those who wrote in Latin but could read Greek well. Augustine's poor Greek made him less valuable as a textual witness in Erasmus' eyes; Jerome's extensive learning and voluminous commentaries ensured his testimony a good hearing. Erasmus could imitate the Fathers' imitation of their pagan predecessors, but not cite it as authoritative on linguistic issues. The matter was complicated by the fact that Erasmus cites them in two capacities: as witnesses to the text of the Old Latin Scriptures, and as authoritative interpreters of the Greek text and consequently fine judges of its Latin translations. The clearest statement of this distinction occurs in Erasmus' *Apologia pro 'In principio erat sermo'*, but the principle pervades his New Testament.[122] When Erasmus suspected that the Greek or Latin manuscripts had been corrupted or that the text of the Vulgate misrepresented the Greek, a new translation might be able to claim a Patristic sanction if they testified that it was old and that it was good.

In his second edition of 1519, Erasmus began a lengthy controversy which went to the heart of the principles behind his Biblical translation and his opponents' objections to it. The Vulgate translates the first words of John's Gospel as 'In principio erat verbum'. In his New Testament, Erasmus translates these words as 'In principio erat sermo'. John's prologue is a particularly sacred part of the sacred text: it was recited at the end of mass and had been the subject of an enormous quantity of exegesis. It would have been familiar to many of his readers because the Greek text was often printed with elementary Greek grammars. Erasmus knew that a new translation of this passage would be controversial. In the accompanying note, he said that he had not made the change in his first edition for two reasons: because he did not want to give his opponents an opportunity to attack him, and 'superstitioso quodam metu'[123] [from some superstitious fear]. In this note he writes that

---

[122] See *Apologia pro 'In principio erat sermo'*. LB IX: 116d ff.
[123] Jn I. A. Reeve (1986) 218. Added 1522.

λόγος Graecis varia significat, *verbum, orationem, sermonem, rationem, modum, supputationem*, nonnunquam et pro *libro* usurpatur, a verbo λέγω, quod est *dico*, sive *colligo*.[124]

[λόγος signifies several things to the Greeks: 'verbum', 'oratio', 'sermo', 'ratio', 'modus', 'supputatio', and sometimes it is used for 'book' from the word λέγω, which means 'I say' or 'I gather together'.]

Erasmus is always reluctant to admit defeat in the search for relevant factors to help make a choice between renderings. It seems that he believed that although some of these factors may be less significant than others, the translator need never run out of considerations on which to base a decision. When there was little to choose between alternatives, Erasmus could resort to less substantial considerations such as gender or euphony:

Levia sunt haec, fateor, sed tamen quamlibet levis accessio huc aut illuc impellit, cum alioqui res est in aequilibrio.[125]

[I grant that these are minor considerations, but when a matter is in all other respects finely balanced even a minor consideration may incline it one way or the other.]

However, Erasmus is at pains to stress that not all of the considerations which inform his version – which inform any version – are equally important. Some, he points out, are quite trivial. Yet if he constantly emphasises that his translation does not always represent all the meanings to be found in the Greek, his annotations do attempt to define the range of semantic possibilities within which he feels that the debate must operate. In subsequent editions of his New Testament Erasmus continued to clarify and define the possibilities he had first suggested in 1516. For every part of the Greek text, his list of possible translations is as exhaustive as he knows how to make it. He does not, in the *Annotations*, set up hierarchies of semantic possibilities, or suggest that a word has many peripheral connotations but one primary meaning. Although some of the meanings inherent in a word may have to be sacrificed to the exigencies of translation, all of its possible meanings are important.

---

[124] Jn I. A. Reeve (1986) 218. From 1516. Manetti retained *verbum*.
[125] *Apologia pro 'In principio erat sermo'*. LB IX: 114a.

The extent of the *Annotations* suggests that Erasmus did not want to lose even one.

More also believed that the translator must draw attention to the limitations of his art, and to his inevitable failures. He saw that Erasmus' new version was only the latest compromise with the original text, that it was a rendering which was not so much intended to provide an alternative to the Vulgate, as to change the way translations were used by theologians. In a letter to Dorp, he defended Erasmus' translation 'in principio erat sermo'. He saw that the difficulty at this point lies in the fact that neither *verbum* nor *sermo* have the range of meanings of the Greek word λόγος, and writes that this Greek word,

quum sanctarum significationum mire foecunda sit, e quibus quam cui praeferas haud proclive sit statuere, fuisset non incautum, eadem servata voce, nullum fecisse praeiudicium . . . Nunc vero quoniam aliter visum est vertentibus, mihi certe videtur proximus esse fructus ut vertant varie, quo nulla significatio τοῦ λόγου quae quidem in Christum competat, aut ignoretur aut obsolescat.[126]

[since it is remarkably productive of holy meanings, amongst which it is not easy to decide which is preferable, it would not have been imprudent to have retained that same word and to have made no decision at all . . . But now, since the translators have thought otherwise, it seems clear to me that the next-best solution is that they translate it in different ways, so that no meaning of λόγος which belongs to Christ remains unknown or falls into disuse.]

More wants a translation which does not seek to hide its own inadequacies. The most straightforward admission of failure is simply not to translate the word. There are precedents for this approach. He notes that some Greek and Hebrew words have been simply transliterated into the gospels: *kyrie eleison, alleluia, amen, hosanna*.[127] Failing that, he argues that successive translators must destabilise the equation between the translation and the archetype. Such renderings draw attention to the translator's art, and encourage the reader to look for their own equations. In the same letter, More sets out the criteria for the perfect translation in a tone that suggests it will never be achieved:

[126] Letter to Dorp, in Kinney (1986) 237–9.
[127] Ibid. 236–7. St Augustine makes a similar observation in *De doctrina christiana* II: 11. *PL* XXXIV: 42.

'Ergo quis vertendi finis erit?' inquis: facillimus si evenerit ut quisquam tam commode verterit, aut ab alio non optime versum alius ita correxerit, ut his manentibus
integris, non inveniant posteri quod immutandum censeant.[128]

['So', you say, 'will there be no end to translating?' The easiest of ends, if it
happens that someone translates so accurately, or if one person corrects another's
imperfect translation so well, that as long as these versions survive later readers
will not find anything they think should be changed.]

He argues that since translation can never be done perfectly someone will always feel the need to do it again. More feels that this
someone should be permitted to do so because the existence of
several translations of a single text expands the ways it may be
read:

quemadmodum nunc evangelistarum varia narratione series rerum in luculen-
tiorem pervenit notitiam, ita in diversorum collatione interpretum, studioso lectori
daretur occasio, si quem, aut verbum fefellit aequivocum, aut orationis amphibologia decepit, aut sermonis proprietas imposuit, ex reliquis conjiciendi quid
verum sit.[129]

[Just as now, through the differing accounts of the Evangelists, the real sequence
of events comes to be understood more distinctly, even so by comparing various
translations the studious reader would be given a chance to note points where
equivocal words or ambivalent syntax or the particular force of an idiom had
misled some translator, and then by consulting the others to grasp the true sense
by conjecture.]

The four Gospel narratives are, he hints, in a manner, translations of
that historical text, the life of Christ. In their turn, the responses of
different translators to the Gospels might contribute to our understanding of the Evangelists' perspectives on that text.

As early as 1499 Erasmus too had talked about the desirability
of multiplying interpretations. In a letter to John Colet, he wrote

Nam quod a me obiter et per occasionem dictum est, ex arcanis litteris, quoniam
fecundissimae sunt, varios sensus elici posse, et nihil reiiciendum quod modo sit
probabile nec a pietate abhorreat, id neque sine argumentis dixi.[130]

[For, as I have said in passing and where the opportunity arose, several senses
can be extracted from the mysteries of the Scriptures since they are very rich

---

[128] Kinney (1986) 83.
[129] Ibid. Erasmus also used *amphibologia*, in Greek characters: see above, 149 and n. 96.
[130] Ep. 111. *EE* I: 255. *CWE* I: 213.

in meanings; and I have argued that nothing should be cast aside provided it is probable and consistent with piety.]

Later, in his controversy with Luther, he hoped that common ground could be defined within which each could take up different positions:

ex his minutiis excitare tragoediam, non arbitror esse Christianae tranquilitatis; praestiterit fortassis permittere ut juxta Paulum hactenus quisque in suo sensu abundet.[131]

[I do not think it befits Christian serenity to make a great fuss over these *minutiae*; it is perhaps better to follow Paul and allow each to overflow with his own understanding of the meaning.]

As I showed earlier, Erasmus grew suspicious of Valla's willingness to multiply distinctions in the New Testament. At best, this approach might make the text a playground for the sort of intellectual exercises he had attacked in the schools. At worst, these distinctions might become banners behind which opposing factions could rally. Luther's *minutiae* and Valla's *elegantiae* are akin. The *grammaticus* is potentially as vulnerable to a loss of perspective in his pursuit of *elegantiae* as the theologian amongst his allegories, or the logician amongst his categories. All of these sciences are limited because they are founded upon language, and Erasmus saw that there are things language cannot be made to do: 'res divinas nullae voces hominum proprie exprimunt'[132] [No human words truly express divine things].

---

[131] *Hyperaspistes diatribae contra servum arbitrium Martini Lutheri.* LB x: 1534c–d, cited in Trinkaus (1976) 25. For the turn of phrase, see Cicero, *Pro Milone*, 7, 18.
[132] *Apologia pro 'In principio erat sermo'.* LB IX: 113c.

4

RENAISSANCE TRANSLATIONS:
SOME CATEGORIES

Over the centuries a number of different treatments of Greek texts had passed for examples of the translator's art. The fortunes of one Greek author may be used to illustrate this here. The works of Eusebius of Caesarea had been popular in the Latin West ever since they had been produced. They attracted different treatments from Latin translators. When Rufinus translated his *Historia ecclesiastica* in late antiquity he compressed, transposed and interpolated material; when St Jerome translated his *Chronicon*, an important reference work, he added material to bring it up to date; and when George of Trebizond translated his *Evangelica praeparatio* he edited his author to remove his Arianism. Rufinus felt that as a rhetorician he could legitimately improve on the author's disposition of his material; Jerome that accuracy and completeness were higher virtues than fidelity to the original; and George that orthodoxy was a basic requirement of a Christian text.[1] This sort of treatment was often the fate of texts which still served the purposes for which they were written. If the works of Aratus and Ptolemy were often brought up to date with interpolations, it was because the names were attached not so much to an author as to a body of knowledge. For translators to take some liberties with the original text was not only not new: in profane texts it was common practice.

Many prefaces to translations are attempts to indicate the relationship between the translation and the original text. Most make some attempt to state what the translator has done to his Greek original. Since antiquity Latin versions had often been located by their authors and their readers somewhere between the poles of *ad verbum* and *ad sensum* translation. Many modern writers still attempt to place translations somewhere on a continuum between

---

[1] Andreas Contrarius criticised Trebizond's translation of the *Evangelica praeparatio* for this reason. See Sabbadini (1916c) 395–6, and Monfasani (1984) 108–12.

the two extremes represented by these terms. In this final chapter, I want to suggest that these Latin translations may be usefully characterised by the attitude they adopt towards the original text. This observation allows several categories to be set up for translations.

The first and most common type of translation is an attempt to replace the Greek text with a Latin equivalent. This substitute text is intended to minimise or eliminate the need to consult the text in the original language. Of course, this intention is seldom plainly stated. Few authors are willing to forgo professions of modesty in their prefaces, or bold enough to claim that their versions are substitutes. Moreover, in Greekless medieval Europe, most versions, whatever the intentions of their translators, came to belong to this category.

That Latin translations might reduce dependence on Greek texts is an ancient idea. Cicero, an inspiration to generations of Hellenists in the fifteenth and sixteenth centuries, wrote in his *Tusculan Disputations*,

hortor omnes . . . ut huius quoque generis laudem iam languenti Graeciae eripiant et perferant in hanc urbem.[2]

[I urge everyone to seize glory of this sort from now ailing Greece and bring it into this city.]

He goes on to anticipate a time when all Greek philosophical literature will have been translated or transformed into Latin, and Greek libraries will no longer be required:

si haec studia traducta erunt ad nostros, ne bibliothecis quidem Graecis egebimus.[3]

[if these works are transferred to us, we shall not even need libraries of Greek books.]

Cicero was a linguistic patriot: in his pride at what had already been written in Latin, and in his optimism at what the language might yet achieve, he may have been exaggerating. However, four centuries later, Boethius' words suggest a similar attitude to his own Latin translations. In the preface to his translation of Porphyry's *Isagoge* he wrote:

---

[2] *Tusc.* II: 5.   [3] Ibid. 6.

multum profecisse videor si, philosophiae libris latina oratione compositis, per integerrimae translationis sinceritatem nihil in Graecorum litteris amplius desideretur.[4]

[I seem to have been very successful if, with books of philosophy written in Latin, through the accuracy of the most thorough translation, no longer will any part of Greek literature be lacking.]

If this strain of thought ever disappeared, it certainly re-emerged in the fifteenth century. Early in the fifteenth century, Giovanni da Ravenna said:

Athice autem si peroraveris, barbarus michi eris . . . Quod si . . . codices habes grecos, interpretare.[5]

[If you declaim at length in Attic Greek, I shall think you a barbarian; but if you have Greek manuscripts then translate them.]

In the first half of the fifteenth century, contempt for the political and cultural pretensions of the Byzantine kingdom accompanied a grudging acceptance of the value of many classical Greek texts. Ancient Latin literature provided a template for this pattern of admiration for the ancient achievements of Greece and scorn for the modern. Projects such as the one undertaken by Pope Nicholas V to create a Latin library of Greek authors encouraged many to think in terms of the comprehensive transference of Greek thought into Latin.

This transference had been largely achieved by the end of the fifteenth century. By 1500 most of the works of the ancient Greek writers which were alluded to or discussed by classical Latin authors were widely available in Latin versions. The fortunes of the Greek historians in their printed editions show that Latin versions tended to consign the Greek originals to the libraries of specialists. The printers, sensitive to the requirements of their readers, knew that the market for these authors in their original language was small, and that the cost of printing such bulky texts was high. Thus, although the two most famous Greek historians, Herodotus and Thucydides, were both printed in Greek at the Aldine Press as early as 1502, the remaining historians were not printed in Greek

---

[4] *In Isagogicon Porphyrii*, cited in Copeland (1989) 30.
[5] Sabbadini (1924) 103.

until much later. Diogenes Laertius' *Lives of the Philosophers* was translated by Traversari by 1433 and his version was first printed in 1472, but the Greek text was not printed until over sixty years later, in 1533.[6] Arrian's history of Alexander, translated by Vergerio about 1440, was not printed in Greek until 1535.[7] Appian's *Roman History* was printed in Decembrio's Latin in 1477, but did not appear in Greek until 1551.[8] The first books of Diodorus Siculus were printed in Poggio Bracciolini's translation in 1472, but the world had to wait until 1559 for a Greek text of most of what survives in Greek.[9] The example of Diodorus is particularly revealing: the inaccuracies of Poggio's version were widely acknowledged, but his popularity was assured because his Latin was very readable. John Skelton, a vocal opponent of Greek studies, valued Poggio's version of this Greek author so highly that he turned it into English.[10] Sometimes the printing of the Greek text provided a stimulus for translators; sometimes the appearance of a Latin translation stimulated an interest in the Greek text. More often, it seems, a printed Latin translation of a voluminous Greek historian supplied its readers with most of what they had wanted from the Greek text. Thus translated, the Greek historians could be read and quarried for moral examples in much the same way as their Latin counterparts had been for centuries.

Religious Greek texts were even more likely to be replaced by their Latin renderings. Translators could sift these Greek works for heterodoxy as they made them into Latin. Of course, the decision whether to translate a text at all is the first element in this process of filtering Greek thought through Latin: the writings of a number of heretical authors only survive because they were wrongly attributed to orthodox pens. Theologically sensitive works can be translated *ad verbum* in order to preserve the translator's distance from, and minimise his responsibility for, the contents of his text. In the middle of the fifth century, for example, Marius Mercator translated heretical sermons of Nestorius into Latin. In his preface he emphasises that he has tried to translate them as literally

---

[6] At Rome and Basle respectively.
[7] At Venice. For the *fortuna* of Arrian, see Stadter (1976).
[8] See Fryde (1983b) 102–7.   [9] Bologna, 1472; Geneva, 1559.
[10] See the edition of Salter and Edwards (1956–7).

as possible, and he may have done this in order to protect himself against the charge of heresy.[11] However, because the translator engages with the meaning of the text he is transmitting, he is more likely to reshape his author than any mere copyist. Cassiodorus, for example, removed passages from Greek texts in order to secure their orthodoxy.[12] If the purpose of translation was to make available to the Latin West only what was good in Greek culture, then censoring texts was a legitimate element of the art. Versions censored like this effectively replaced the original because they were better works in every way that mattered to contemporary readers.

If the only reason to study Greek was to exploit the utility of the texts available in that language, then when enough translations were available Greek would no longer be needed. In the fifteenth century, Michael Apostolis, an impoverished Greek teacher, complained that Latin translations, and Latin methods of teaching, would eventually wipe out the Greek language in the West altogether:

Εἰ δέ τις φαίη τοὺς τῶν Ῥωμαίων πορθμέας εὐθέτως καὶ ὡς προσήκει διερμηνεύειν τὸν ἕλληνα ἐς τὴν σφετέραν φώνην τε καὶ συνήθειαν, τί τοῦτο πρὸς Ἕλληνας καὶ σοφίαν αὐτῶν; μᾶλλον μὲν οὖν καὶ ἀδικία μεγίστη καὶ πολλῶν ἀξία τιμωρίων. τούτῳ δὴ τῷ τρόπῳ κατὰ μικρόν τἀκείνων ἀφανίζειν ἐπιχειροῦσι, καὶ οὕτως ἀνθ᾽ Ἑλλήνων ὅσον οὐκ ἤδη Ῥωμαίους πεποιήκασι.[13]

[If someone were to say that the Italian teachers translate Greek into their own language and manner very ably and appropriately, what does this have to do with the Greeks and their learning? It is rather a great offence which deserves strong penalties. In this way they are trying gradually to obliterate the Greek language, and have practically made the Greeks into Romans.]

He suggests that those who palm off Greek works in translation as their own should be compelled to pay a fine of 10,000 talents. This angry and slightly absurd proposal illustrates the fears of a contemporary and lettered Greek that his culture is being appropriated by unscrupulous Latins. Apostolis' complaints are not entirely without substance. In the 1450s, for example, Lorenzo Ghiberti began his *commentarii* with an unacknowledged translation of

---

[11] Blatt (1938) 221.   [12] Ibid. 237.

[13] Noiret (1889) 148–53, 151. I have adopted an adjustment of Noiret's text proposed by Michael Reeve.

Athenaeus' preface to his work on siege engines.[14] But Apostolis' words are also part of a broader current of anxiety about intellectual property. In the 1470s Francesco Zambeccari was able to pass off hundreds of his own compositions as works of Libanius.[15] At a time when new Greek works were still regularly appearing in translation, readers were susceptible to such plausible frauds. Moreover, in the fifteenth century few people were in a position to assess the claims of those who called themselves Greek scholars.[16] In such a situation, Greek texts often provided a field for scholarly rivalries. Filelfo's letters, for example, claim knowledge of a dazzling array of Greek writers, but he neglects to point out that he knew many of these only from the notices in the Suda lexicon. A few years later, Angelo Poliziano had harsh words for Domizio Calderini's claims to have used Greek sources:

Enarravit Domitius libellum Nasonis in Ibin, praefatus ex Apollodoro se, Lycophrone, Pausania, Strabone, Apollonio, aliisque Graecis, etiamque Latinis accepta scribere. Multa in eo commentario vana ridiculaque confingit, et comminiscitur ex tempore commodoque suo.[17]

[Domizio expounded Ovid's book, *Ibis*, and he began by saying that he drew his material from Apollodorus, Lycophron, Pausanias, Strabo, Apollonius, and other Greeks, and from Latin writers too. In that commentary he fabricates many meaningless and absurd things, and invents them as he goes and for his own convenience.]

Most of Calderini's readers would not have been able to check the sources he cites; but neither could they have tested Poliziano's charges. The Latins not only took the ancient Greeks from their Byzantine descendants: they even stole the Greeks from each other. Richard Pace says that he translated Simplicius' commentary on Aristotle's *Categories* into Latin while he was at Ferrara. He describes how he showed it to a lecturer who subsequently presented the material as if it were his own.[18] In fact, translations

---

[14] Stinger (1977) 35–6. [15] See Breen (1964).
[16] Compare the situation at Salamanca in 1511: when Hernán Núñez applied for the chair of Oriental languages it was difficult to find someone able to assess his qualifications. See Bataillon (1935) 4ff.
[17] Grafton (1977) 158.
[18] Pace says that he did not expose the fraud: 'continui me tamen, et gratulatus sum amico, quod tam feliciter ex aliena semente, id est, graeca, messem sibi fecerit' (Manley and Sylvester (1967) 132).

very often figure prominently in scholarly myths. The charge that Bruni had attempted to pass off Procopius' work as his own was eventually transformed into one such legend. Bruni, it was said, having come upon what he believed to be a unique manuscript of Procopius' history, translated it into Latin and burnt the original.[19] Niccolò Perotti's translation of Polybius nearly suffered a similar fate. According to Giovio, such was the Latinity of this version

Non defuere tamen ex aemulis, qui eius auctoris traductionem antiquissimam fuisse, furtoque surreptam existimarit.[20]

[There were, however, some of his rivals who thought that his translation of this author was very ancient, and that he had stolen it.]

This observation, which probably took its inspiration from a piece of rhetorical praise of Perotti's version, is well on its way to becoming another tale of literary theft.

In this climate, another type of translation flourished. The fifteenth century saw the emergence, or rather the re-emergence, of translations constructed to compete with the original Greek texts. The translation of Greek authors had been recommended in antiquity not to make them available to Latin readers, but as part of a broader educational programme. Thus Cicero says that in his youth he would translate Greek orators;[21] and Quintilian, too, talked of the use of translation for training young men in the rhetorical arts.[22] For both men, one of the reasons for studying Greek was to analyse the practices of the Greek orators so that their techniques could be used in Latin productions. In such versions, students attempted to reproduce not only the meaning, but also the persuasive effect of the original text. Such translators measure their skill in their own language against the skill of the author of the original text, or against the virtues of other Latin versions. The pseudo-Cicero in *De optimo genere oratorum* proposes this model for translations of Demosthenes and Aeschines. Bruni's version of these speeches, noticed in chapter I, competed with these lost translations, and he

---

[19] The story is recounted in Mehus (1741) I: liv.   [20] Cited in Pace (1989) 222.
[21] Cicero, *De oratore* I: 155: 'mihi placuit, eoque sum usus adolescens, ut summorum oratorum Graecas orationes explicarem'.
[22] Quintilian, *Inst. orat.* X: 5.

did more than any other to revive this type of competitive translation. Lorenzo Valla later produced a version of Demosthenes' *De corona* in emulation of Bruni's. He argues that, since it is often impossible to keep to the *via media*, the translator should strike out on his own when he sees a better path:

Nam cum medium tenere nequeas ut nec melius illo nec peius dicas, nimirum, si fieri potest, melius dicendum est, eo quidem libentius quod plus honoris greco auctori habes si superasse illum, quam si ab eo superatus esse videare.[23]

[When you cannot keep to the middle way, and speak no better and no worse than the original, you must speak better if at all possible. And you will do so more willingly because you do your author more honour by appearing to surpass him than by appearing to have been surpassed by him.]

George of Trebizond and Nicholas Secundinus produced translations of this speech, and there are two anonymous translations of it, both dating from the middle years of the fifteenth century.[24] I have already discussed Bruni's rivalry with Plutarch's *Cicero* and with Angeli's translation of it.[25] The friendly rivalry between Thomas More and Erasmus in their translations of Lucian's *Tyrannicida* is well documented.[26] Erasmus depicted his version of Euripides' *Hecuba* as an exercise in the Greek language, and as an attempt to surpass Filelfo's earlier version.[27] Multiple translations of Greek texts are common in the fifteenth and early sixteenth centuries: between 1400 and 1530 there are, for example, seven extant Latin versions of Plutarch's *Quomodo ab adulatore discernatur amicus*;[28] at least seven of his *De utilitate quae habetur ex amicis*;[29]

---

[23] Valla's preface is edited in Lo Monaco (1986) 162–4.
[24] For the extant versions of *De corona*, see Monfasani (1976) 61–8. Trebizond criticises Bruni's version without naming him. See Monfasani (1984) 93–6. Valla praises Bruni's version in his preface (Lo Monaco (1986) 162–4).
[25] See chapter 2, 'Greek biography'.
[26] See Thompson (1974).
[27] See Waszink (1969a) 193–359. Erasmus' preface to Warham is Ep. 188, *EE* I: 417–20.
[28] Four versions are noticed in Resta (1959) 230–2 nn. 1–3. For Guarino Veronese's partial rendering, see Sabbadini (1896) 135–6. For Giovanni Lorenzi's versions (Rome, 1514), see Paschini (1943) 140; for Erasmus' version (Basle, 1514), see *EE* I: 529–30.
[29] All noticed in Resta (1959) 234–6, 140 and nn. 1–2. For Erasmus' version, see also *EE* I: 548–9. For the anonymous translation in Florence, Riccardiana 906, see Bevegni (1994) 84.

twelve of Isocrates' *Ad Demonicum*;[30] and no fewer than twenty of his *Ad Nicoclem*.[31] The Planudean Anthology, a vast collection of competing treatments of common themes, also provided a playground for Latin versifiers. In a lecture delivered about 1493, Janus Lascaris, the first editor of the Anthology, wrote:

Haec itaque transferat unusquisque, et in his se oblectet, haec imitetur, in his se exerceat qui praeter alias utilitates tale quid etiam et tentare cupit et perficere.[32]

[And so let everyone translate these verses, amuse himself with them, imitate them; let that person practise his art among them who (besides other advantages which may accrue) wants to attempt and to complete a similar poem.]

Not a few students took this to heart. In 1494 Poliziano wrote to Antonio Urceo Codro:

Mitto interim quaedam tibi . . . quibus cum veteribus Graecis, nisi tamen hoc nimis improbum, certavi.[33]

[Meantime I am sending you certain of these epigrams . . . those in which I have sought to rival the ancient Greeks – if that is not too shameless.]

Thomas More and William Lily produced rival versions of eighteen of the simpler epigrams from the Anthology, a collection apparently intended for use in the classroom.[34] By the beginning of the sixteenth century, the notion of competitive translation had become a commonplace of the schools once again.

These competitive translations took their inspiration from antiquity. The final type of translation I want to look at developed during the fifteenth century. About 1406, Roberto Rossi proposed that his

---

[30] For nine fifteenth-century versions, see Sabbadini (1905), Allen (1906) 312, Gualdo Rosa (1973c) and Gualdo Rosa (1984) 64 n. 27, 185, 188–9. Willibald Pirckheimer refers to a completed Latin version in a letter of 17 November 1503 (Rupprich (1934) no. 302). Ottomar Nachtgall's version was printed at Strasbourg in 1515, and Erasmus' at Louvain in 1517.

[31] Fourteen fifteenth-century versions of *Ad Nicoclem* are recorded in Gualdo Rosa (1973b). At least five more versions reached print by 1516: Dominicus Bonominus (Brescia, 1503); Martino Filetico (Strasbourg, 1514); Ottomar Nachtgall (Strasbourg, 1515); Iacobus Marinus Weertensis ('s-Hertogenbosch, 1516); Erasmus (Louvain, 1516). A British Library manuscript, Add.19553, contains a Latin version made by Erasmus' pupil, Boerio, c.1506 (*EE* VII: 324).

[32] Hutton (1935) 116. The *editio princeps* of the Anthology was printed at Florence in 1494. Legrand (1885–1906) no. 13; Botfield (1861) 185–92.

[33] Poliziano (1553) 66. This undated letter was written in 1494, before 5 July.

[34] See Miller *et al.* (1984) 2.

version of the *Posterior Analytics* be regarded as a supplement to the other Latin translations of the work available in his day. He writes in the preface to his translation:

forsan avidiusculus quidam Aristotelis, cum prisce novam istam interpretationem nostram iniunxerit, abundantior factus in legendo, quandoque labori nostro gratias aget.[35]

[perhaps one of Aristotle's keener students, reading more profitably by joining this new translation of mine with the old one, will sometimes thank me for my work.]

He says that more versions may help the reader:

Dignus enim vir ille ut cunctis modis humanitatis auribus insinuetur . . .

[Because Aristotle should be introduced to the ears of the world in every possible way . . .]

Though Rossi has some hard words for the earlier versions, his attitude here is rather different from Bruni's contempt for the medieval translator of the *Ethics*. Perhaps the fact that Boethius' name was attached to the version of the *Posterior Analytics* current in his day preserved it from harsher criticism. Nevertheless, said Rossi, even if the extant Latin version of the *Posterior Analytics* had been a more agreeable piece of prose, another version might still be helpful.[36] The notion that a reader with no knowledge of Greek might deepen his understanding of a Greek author by collating a number of translations of the original text seems to have emerged in the fifteenth century because, for the first time, Latin readers had access to a number of translations of the same text. Rossi's view that a new Latin translation might supplement an earlier translation was certainly shared by Manetti. Manetti's Psalter translation, set alongside the versions of Jerome, functioned not as a replacement for the earlier versions, but as a commentary or a key to open up the meaning of the original text to the reader.

The parallel Latin versions which accompanied many elementary Greek texts are also supplementary in this sense. This new variety of translation emerged in the language schools, and it is a modest but distinctive contribution of the fifteenth century to

---

[35] Manetti (1951) 53.   [36] Ibid. 54.

translation practices. This development is significant for two reasons. Most important is the fact that these translations acknowledge the permanent value of the original Greek text. Less obviously, these translations are significant because they are self-consciously impermanent constructions. Students of Greek found that the most useful Latin translations were the most literal, and these literal translations did not make attractive specimens of Latin prose. As such, these translations were regarded as temporary and replaceable accommodations with the Greek text. After all, if they taught their readers how to read the Greek text that they rendered, they made themselves redundant. Aldine parallel translations exemplify this tendency: Aldus arranged some of his Greek editions so that the Latin versions could be removed and discarded once they had served their purpose.[37] Thomas More, we have seen, thought that the imperfections of any translation rendered it liable to replacement. In his note on 'in principio erat sermo' Erasmus made a virtue of this necessity to justify a number of renderings of the same text:

in hoc meo proposito, quo major est varietas, hoc plus est fructus.[38]

[this is my point: where there is greater variety, there is more profit.]

Erasmus frequently claimed that his version of the New Testament was not intended as a competitor to the Vulgate translation, but as a supplement to the Greek text printed alongside it. This may have been a little disingenuous, but it was a distinction he expected his critics to understand. He insisted that the New Testament was among those Greek texts which could not be replaced by their Latin renderings. In these circumstances, it became the duty of every theologian to grapple with the text in its original language.

Yet if the products of the new Greek presses did a great deal to spread knowledge of the Greek language, they also ensured that a little knowledge could be made to go a very long way. Clearly, some scholars studied Greek to dispense with translations altogether. There were some whose Greek was so good that translations were not needed at all. In 1508, Erasmus wrote to William Blount, Lord Mountjoy:

---

[37] See Botley (2002).   [38] A. Reeve (1986) 220. Added 1522.

Utinam Graecanicae literaturae peritia sic ubique propagetur ut is labor meus tanquam supervacaneus merito contemnatur.[39]

[If only the knowledge of Greek literature were so widespread that this labour of mine in translating could justly be despised as superfluous.]

The ideal scholar was fluent in both the learned languages. Thomas More painted this ideal into his *Utopia*: there, they do not translate Greek works into their own language, but learn Greek instead. More also makes of his narrator, Hythlodaeus, a specimen of erudition unheard of in the sixteenth century: his Greek was better than his Latin.[40] These Utopian elements are provocative because they show Greek as an alternative rather than a supplement to Latin culture.

Back in Europe, however, Erasmus knew that the wider readership would never read in Greek. He admitted as much in his *Methodus* when he said that only a middling ability in the language, *mediocritas aliqua*, is required of the reader.[41] In fact, Erasmus gave his New Testament to a world in which knowledge of Greek was common, but usually superficial. An abundance of preliminary texts and few more complex ones suggests that most did not take their Greek studies very far. The slowness with which substantial, scholarly, Greek texts sold is attested by the persistence of these volumes in successive Aldine catalogues: in the third extant Aldine catalogue of 1512, the Press advertised its third edition of Lascaris' Greek grammar alongside those copies of Theocritus, Aristophanes and Aristotle it had printed between 1495 and 1498.[42] Only a little knowledge of Greek was required to claim the benefits of the language outlined by the advocates of Greek studies. The interest of many Latins in the Greek language was exclusively lexicographical. They were interested in the origins of Latin words, and in the technical vocabularies of the political, philosophical and physical sciences. Greek words could certainly be studied without Greek grammar. Only a little more Greek was necessary in order to use Greek texts to elucidate ambiguous or corrupt passages in

---

[39] Ep. 211. *EE* i: 446. *CWE* ii: 142.
[40] Surtz and Hexter (1965) 38, 48–50, 180–2.   [41] See chapter 3, 131.
[42] The catalogues of the Aldine Press are edited in Renouard (1834) 329–38. The three catalogues produced in Aldus' lifetime are in facsimile in Orlandi (1975) figs ix–xviii.

established Latin translations. Greek texts, it would seem, were more often consulted than read. It is likely, for example, that many of those who bought the expensive Aldine Aristotle first used it to solve the problems thrown up by their Latin translations.[43] It is also likely that many went little further than this.

Nevertheless, the work of the printers had helped to create a large number of Latin readers with a rudimentary grasp of Greek by multiplying the basic tools of the language, and by making self-instruction a practical proposition. By 1516, Greek was no longer the exclusive province of a small number of specialists. Neither Bruni nor Manetti had had any missionary zeal for the propagation of Greek studies. They did not encourage, and they did not expect, their readers to learn Greek. Erasmus, however, hoped that every one of his readers would take up as much Greek as they could master. Shortly after the publication of his *Novum instrumentum*, he wrote to John Fisher:

Multi legunt hac occasione divinas litteras, nunquam alias lecturi, quod ipsi fatentur; complures graecari coeperunt, imo passim.[44]

[Many are taking this opportunity to read the Scriptures who would otherwise never read them, as they themselves admit; many people have begun to learn Greek, indeed they are doing so everywhere.]

In Italy in the early years of the fifteenth century, Bruni had attempted to surpass his Greek sources in his translations of Greek rhetoric; he had sifted a number of Greek historians in order to present the sort of material which might be of interest to a Latin historian. In the middle of the century, as Greek became more widely known in Italy, Manetti produced translations of Aristotle which refused to hide the difficulties of the language of the original text; he made a translation of the Psalter which was not a replacement for the ancient versions, but a critical tool with which to assess their virtues and limitations. At the beginning of the sixteenth century Erasmus set out to make converts to Greek studies. Not all who took up Greek under his influence were Erasmian enthusiasts: some of those who learnt the language did so in order to be

[43] The Aldine Aristotle was printed in five volumes from November 1495 to June 1498.
[44] Ep. 413. *EE* II: 245. *CWE* III: 295.

able to confront Erasmus on his own ground; some who felt that the reliability of the Vulgate translation had rendered knowledge of the Biblical languages unnecessary nevertheless set themselves to learn Greek in order to defend the Vulgate translator. Erasmus made the study of Greek desirable by showing the sort of claims it enabled its students to make.

APPENDIX

THE PREFACE TO MANETTI'S VERSION
OF THE PSALTER

This preface is extant in two versions. The longer text, found in the dedication manuscript, has a description of the arrangement of the three Latin Psalters. The other version, found in manuscripts containing Manetti's translation alone, omits this description. It is likely that Manetti composed both versions.

Some excerpts from this preface were edited by Garofalo (1946) 367–8. There is a photograph of Vatican Library Pal.lat.41, fol. 2ʳ in Garofalo (1953) facing page 232. There are photographs of Pal.lat.41, fols 2ʳ and 3ᵛ in Mittler (1986) 117–18. The complete text has not been edited before.

There are five manuscripts of Manetti's Psalter translation in the Vatican Library:

1   Pal.lat.40 (preface, triple Psalter, and *Apologeticus*) written by Agnolo Manetti with additions by Pietro Ursuleo
2   Pal.lat.41 (preface, triple Psalter, and *Apologeticus*) written for Alfonso of Aragon by Pietro Ursuleo.
3   Pal.lat.42 (Manetti's version only) written by Agnolo Manetti.
4   Pal.lat.43 (Manetti's version only) written by Agnolo Manetti.
5   Urb.lat.5 (Manetti's chief works, including his Psalter) written at Florence under the supervision of Vespasiano da Bisticci, for the duke of Urbino, Federico da Montefeltro.

This information is taken from Garofalo (1953) 230. De Petris states that Pal.lat.40 is in Giannozzo Manetti's hand (de Petris (1981) xliii). To these manuscripts may be added Bologna, Bibl. Univ. MS 2948, which contains Manetti's Psalter (de Petris (1981) xv n. 33); Brussels, B. R. MS 10745 (Psalter) and Florence, Marucelliana C 336 (to Ps. 36 only). See Trinkaus (1970) 584, 818. *Iter Italicum* records another fifteenth-century manuscript of Manetti's version: Lisbon, Bibl. Nac. Geral. 5620 (preface and Psalter).

For this dedicatory preface, I have preferred the text of the dedication manuscript, Pal.lat.41, fols 2ʳ–3ʳ, prepared during Manetti's lifetime. The scribe, Pietro Ursuleo of Capua, commends himself to the king in the colophon. For Ursuleo, see Banti (1939) 384–93. He was in Manetti's debt in 1458. See Cagni (1971) 301 n. 2. I have collated this text with the copies preserved in Pal.lat.40, fols 2ʳ–2ᵛ, Pal.lat.42, fols 3ʳ–5ʳ, Pal.lat.43, fols 1ʳ–11ᵛ, and Urb.lat.5, fols 7ʳ–8ʳ. The relationship between these manuscripts cannot be firmly established on the basis of this sample. In the text below, I have expanded all contractions and modernised the punctuation.

Ad Alfonsum clarissimum Aragonum regem Iannozii Manetti prefatio in noua totius Psalterii de Hebraica ueritate traductione incipit feliciter.[1]

Quanto ingentiora, gloriosissime princeps, excellentium uirorum erga quoscunque homines extant beneficia, tanto profecto secundum celebratam ueterum philosophorum sententiam maiora apud illos qui ea susceperunt obligationum uincula remanere restareque uidentur. Cum igitur maiestati tue, tum[2] ob excellentiam uirtutum tuarum, quibus deditissimus sum, partim etiam ob plurima ac maxima beneficia uariis temporibus[3] abste suscepta, omnia debeam, nimirum uehementia et efficacia quedam solide ac uere gratitudinis[4] inditia non solum tibi, sed cunctis quoque presentibus et posteris hominibus ad quorum manus hec nostra litterarum monumenta peruenerint, nuper ostendere ac demonstrare constitui.

Nam cum poetis, oratoribus et historicis, ac ceteris huiusmodi humanitatis studiis quibus in adolescentia assiduam operam nauaueras penitus et omnino pretermissis, te ad gymnasia philosophie ac diuine sapientie (que grece unico uerbo *theologia* appellatur) omnibus animi et corporis ceu dicitur uiribus merito, cum ob illius uere et non adumbratilis sapientie dignitatem, tum quoque ob persone tue sublimitatem, conuersum fuisse intelligerem ac plane aperteque aspicerem,[5] nempe maioribus, grauioribus, dignioribus, atque sane his nouis facultatibus tuis accommodatioribus litterariis laboribus nostris quam antea tecum dum inter poetica uersabamur ludere consueueram deinceps agere operarique decreui.

Cum enim uere ac solide utriusque et prisce et[6] moderne (ut ita dixerim)[7] theologie fundamenta in cunctis ueteris ac[8] noui testamenti codicibus tantum modo omnium doctorum hominum consensu iaciantur, atque ambo illa a ueris hebreorum ac grecorum fontibus in latinam linguam traducta ab ipsis a quibus ea suscepimus quotidie carpi lacerarique acciperem, pro uirili mea ulterius equo animo ferre ac tolerare non potui.

Quocirca, hac precipua causa adductus, laborem noue amborum testamentorum traductionis non iniuria nuper assumpsi. Licet uero hoc quodcunque est opus magnum et arduum ac mea quidem sententia herculeum proprias uires longe excellere [fol. 2ᵛ] atque admodum superare uideatur, si tamen deus ut spero, quando boni

[1] VERITATE IN LATINUM TRADUCTIONE . . . Pal.lat.43.
  IANOTII MANETTI FLORENTINI PREFATIO IN NOVA TOTIVS PSALTERII DE HEBRAICA VERITATE IN LATINVM TRADVCTIONE AD ALFONSVM CLARISSIMVM ARAGONVM REGEM FELICITER INCIPIT. Urb.lat.5.
[2] partim. Pal.lat.42.   [3] beneficia atque uariis abste. Urb.lat.5.
[4] gratitudinis mee. Pal.lat.42.   [5] conspicerem. Pal.lat.42.
[6] prisce et. Lacking in Urb.lat.5.
[7] et prisce et moderne ut ita dixerim. This is a correction in Pal.lat.42. It is longer than the text it replaced since it spills into the margin.
[8] et. Urb.lat.5.

gratia hoc quodcumque laboris est magnanimiter aggredi atque libenter assumere uoluerim, adiutor noster erit, optatos forsitan sortietur effectus. Quod si nobis diuina ope patrocinioque suffultis euenire contigerit, quicquid laboris in hac nostra translatione assumptum et exanclatum fuerit, saltem, ut sine arrogantia dictum uelim, ab omnibus doctis et eruditis uiris qui nulla animi perturbatione ducti iudicabunt non inutile propterea fuisse censebitur,[9] ut hebreis et grecis latina nostra, quasi a primeuis eorum fontibus deprauata plurimum degenerassent, passim carpentibus et calumniantibus iure respondere ac etiam eis perpetuum silentium iniungere atque indicere ualeamus.

Sed cum huiusmodi opus, quod ego in certum[10] quoddam et euidens ac perpetuum tantorum tuorum erga me meritorum signum celsitudini tue consulto et de industria dedicaui, partim ob magnam eius longitudinem, partim etiam ob nimiam difficultatem diuturnum fore uideatur et sit, ut paruulam interea reliquorum omnium degustationem tibi absque longa dilatione preberem, accuratam quandam ac integram solius Psalterii interpretationem nuper edere atque ad te mittere constitui. Tu uero pro tua singulari ac[11] precipua in examinandis et perpendendis cunctis paulo grauioribus rebus diligentia hanc commemorati Psalterii interpretationem cum duabus aliis celebratis Hieronymi nostri traductionibus parumper conferre ac comparare dignaberis. Due enim predicti Psalterii translationes ceteris celebratiores reperiuntur atque extant, quarum una est de greca in latinam linguam a Hieronymo ex septuaginta duobus illis primis famosissimisque interpretibus transumpta: hec est illa qua romana ecclesia in orationibus suis iampridem usque ad tempora nostra uti consueuit; altera eiusdem Hieronymi perhibetur et est, cuius titulus fertur de hebraica ueritate. Ac due dicte traductiones simul collate usque adeo ab inuicem differunt diuerseque cernuntur ut mirabile quiddam uideatur et sit, atque hac comparatione diligenter et accurate habita qualis hec nostra fuerit pro tua sapientia facile diiudicare poteris.

Ceterum de ista noua Psalterii traductione hec impresentiarum dicta sufficiant, cum plura alia in totius operis, si diuino fauore adiuti ultimas ei manus tandem aliquando imponere ualuerimus, prefatione non temere suis locis dicenda reseruentur. Tu autem, gloriosissime princeps, libenti gratoque animo hanc tam singularem ac tam precipuam et pene incredibilem mentis mee erga celsitudinem tuam **[fol. 3ʳ]** in huiusmodi tam animosis et tam magnanimis ceptis deuotionem benigne capere ac suscipere digneris maiorem in modum et rogo et obsecro. In hoc namque arduo pioque opere – ut cetera omittam – non paruam inter legendum uoluptatem et consolationem assequeris cum eiusmodi litterarum monumenta sacra ac diuina post mille circiter annorum curricula tuo regio regalique nomini nuper dedicata cognoueris, presertim cum Ptolemeum cognomine Philadelphum secundum Egyptiorum regem multo plus glorie ex sola et unica ueteris duntaxat testamenti translatione a commemoratis septuaginta duobus interpretibus nomini eius consecrata quam ex ceteris omnibus ipsius gloriosissime gestis non

---

[9] censebitur. Pal.lat.40; Pal.lat.42; Pal.lat.43; Urb.lat.5. censebuntur. Pal.lat.41.
[10] incertum. Pal.lat.40; Pal.lat.43; Urb.lat.5.   [11] et. Pal.lat.42; Pal.lat.43; Urb.lat.5.

immerito consecutum fuisse animaduerteris. Sed hec hactenus. Nunc dauidicam[12] tubam mirabiliter diuinitusque canentem accurata attentione sinceraque deuotione parumper audiamus, si prius de triplici descriptarum columnarum dispositione breuissime dixerimus. In primo nanque ordine septuaginta duorum, in secundo Hieronymi de hebraica ueritate, in tertio translatio nostra collocatur et ponitur, ut singule queque predictarum traductionum differentie e regione adinuicem posite facilius discernantur.[13]

Explicit prefatio Iannozii Manetti in noua Psalterii traductione ad Alfonsum clarissimum Aragonum regem.[14]

---

[12] dauiticam. Pal.lat.43; Urb.lat.5.
[13] si prius . . . discernantur. Lacking in Pal.lat.42, Pal.lat.43 and Urb.lat.5.
[14] Pal.lat.40 lacks explicit . . . Psalterii de Hebraica veritate traductione . . . Pal.lat.43. Prefacio psalterii Iannocii manetti in noua de hebraica ueritate traductione feliciter finit. Urb.lat.5.

REFERENCES

Abbreviations for journal titles are to be found in *L'Année philologique*.

Accame Lanzillotta, M. (ed.) (1986) *Leonardo Bruni traduttore di Demostene: La 'Pro Ctesiphonte'*, Pubblicazioni dell'Istituto di filologia classica e medievale dell' Università di Genova 96, Genoa

Alexander, J. J. G. (1977) *Italian Renaissance Illuminations*, New York

Allen, P. S. (1906) 'The letters of Rudolf Agricola', *English Historical Review* 21: 302–17

Allen, P. S., H. M. Allen and H. W. Garrod (eds) (1906–47) *Opus epistolarum Des. Erasmi Roterodami* (12 vols.), Oxford

Aristotle (1510) *Decem librorum moralium Aristotelis tres conversiones. Prima Argyropili Byzantii, secunda Leonardi Aretini, tertia vero antiqua per capita et numeros conciliate communi familiarique commentario ad Argyropilum adjecto*, Paris

   (1831–70) *Aristotelis opera*, ed. Academia Regia Borussica (5 vols.), Berlin

   (1962) *Aristotelis opera cum Averrois commentariis* (12 vols.), facsimile of Venice edition, 1562–74, Frankfurt

Bainton, R. H. (1969) *Erasmus of Christendom*, London

Balbi, G. P. (ed.) (1974) *Giannozzo Manetti: Elogi dei Genovesi*, Milan

Banti, L. (1939) 'Agnolo Manetti e alcuni scribi a Napoli', *Annali della R. Scuola normale superiore di Pisa*, ser. 2, no. 8: 382–94

Baron, H. (1928) *Leonardo Bruni Aretino: Humanistisch-philosophische Schriften, mit einer Chronologie seiner Werke und Briefe*, Leipzig and Berlin

   (1955a) 'Bruni's development as a translator from the Greek (1400–1403/04): the date of his epistola I, 8', in H. Baron, *Humanistic and Political Literature in Florence and Venice at the Beginning of the Quattrocento: Studies in Criticism and Chronology*, Cambridge, Mass.: 114–25

   (1955b) 'The genesis of Bruni's annotated Latin version of the (pseudo-) Aristotelian Economics (1420–1421)', in H. Baron, *Humanistic and Political Literature in Florence and Venice at the Beginning of the Quattrocento: Studies in Criticism and Chronology*, Cambridge, Mass.: 166–72

   (1966) *The Crisis of the Early Italian Renaissance: Civic Humanism and Republican Liberty in an Age of Classicism and Tyranny*, 2nd edn, Princeton

   (1967) 'Leonardo Bruni: "professional rhetorician" or "civic humanist"?', *Past and Present* 36: 21–37

REFERENCES

(1968) 'Aulus Gellius in the Renaissance: his influence and a manuscript from the school of Guarino', in H. Baron, *From Petrarch to Leonardo Bruni: Studies in Humanistic and Political Literature*, Chicago: 196–215

(1971) 'The date of Leonardo Bruni's *Isagogicon moralis disciplinae* and the recovery of the *Eudemian Ethics*', *Yearbook of Italian Studies* 1: 64–74

(1981) 'Progress in Bruni scholarship: à propos of F. P. Luiso's *Studi su l'epistolario di Leonardo Bruni*', *Speculum* 56: 831–9

Bataillon, M. (1935) 'L'arabe à Salamanque au temps de la Renaissance', *Hesperis* 21: 1–17

(1937) *Érasme et l'Espagne*, Paris

Bentley, J. H. (1983) *Humanists and Holy Writ: New Testament Scholarship in the Renaissance*, Princeton

(1987) *Politics and Culture in Renaissance Naples*, Princeton

Bernardinello, S. (1973) 'La traduzione greca di *Rhetorica ad Herennium* III, 16–24', *Aevum* 47: 387–416

Bertalot, L. (1975a) 'Zwölf Briefe des Ambrogio Traversari', in *Studien zum italienischen und deutschen Humanismus*, ed. P. O. Kristeller (2 vols.), Rome: I: 251–67

(1975b) 'Zur Bibliographie der Übersetzungen des Leonardus Brunus Aretinus', in L. Bertalot, *Studien zum italienischen und deutschen Humanismus*, ed. P. O. Kristeller (2 vols.), Rome: II: 265–83

(1975c) 'Zur Bibliographie des Leonardus Brunus Aretinus', in L. Bertalot, *Studien zum italienischen und deutschen Humanismus*, ed. P. O. Kristeller (2 vols.), Rome: II: 285–303

(1975d) 'Forschungen über Leonardo Bruni Aretino', in L. Bertalot, *Studien zum italienischen und deutschen Humanismus*, ed. P. O. Kristeller (2 vols.), Rome: II: 375–420

Berti, E. (1978) 'La traduzione di Leonardo Bruni del *Fedone* di Platone ed un codice greco della Biblioteca Bodmer', *MH* 35: 125–48

(1987) 'Alla scuola di M. Crisolora: lettura e commento di Luciano', *Rinascimento*, ser. 2, 27: 3–73

Besomi, O. and M. Regoliosi (eds) (1984) *Laurentii Valle epistolae*, Padua

Bevegni, C. (1994) 'Appunti sulle traduzioni latine dei *Moralia* di Plutarco nel Quattrocento', *Studi umanistici piceni* 14: 71–84

Beza, T. (1642) *Jesu Christi domini nostri Novum Testamentum sive Novum Foedus cuius graeco contextui respondent interpretationes duae: una, vetus; altera, Theodori Bezae. Eiusdem Theod. Bezae annotationes*, Cambridge

Bianca, C. (1999) 'Gaza, Teodoro', *Dizionario biografico degli Italiani* 52: 737–46

Bietenholz, P. G. (ed.) and Thomas B. Deutscher (asst. ed.) (1985–7) *Contemporaries of Erasmus: A Biographical Register of the Renaissance and Reformation* (3 vols.), Toronto

Binns, J. W. (1978) 'Latin translations from Greek in the English Renaissance', *HumLov* 27: 128–59

Birkenmajer, A. (1922) 'Der Streit des Alonso von Cartagena mit Leonardo Bruni Aretino', *Beiträge zur Geschichte der Philosophie des Mittelalters* 20, part 5: 129–210

Blatt, F. (1938) 'Remarques sur l'histoire des traductions latines', *C&M* 1: 217–42

Bolgar, R. R. (1954) *The Classical Heritage and its Beneficiaries*, repr. 1973, Cambridge

Botfield, B. (ed.) (1861) *Prefaces to the First Editions of the Greek and Roman Classics and of the Sacred Scriptures*, Cambridge

Botley, P. (2002) 'Learning Greek in Western Europe 1476–1516', in *Literacy, Education and Manuscript Transmission in Byzantium and Beyond*, ed. C. Holmes and J. Waring, Leiden: 199–223

Bouyer, L. (1963–70) 'Erasmus in relation to the medieval biblical tradition', in *The Cambridge History of the Bible* (3 vols.), Cambridge: II: 492–505

Brandes, P. D. (1989) *A History of Aristotle's Rhetoric with a Bibliography of Early Printings*, Metuchen, N.J., and London

Breen, Q. (1952) 'Rhetoric vs philosophy: texts of E. Barbaro, Pico, and Melanchthon, translated, with an introduction', *JHI* 13: 384–426

   (1964) 'Francesco Zambeccari: his translations and fabricated translations of Libanian letters', *SR* 11: 46–75

Bretschneider, C. G. (ed.) (1842) *Philippi Melanthonis Opera quae supersunt omnia*, Corpus Reformatorum (28 vols.), Halis Saxonum

Brown, A. (1992) *The Medici in Florence: The Exercise and Language of Power*, Italian Medieval and Renaissance Studies 3, Florence and Perth

Brown, A. J. (1984) 'The date of Erasmus' Latin translation of the New Testament', *Transactions of the Cambridge Bibliographical Society* 8: 351–80

Brucker, G. A. (1969) 'Florence and its university, 1348–1434', in *Action and Conviction in Early Modern Europe: Essays in Memory of E. H. Harbison*, ed. T. K. Rabb and J. E. Seigel, Princeton: 220–36

Burke, P. (1966) 'A survey of the popularity of ancient historians, 1450–1700', *H&T* 5: 135–52

   (1992) 'The Renaissance', in *Perceptions of the Ancient Greeks*, ed. K. J. Dover, Oxford and Cambridge, Mass.: 128–46

Cagni, G. M. (1960) 'I codici vaticani palatino-latini appartenuti alla biblioteca di Giannozzo Manetti (1396–1459)', *Bibliofilía* 62: 1–43

Cagni, G. M. (ed.) (1969) *Vespasiano da Bisticci e il suo epistolario*, Temi e testi 15, Rome

   (1971) 'Agnolo Manetti e Vespasiano da Bisticci', *IMU* 14: 293–312

Cameron, A. (1985) *Procopius and the Sixth Century*, London

Cammelli, G. (1941) *Giovanni Argiropulo*, I dotti bizantini e le origini dell' Umanesimo, vol. II, Florence

Camporeale, S. (1972) *Lorenzo Valla: Umanesimo e teologia*, Florence

Carvajal, T. G. (1832) 'Elogio histórico del doctor Benito Arias Montano', *Memorias de la Real Academia de la Historia* 8: 144

Cassuto, U. (1918) *Gli Ebrei a Firenze nell'età del Rinascimento*, Florence

(1935) *I manoscritti palatini ebraici della biblioteca apostolica vaticana e la loro storia*, Studi e testi 66, Vatican City

Cast, D. (1974) 'Aurispa, Petrarch, and Lucian: an aspect of Renaissance translation', *RenQ* 27: 157–73

Cecchini, E. and A. C. Cassio (1972) 'Due contributi sulla traduzione di Leonardo Bruni del "Pluto" di Aristofane', *GIF* n.s. 3: 472–82

Celenza, C. S. (1994) 'Renaissance humanism and the New Testament: Lorenzo Valla's annotations to the Vulgate', *Journal of Medieval and Renaissance Studies* 24: 33–52

Chomarat, J. (1978) 'Les Annotations de Valla, celles d'Erasme et la grammaire', in *Histoire de l'exégèse au XVIe siècle: Textes du Colloque international tenu à Genève en 1976*, ed. O. Fatio and P. Fraenkel, Etudes de philologie et d'histoire 34, Geneva: 202–28

(1979) 'Erasme lecteur des *Elegantiae* de Valla', in *Acta Conventus Neo-Latini Amstelodamensis: Proceedings of the Second International Congress of Neo-Latin Studies, Amsterdam 19–24 August 1973*, ed. P. Tuynman, G. C. Kuiper and E. Kessler, Munich: 206–43

Comparetti, D. (ed.) (1895) *La guerra gotica di Procopio di Cesarea: Testo greco emendato sui manoscritti con traduzione italiana*, Rome

Connell, W. J. (2000) 'The humanist citizen as provincial govenor', in *Florentine Tuscany: Structures and Practices of Power*, ed. W. J. Connell and A. Zorzi, Cambridge: 144–64

Conti, E. (1984) *L'imposta diretta a Firenze nel Quattrocento (1427–1494)*, Rome

Coogan, R. (1986) 'The Pharisee against the Hellenist: Edward Lee versus Erasmus', *RenQ* 39: 476–506

Copeland, R. (1989) 'The fortunes of "non verbum pro verbo": or, why Jerome is not a Ciceronian', in *The Medieval Translator: The Theory and Practice of Translation in the Middle Ages*, ed. R. Ellis, Cambridge: 15–35

Copenhaver, B. P. (1988) 'Translation, terminology and style in philosophical discourse', in *The Cambridge History of Renaissance Philosophy*, ed. C. B. Schmitt, with Q. Skinner, E. Kessler and J. Kraye, Cambridge: 77–110

Coppens, J. (ed.) (1969) *Scrinium Erasmianum: Mélanges historiques publiés sous le patronage de l'Université de Louvain à l'occasion du cinquième centenaire de la naissance d'Erasme* (2 vols.), Leiden

Cortesi, M. (1995) 'La tecnica del tradurre presso gli umanisti', in *The Classical Tradition in the Middle Ages and the Renaissance: Proceedings of the First European Science Foundation Workshop on 'The Reception of Classical Texts' (Florence: Certosa del Galluzzo, 26–27 June 1992)*, ed. C. Leonardi and B. M. Olsen, Biblioteca di Medioevo Latino 15, Spoleto: 143–67

Coulter, G. G. (1926) 'Boccaccio's acquaintance with Homer', *PhQ* 5: 44–53

Courcelle, P. (1969) *Late Latin Writers and their Greek Sources*, tr. H. E. Wedeck, Cambridge, Mass.

Crahay, R. (1969) 'Les censeurs louvanistes d'Erasme', in Coppens (1969): I: 221–49

REFERENCES

Cuendet, G. (1933) 'Cicéron et s. Jérôme traducteurs', *REL* 11: 380–400
Cytowska, M. (ed.) (1973) *De recta latini graecique sermonis pronuntiatione*, in *Opera Omnia Desiderii Erasmi Roterodami recognita et adnotatione critica instructa notisque illustrata*, vol. 1, part 4, Amsterdam: 1–103
Davies, M. C. (1984) 'The senator and the schoolmaster: friends of Leonardo Bruni Aretino in a new letter', *HL* 33: 1–21
(1987) [Review of De Petris (1981)] *Wolfenbütteler Renaissance Mitteilungen* 11: 23–8
(1988) 'Leonardo Bruni and Demosthenes', *CR* n.s. 38: 131–4
Dekkers, E. (1953) 'Les traductions grecques des écrits patristiques latins', *SEJG* 5: 193–233
Delaruelle, L. (1899) 'Une vie d'humaniste au XVe siècle: Gregorio Tifernas', *MEFRA* 19: 9–33
Delcourt, M. (1969) 'Erasme traducteur de Lucien', in *Hommages à Marcel Renard*, ed. J. Bibauw (3 vols.), Collection Latomus 101–3, Brussels: 1: 303–11
Delègue, Y. (ed.) (1990) *Les préfaces au Novum Testamentum (1516) avec textes d'accompagnement présentées, traduites et commentées par Yves Delègue avec la collaboration de J. P. Gillet*, Geneva
Dewing, H. B. (1914–40) *Procopius*, Loeb Classical Library (7 vols.), London
Dihle, A. (1955) 'Ein Spurium unter den rhetorischen Werken Ciceros', *Hermes* 83: 303–14
Diller, A. (1961) 'Greek codices of Palla Strozzi and Guarino Veronese', *JWI* 24: 313–21, repr. in Diller (1983), 405–13
(1964) 'Petrarch's Greek codex of Plato', *CPh* 59: 270–2, repr. in Diller (1983), 349–51
(1979) 'The manuscript tradition of Aeschines' orations', *ICS* 4: 34–64, repr. in Diller (1983), 219–49
(1983) *Studies in Greek Manuscript Tradition*, Amsterdam
Dionisotti, A. C. (1992) 'The medieval West', in *Perceptions of the Ancient Greeks*, ed. K. J. Dover, Oxford and Cambridge, Mass.: 100–27
Dobson, G. S. (1828) *Lysiae quae exstant omnia indicibus locupletissimis varietate lectionis continua interpretatione latina Taylori lectionibus lysiacis annotationibus variorum H. Stephani Schotti Scaligeri Contii Taylori Marklandi Reiskii Augeri Sluiteri aliorumque et suis illustravit Gulielmus Stephanus Dobson. Praefiguntur Adversaria... Petri Pauli Dobree* (2 vols.), London
Dröge, C. (1987) *Giannozzo Manetti als Denker und Hebraist*, Frankfurt, Bern and New York
Duran, E. (ed.) (1990) *Antonio Beccadelli el Panormita: Dels Fets e Dits del Gran Rey Alfonso, Versio catalana del segle XV de Jordi de Centelles*, Barcelona
Düring, I. (1957) *Aristotle in the Ancient Biographical Tradition*, Göteborg
Elaut, L. (1958) 'Erasme traducteur de Galien', *BiblH&R* 20: 36–43

Eleuteri, P. (1991) 'Francesco Filelfo copista e possessore di codici greci', in *Paleografia e codicologia greca*, ed. D. Harlfinger and G. Prato (2 vols.), Alexandria: I: 163–79

Fanfani, P. (ed.) (1862) *Commentario della vita di Messer Giannozzo Manetti scritto da Vespasiano Bisticci aggiuntevi altre vite inedite del medesimo e certe cose volgari di esso Giannozzo*, Collezione di opere inedite o rare dei primi tre secoli della lingua 2, Turin

Fiocco, G. (1964) 'La biblioteca di Palla Strozzi', in *Studi di bibliografia e storia in onore di Tammaro de Marinis*, ed. G. Mardersteig (4 vols.), Verona: II: 289–310

Fioravanti, G. (1983) 'L'apologetica anti-giudaica di Giannozzo Manetti', *Rinascimento* ser. 2, 23: 3–32

Franceschini, E. (1953) 'Una nuova testimonianza su Roberto Grossatesta traduttore dell' *Etica a Nicomaco*', *Aevum* 27: 370–1

(1955) 'Leonardo Bruni e il "vetus interpres" dell' *Etica Nicomachea* di Aristotele', in *Medioevo e rinascimento: Studi in onore di Bruno Nardi* (2 vols.), Pubblicazioni dell'Istituto di filosofía dell'Università di Roma 1–2, Florence: I: 300–19

Frati, L. (1933) 'Lianoro de' Lianori ellenista bolognese', *Studi e memorie per la storia dell'Università di Bologna* 10: 166–73

Fryde, E. B. (1983a) 'The beginnings of Italian humanist historiography: the "New Cicero" of Leonardo Bruni', in E. B. Fryde, *Humanism and Renaissance Historiography*, London: 33–53

(1983b) 'Some fifteenth-century Latin translations of ancient Greek historians', in E. B. Fryde, *Humanism and Renaissance Historiography*, London: 83–113

(1988) 'The first humanistic life of Aristotle: the "Vita Aristotelis" of Leonardo Bruni', in *Florence and Italy: Renaissance Studies in Honour of Nicolai Rubinstein*, ed. P. Denley and C. Elam, London: 287–96

Fubini, R. (ed.) (1964–9) *Poggio Bracciolini: Opera Omnia* (4 vols.), Monumenta politica et philosophica rariora, ser. 2, 4–7, Turin

(1986) 'Una sconosciuta testimonianza manoscritta delle *Annotationes in Novum Testamentum* del Valla', in *Lorenzo Valla e l'umanesimo italiano*, ed. O. Besomi and M. Regoliosi, Padua: 179–96

Galletti, G. C. (ed.) (1847) *Philippi Villani liber de civitatis Florentiae famosis civibus . . . et de Florentinorum litteratura principes fere synchroni scriptores*, Florence

Gambaro, A. (ed.) (1965) *Desiderio Erasmo da Rotterdam: Il Ciceroniano o Dello stile migliore, Testo latino critico, traduzione italiana, prefazione, introduzione e note a cura di Angiolo Gambaro*, Brescia

García, J. M. M. (ed. and tr.) (1995) *Vita Nicolai V summi pontificis de Giannozzo Manetti*, Malaga

Garin, E. (1949–50) 'Le traduzioni umanistiche di Aristotele nel secolo XV', *Atti e memorie dell'Accademia fiorentina di scienze morali* 16: 55–104

Garin, E. (ed.) (1952) 'Ad Petrum Paulum Histrum dialogus', in *Prosatori latini del quattrocento*, ed. E. Garin, Milan and Naples: 44–99

(1955) 'Ricerche sulle traduzioni di Platone nella prima metà del secolo XV', in *Medioevo e Rinascimento: studi in onore di Bruno Nardi* (2 vols.), *Pubblicazioni dell'Istituto di filosofia dell'Università di Roma* 1–2, Florence: 1: 341–74

(1957) 'Il pensiero morale d'Aristotele nell'umanesimo fiorentino', in *Estudios de la historia de la filosofía en homenaje al profesor Rodolfo Mondolfo*, Argentina: 417–30

(1972) 'The humanist chancellors of the Florentine Republic from Coluccio Salutati to Bartolomeo Scala', in E. Garin, *Portraits from the Quattrocento*, tr. V. A. and E. Valen, New York, Evanston, San Francisco and London: 1–29

Garofalo, S. (1946) 'Gli umanisti italiani del secolo XVe la Bibbia', *Biblica* 27: 338–75

(1953) 'Il Salterio di Asaf in una traduzione umanistica inedita dall'ebraico', *Miscellanea Biblica B. Ubach*, ed. R. M. Díaz, Scripta et Documenta 1, Montisserrati: 227–41

Gasquet, F. A. (1914) 'Roger Bacon and the Latin Vulgate', in *Roger Bacon Essays, Contributed by Various Writers on the Occasion of the Commemoration of the Seventh Centenary of his Birth*, ed. A. G. Little, Oxford: 89–99

Gauthier, R. A. (ed.) (1973) *Ethica Nicomachea: Translatio Roberti Grosseteste Lincolniensis sive 'Liber Ethicorum' B. recensio recognita, Aristoteles Latinus* 26, part 4, Leiden and Brussels

Geanakoplos, D. J. (1958) 'A Byzantine looks at the Renaissance: the attitude of Michael Apostolis towards the rise of Italy to cultural eminence', *GRBS* 1: 157–62

(1960) 'Erasmus and the Aldine Academy of Venice: a neglected chapter in the transmission of Graeco-Byzantine learning to the West', *GRBS* 3: 107–34

(1962) 'Michael Apostolis: Byzantine copyist and manuscript collector in Crete', in D. J. Geanakoplos, *Greek Scholars in Venice: Studies in the Dissemination of Greek Learning from Byzantium to Western Europe*, Cambridge, Mass.: 73–110

(1974) 'The discourse of Demetrius Chalcondyles on the inauguration of Greek studies at the University of Padua in 1463', *Studies in the Renaissance* 21: 118–44

(1989) 'Theodore Gaza, a Byzantine scholar of the Palaeologan "renaissance" in the early Italian Renaissance (c.1400–1475)', in D. J. Geanakoplos, *Constantinople and the West: Essays on the Late Byzantine (Palaeologan) and Italian Renaissances and the Byzantine and Roman Churches*, Madison, Wis.: 68–90

Geiger, L. (ed.) (1875) *Johann Reuchlins Briefwechsel, Bibliothek des Litterarischen Vereins in Stuttgart* 126, Tübingen

Gentile, S. (ed.) (1997) *Umanesimo e Padri della Chiesa: Manoscritti e incunaboli di testi patristici da Francesco Petrarca al primo Cinquecento*, Florence

George, W. and E. Waters (tr.) (1963) *Renaissance Princes, Popes and Prelates: The Vespasiano Memoirs*, intro. by M. P. Gilmore, New York, Evanston and London

Gibaud, H. (1986) 'Verbal subordination in the Vulgate and in Erasmus' first version of the New Testament as sampled in Acts 15 (1506–09)', in *Acta Conventus Neo-Latini Sanctandreani: Proceedings of the Fifth International Congress of Neo-Latin Studies, St Andrews 24 August to 1 September 1982*, ed. I. D. McFarlane, Medieval and Renaissance Texts and Studies 38, Binghamton, N.Y.: 225–7

Gilly, C. (1986) 'Una obra desconocida de Nebrija contra Erasmo y Reuchlin', in *El Erasmismo en España: ponencias del Coloquio celebrado en la biblioteca de Menendez Pelayo del 10 al 14 de Junio de 1985*, ed. M. Revuelta Sañudo and C. Morón Arroyo, Santander: 195–218

Gilmore, M. P. (1971) '*De modis disputandi*: the apologetic works of Erasmus', in *Florilegium Historiale: Essays Presented to Wallace K. Ferguson*, ed. J. G. Rowe and W. H. Stockdale, Toronto: 63–88

Giustiniani, V. R. (1961) 'Sulle traduzioni latine delle "Vite" di Plutarco nel quattrocento', *Rinascimento* ser. 2, 1: 3–62

Godin, A. (1978) 'Fonction d'Origène dans la practique exégétique d'Erasme: les Annotations sur l'Épitre aux Romains', in *Histoire de l'exégèse au XVIe siècle: Textes du Colloque international tenu à Genève en 1976*, ed. O. Fatio and P. Fraenkel, Etudes de philologie et d'histoire 34, Geneva: 17–44

Goguel, M. (1920) 'Le texte et les éditions du Nouveau Testament grec', *RHR* 82: 1–75

Gordan, P. W. G. (1991) *Two Renaissance Book Hunters: The Letters of Poggio Bracciolini to Nicolaus de Niccolis*, New York

Grabmann, M. (1926) 'Eine ungedruckte Verteidigungsschrift der scholastischen Übersetzung der Nikomachischen Ethik gegenüber dem humanisten Lionardo Bruni', in *Mittelalterliches Geistleben: Abhandlungen zur Geschichte der Scholastik und Mystik*, Munich: 440–8

Grafton, A. (1977) 'On the scholarship of Politian and its context', *JWI* 40: 150–88

Gravelle, S. S. (1982) 'Lorenzo Valla's comparison of Latin and Greek and the humanist background', *BiblH&R* 44: 269–89

(1993) 'The Latin–vernacular question and humanist theory of language and culture', in *Renaissance Essays*, ed. W. J. Connell (2 vols.), Rochester: II: 110–29

Gray, H. H. (1963) 'Renaissance humanism: the pursuit of eloquence', *JHI* 24: 497–514

Graziosi, M. T. (1969) 'Cinque lettere inedite di Giannozzo Manetti', *Atti e memorie dell'Arcadia* ser. 3, 5: 149–60

Greco, A. (ed.) (1970–6) *Vespasiano da Bisticci: Le vite* (2 vols.), Florence

(1983) 'Giannozzo Manetti nella biografia di un contemporaneo', *RPL* 6: 155–70

Griffiths, G. (1973) 'Leonardo Bruni and the restoration of the University of Rome (1406)', *RenQ* 26: 1–10

Griffiths, G., J. Hankins and D. Thompson (1987) *The Humanism of Leonardo Bruni: Selected Texts, Translations and Introductions*, Medieval and Renaissance Texts and Studies 46, Renaissance Society of America Renaissance Texts Series 10, Binghamton, N.Y.

Griggio, C. (1986) 'Due lettere inedite del Bruni a Salutati e a Francesco Barbaro', *Rinascimento* 26: 27–50

Grimm, C. L. W. and J. H. Thayer (1898) *A Greek–English Lexicon of the New Testament*, 4th edn, Edinburgh

Gualdo Rosa, L. (1973a) 'Le lettere di dedica delle traduzioni dal greco nel '400: Appunti per un analisi stilistica', *Vichiana* n.s. 2: 68–85

    (1973b) 'Le traduzioni latine dell' *A Nicocle* di Isocrate nel secolo XV', in *Acta Conventus Neo-Latini Lovaniensis*, ed. J. IJsewijn and E. Kessler, Louvain: 275–303

    (1973c) 'Niccolò Loschi e Pietro Perleone e le traduzioni dell'orazione pseudo-isocratea "A Demonico" ', *Atti dell'Istituto veneto di scienze, lettere, ed arti* 131: 825–56

    (1983) 'Una nuova lettera del Bruni sulla sua traduzione della "Politica" di Aristotele', *Rinascimento* ser. 2, 23: 113–24

    (1984) *La fede nella 'Paideia': Aspetti della fortuna europea di Isocrate nei secoli XV e XVI*, Rome

    (1985) 'Le traduzioni dal greco nella prima metà del '400: alle radici del classicismo europeo', in *Hommages à Henri Bardon*, ed. M. Renard and P. Laurens, Collection Latomus 187, Brussels: 177–93

    (1994) 'Due nuove lettere del Bruni e il ritrovamento del "materiale Bertalot" ', *Rinascimento* ser. 2, 34: 115–41

Gutkind, C. S. (1938) *Cosimo de' Medici Pater Patriae, 1389–1464*, Oxford

Hadot, J. (1972) 'La critique textuelle dans l'édition du Nouveau Testament d'Erasme', in *Colloquia Erasmiana Turonensia*, ed. J. C. Margolin (2 vols.), Toronto: II: 749–60

Hall, B. (1969) 'The trilingual college of San Ildefonso and the making of the Complutensian Polyglot Bible', *Studies in Church History* 5: 114–46

Hankins, J. (1990) *Plato in the Italian Renaissance* (2 vols.), Columbia Studies in the Classical Tradition 17, Leiden

    (1995) 'The "Baron thesis" after forty years and some recent studies on Leonardo Bruni', *JHI* 56: 309–38

    (1997) *Repertorium Brunianum: A Critical Guide to the Writings of Leonardo Bruni*, vol. I: *Handlist of MSS*, Fonti per la storia dell'Italia medievale subsidia 5, Rome

Hankins, J. (ed. and tr.) (2001) *Leonardo Bruni: History of the Florentine People*, vol. I: Books 1–4, Cambridge, Mass., and London

Harth, H. (ed.) (1984–7) *Poggio Bracciolini: Lettere* (3 vols.), Florence

Haury, J. (ed.) (1962–4) *Procopius caesariensis omnia opera* (4 vols.), Leipzig

Heesakkers, C. L. and J. H. Waszink (eds) (1973) *Paraphrasis seu potius epitome in Elegantiarum libros Laurentii Vallae*, in *Opera omnia Desiderii Erasmi Roterodami recognita et adnotatione critica instructa notisque illustrata*, vol. I, part 4, Amsterdam: 187–351

Herbermann, C. G., E. A. Pace, C. B. Pallen, T. J. Shahan and J. J. Wynne (eds) (1907–14) *The Catholic Encyclopedia: An International Work of Reference on the Constitution, Doctrine, Discipline, and History of the Catholic Church* (16 vols.), New York

Hetzenauer, P. M. (ed.) (1922) *Biblia sacra vulgatae editionis Sixti V Pont. Max. iussu recognita et Clementis VIII auctoritate edita*, Ratisbon and Rome

Hibbert, C. (1975) *The Rise and Fall of the House of Medici*, Newton Abbot

Highet, G. (1949) *The Classical Tradition: Greek and Roman Influences on Western Literature*, Oxford

Hirsch, R. (1978) 'Early printed Latin translations of Greek texts', in R. Hirsch, *The Printed Word: Its Impact and Diffusion*, London: no. 6

Hody, H. (1705) *De Bibliorum textibus originalibus, versionibus graecis, et latina Vulgata, libri IV . . . Praemittitur Aristeae historia graece et latine*, Oxford

Holmes, G. (1992) *The Florentine Enlightenment, 1400–1450*, Oxford

Hunt, R. W. (1966) 'Greek manuscripts in the Bodleian Library from the collection of John Stokovic of Ragusa', *Studia Patristica* 7: 75–82

Hutton, J. (1953) *The Greek Anthology in Italy to the Year 1800*, Ithaca, N.Y.

Hyma, A. (1932) 'Erasmus and the Oxford reformers', *Nederlands Archief voor Kerkgeschiedenis* 15: 69–92, 97–134

IJsewijn, J. (1969) 'Erasmus ex poeta theologus sive de literarum instauratarum apud Hollandos incunabulis', in Coppens (1969) I: 375–84

The Illustrated Incunabula Short Title Catalogue, Primary Source Media, in association with the British Library (CD Rom), VBIA Ver. 1.5

Jarrott, C. A. L. (1964) 'Erasmus' *in principio erat sermo*: a controversial translation', *Studies in Theology* 61: 35–40

   (1978) 'Erasmus' annotations and Colet's commentaries on Paul', in *Essays on the Works of Erasmus*, ed. R. L. de Molen, New Haven and London: 125–44

Jones, D. M. (1959) 'Cicero as a translator', *Institute of Classical Studies Bulletin* 6: 22–33

de Jonge, H. J. (1980) 'Erasmus and the *Comma Johanneum*', *Ephemerides Theologiae Lovanienses* 56: 381–9

   (ed.) (1983) *Apologia respondens ad ea quae Iacobus Lopis Stunica taxaverunt in prima duntaxat Novi Testamenti aeditione*, in *Opera omnia Desiderii Erasmi Roterodami recognita et adnotatione critica instructa notisque illustrata*, vol. IX, part 2, Amsterdam and Oxford

   (1984a) '*Novum Testamentum a nobis versum*: the essence of Erasmus' edition of the New Testament', *JThS* n.s. 35: 394–413

(1984b) 'The character of Erasmus' translation of the New Testament as reflected in his translation of Hebrews 9', *Journal of Medieval and Renaissance Studies* 14: 81–7

(1988) 'The date and purpose of Erasmus' *Castigatio Novi Testamenti*: a note on the origins of the *Novum Instrumentum*', in *The Uses of Greek and Latin: Historical Essays*, ed. A. C. Dionisotti, A. Grafton and J. Kraye, London: 97–110

Kallendorf, C. W. (ed. and tr.) (2002) *Humanist Educational Treatises*, Cambridge, Mass., and London

Keil, H. (1855–80) *Grammatici Latini* (8 vols.), Leipzig

Kelly, J. N. D. (1986) *The Oxford Dictionary of Popes*, Oxford

Kelly, L. (1979) *The True Interpreter: A History of Translation Theory and Practice in the West*, Oxford

Kessler, E. (1990) 'The transformation of Aristotelianism during the Renaissance', in *New Perspectives on Renaissance Thought*, ed. J. Henry and S. Hutton, London: 137–47

Kibbee, D. A. (1992) 'Renaissance notions of medieval language and the development of historical linguistics', *Journal of Medieval and Renaissance Studies* 22: 41–54

Kinney, D. (ed.) (1986) *The Yale Edition of the Complete Works of St Thomas More*, vol. XV: *In Defense of Humanism*, New Haven and London

Knott, B. I. (ed.) (1983) *De copia verborum ac rerum*, in *Opera omnia Desiderii Erasmi Roterodami recognita et adnotatione critica instructa notisque illustrata*, vol. I, part 6, Amsterdam and Oxford

Kraye, J. (1988) 'Daniel Heinsius and the author of *De mundo*', in *The Uses of Greek and Latin: Historical Essays*, ed. A. C. Dionisotti, A. Grafton and J. Kraye, London: 171–97

(1990a) 'Erasmus and the canonisation of Aristotle: the letter to John More', in *England and the Continental Renaissance: Essays in Honour of J. B. Trapp*, ed. E. Cheney and P. Mack, Woodbridge: 37–49

(1990b) 'Aristotle's god and the authenticity of *De mundo*: an early modern controversy', *JHPh* 28: 339–58

(1996) 'Philologists and philosophers', in *The Cambridge Companion to Renaissance Humanism*, ed. J. Kraye, Cambridge: 142–60

Kristeller, P. O. (1963–97) *Iter Italicum: A Finding List of Uncatalogued or Incompletely Catalogued Humanistic Manuscripts of the Renaissance in Italian and Other Libraries* (7 vols.), Leiden

Kristeller, P. O., F. E. Cranz and V. Brown (eds) (1960–92) *Catalogus Translationum et Commentariorum: Medieval and Renaissance Latin Translations and Commentaries* (7 vols. to date), Washington D.C.

Lardet, P. (1988) 'Un lecteur de Jérôme au XIIIe siècle: langues et traduction chez Roger Bacon', in *Jérôme entre l'Occident et l'Orient: Actes du Colloque de Chantilly (septembre 1986)*, ed. Y.-M. Duval, Paris: 445–63

(1989) 'Les traductions de la *Rhétorique* d'Aristote à la Renaissance', in *Traduction et traducteurs au Moyen Âge: Actes du Colloque international du CNRS organisé à Paris, Institut de recherche et d'histoire des textes, les 26–8 mai 1986*, ed. G. Contamine, Paris: 15–30

Lawrance, J. N. H. (ed.) (1989) *Tres opúsculos de Nuño de Guzman y Giannozzo Manetti: un episodio del protoumanismo español*, Salamanca

LeClerc, J. (ed.) (1961) *Omnia opera Desiderii Erasmi Roterodami* (10 vols.), Leiden, 1703–6, facsimile, Hildesheim

Legrand, E. (1885–1906) *Bibliographie hellénique ou description raisonnée des ouvrages publiés en grec par des grecs aux XVᵉ et XVIᵉ siècles* (4 vols.), Paris

Legrand, E. (ed. and tr.) (1892) *Cent-dix lettres grecques de François Filelfe*, Paris

Leonard, E. R. (ed.) (1975) *Ianotii Manetti: De dignitate et excellentia hominis*, Padua

Lerz, N. (1959) 'Il diario di Griso di Giovanni', *Archivio storico italiano* 117: 247–78

Levi, A. H. T. (tr.) (1986) *Ciceronianus*, CWE 28, Toronto, Buffalo and London

Lockwood, D. P. (1913) 'De Rinucio Aretino graecarum litterarum interprete', *HSPh* 24: 51–109

(1931) 'Leonardo Bruni's translation of act I of the *Plutus* of Aristophanes', in *Classical Studies in Honor of J. C. Rolfe*, ed. G. Depue Hadzsits, Philadelphia: 163–72

(1933) 'Plutarch in the fourteenth century: new evidence concerning the transition from the middle ages to the Renaissance', *TAPhA* 64: lxvi–lxvii

(1938) 'In domo Rinucii', in *Classical and Medieval Studies in Honour of Edward Kennard Rand: Presented upon the Completion of his Fortieth Year of Teaching*, ed. L. W. Jones, New York: 177–91

(1951) *Ugo Benzi, Medieval Philosopher and Physician, 1376–1439*, Chicago

Loewe, R. (1969) 'The medieval history of the Latin Vulgate', in *The Cambridge History of the Bible*, ed. G. W. H. Lampe (3 vols.), Cambridge: II: 102–54

Lo Monaco, F. (1986) 'Per la traduzione valliana della "Pro Ctesiphonte" di Demostene', in *Lorenzo Valla e l'umanesimo italiano: Atti del convegno internazionale di studi umanistici*, ed. O. Besomi and M. Regoliosi, Padua: 141–64

Loomis, L. R. (1927) 'The Greek studies of Poggio Bracciolini', in *Medieval Studies in Memory of Gertrude Schopperle Loomis*, Paris and New York: 489–512

Lowry, M. (1988) 'Erasmus as translator', *CR* n.s. 38: 134–6

Luiso, F. P. (1904) *Firenze in Festa per la consecrazione di Santa Maria del Fiore, 1436*, Lucca

(1980) *Studi su l'epistolario di Leonardo Bruni*, ed. L. Gualdo Rosa, Studi storici: Istituto storico italiano per il medio evo 122–24, Rome

Luttrell, A. (1960) 'Greek histories translated and compiled for Juan Fernández de Heredia, master of Rhodes, 1377–96', *Speculum* 35: 401–7

Lyell, J. P. R. (1917) *Cardinal Ximenes: Statesman, Ecclesiastic, Soldier and Man of Letters*, London

Manetti, A. (1951) 'Roberto de Rossi', *Rinascimento* 2: 33–55

Manley, F. and R. S. Sylvester (ed. and tr.) (1967) *De fructu qui ex doctrina percipitur (The Benefit of a Liberal Education)*, New York

Mara, M. G. (1973–4) 'La II Epistola di Pietro: testo e annotazioni erasmiane', *ArchClass* 25–6: 376–94

Marc'Hadour, G. (1979) 'The Latin Vulgate in the prose of sixteenth-century humanists', in *Acta Conventus Neo-Latini Amstelodamensis: Proceedings of the Second International Congress of Neo-Latin Studies, Amsterdam, 19–24 August 1973*, ed. P. Tuynman, G. C. Kuiper and E. Kessler, Munich: 682–9

(1988) 'Thomas More in emulation and defense of Erasmus', in *Erasmus of Rotterdam: The Man and the Scholar, Proceedings of the Symposium held at the Erasmus University, Rotterdam, 9–11 November 1986*, ed. J. Sperna Weiland and W. Th. M. Frijhof, Leiden: 203–14

Marchesi, C. (1904) *L'Etica Nicomachea nella tradizione latina medievale: documenti ed appunti*, Messina

Marco, F. de (1958) 'Di alcune traduzioni dal greco di Leonardo Bruni', *Aevum* 32: 187–90

Marcovich, M. (ed.) (1999) *Diogenes Laertius: Vitae Philosophorum* (2 vols.), Stuttgart and Leipzig

Mare, A. C. de la, P. K. Marshall and R. H. Rouse (1976) 'Pietro da Montagnana and the text of Aulus Gellius', *Scriptorium* 30: 219–25

Marsh, D. (1979) 'Grammar, method, and polemic in Lorenzo Valla's "Elegantiae"', *Rinascimento* ser. 2, 19: 91–116

(1984) 'Lorenzo Valla in Naples: the translation from Xenophon's *Cyropaedia*', *BiblH&R* 46: 407–20

(1992) 'Xenophon', in Kristeller, Cranz and Brown (1960–92) VII: 75–196

Martellotti, G. (1964) 'La *Collatio inter Scipionem Alexandrum Hanibalem et Pyrrum*: Un inedito del Petrarca nella biblioteca della University of Pennsylvania', in *Classical, Mediaeval and Renaissance Studies in Honor of Berthold Louis Ullman*, ed. C. Henderson (2 vols.), Rome: II: 145–68

Martinelli, L. C. (1980) 'Note sulla polemica Poggio–Valla e sulla fortuna delle *Elegantiae*', *Interpres* 3: 29–79

Martines, L. (1963) *The Social World of the Florentine Humanists*, London

McConica, J. K. (1969) 'Erasmus and the grammar of consent', in Coppens (1969) II: 77–99

McManamon, J. (1996) *Pierpaolo Vergerio the Elder: The Humanist as Orator*, Medieval and Renaissance Texts and Studies 163, Tempe, Ariz.

Mehus, L. (ed.) (1741) *Leonardi Bruni Aretini Epistolarum Libri VIII . . . recensente Laurentio Mehus . . . qui Leonardi vitam scripsit, Manetti et Poggii orationes praemisit, indices, animadversiones, praefationemque adjecit, librumque nonum, ac decimum in lucem protulit* (2 vols.), Florence

(1759) *Ambrosii Traversarii epistolae a domno Petro Canneto in libros XXV tributae variorum opera distinctae, et observationibus illustratae . . . ex monumentis potissimum nondum editis deducta est a Laurentio Mehus* (2 vols.), Florence

Mengaldo, P. V. (ed.) (1968) *Dante Alighieri: De Vulgari Eloquentia*, Padua

Mercati, G. (1916) *Se la versione dall'ebraico del codice veneto greco VII sia di Simone Atumano, Arcivescovo di Tebe*, Studi e testi 30, Rome

Mesnard, P. (1963) 'Humanisme et théologie dans la controverse entre Erasme et Dorpius', *Filosofia* 14: 885–900

Migne, J.-P. (ed.) (1844–90) *Patrologiae Cursus Completus: Series Latina* (221 vols.), Paris

Migne, J.-P. (ed.) (1857–66) *Patrologiae Cursus Completus: Series Graeca* (161 vols.), Paris

Miller, C. H., L. Bradner, C. A. Lynch and R. P. Oliver (eds) (1984) *The Yale Edition of the Complete Works of St Thomas More*, vol. III, part 2: *Epigrams*, New Haven

Minio-Paluello, L. (ed.) (1950) *Phaedo, interprete Henrico Aristippo*, in *Corpus Platonicum Medii Aevi*, ed. R. Klibansky (4 vols.), London: vol. II

(1952) 'Iacobus Veneticus Grecus: canonist and translator of Aristotle', *Traditio* 8: 265–304

(1972) 'Il "Fedone" latino con note autografe del Petrarca', in L. Minio-Paluello, *Opuscula: The Latin Aristotle*, Amsterdam: 87–93

Minio-Paluello, L. and H. Klos (1972) 'The text of the *Phaedo* in *W* and in Henricus Aristippus' translation', in L. Minio-Paluello, *Opuscula: The Latin Aristotle*, Amsterdam: 94–7

Mittler, E. *et al.* (eds) (1986) *Biblioteca Palatina: Katalog zur Ausstellung vom 8 Juli bis 2 November 1986 Heiliggeistkirche Heidelberg*, Heidelberg

Modigliani, A. (tr. and comm.) (1999) *Giannozzo Manetti: Vita di Niccolò V*, pref. M. Miglio, Rome

Momigliano, A. D. (1977) 'Polybius' reappearance in Western Europe', in A. D. Momigliano, *Essays in Ancient and Modern Historiography*, Oxford: 79–98

Monfasani, J. (1976) *George of Trebizond: A Biography and Study of his Rhetoric and Logic*, Columbia Studies in the Classical Tradition 1, Leiden

Monfasani, J. (ed.) (1984) *Collectanea Trapezuntiana: Texts, Documents, and Bibliographies of George of Trebizond*, Medieval and Renaissance Texts and Studies 25, Binghamton, N.Y.

Montuori, M. (ed.) (1974) *Jannotius Manetti: Vita Socratis*, Biblioteca di *De Homine* 6, Florence

Moreschini, C. (ed.) (1976) 'La *Vita Senecae* di Giannozzo Manetti', *ASNP* ser. 3, 6: 847–75

Morisi, A. (1964) 'La filologia neotestamentaria di Lorenzo Valla', *NRS* 48: 35–49

(1967) 'A proposito di due redazioni della *Collatio Novi Testamenti* di Lorenzo Valla', *Bullettino dell'Istituto storico italiano per il Medio Evo e Archivio muratoriano* 78: 345–81

Moulakis, A. (ed.) (1986) 'Leonardo Bruni's constitution of Florence', *Rinascimento* ser. 2, 26: 141–90

Muckle, J. T. (1942–3) 'Greek works translated directly into Latin before 1350', *MS* 4: 33–42 and 5: 102–14

Müllner, K. (1899) *Reden und Briefe italienischer Humanisten*, Vienna

Muratori, L. A. (ed.) (1731) *Chronicon Pistoriense a condita urbe usque ad annum 1446*, Rerum Italicarum Scriptores 19, Milan: 989–1076

Muratori, L. A. (ed.) (1734) *Vita Nicolai summi pontificis auctore Jannotio Manetto Florentino*, Rerum Italicarum Scriptores 3, part 2, Milan: 905–60

Murdoch, J. E. (1990) 'From the medieval to the Renaissance Aristotle', in *New Perspectives on Renaissance Thought*, ed. J. Henry and S. Hutton, London: 163–76

Naldini, M. (ed.) (1984) *Basilio di Cesarea: Discorso ai giovani / Oratio ad adolescentes, con la versione latina di Leonardo Bruni*, Biblioteca patristica 3, Florence

Nida, E. A. (1964) 'The tradition of translation in the western world', in E. A. Nida, *Toward a Science of Translating with Special Reference to Principles and Procedures involved in Bible Translating*, Leiden: 11–29

(1972) 'Linguistic theories and Bible translating', *Bible Translator* 23: 301–7

Noiret, H. (1889) *Lettres inédites de Michel Apostolis publiées d'après les manuscrits du Vatican avec des opuscules inédits du même auteur*, Paris

Novati, F. (ed.) (1891–1911) *Epistolario di Coluccio Salutati* (4 vols.), Rome

Oliger, P. L. (1912) *Expositio regulae fratrum minorum auctore Fr. Angelo Clareno*, Quaracchi, nr Florence

Oliver, R. P. (1940) 'Plato and Salutati', *TAPhA* 71: 315–34

Omont, H. (1887) 'Catalogue des manuscrits grecs des bibliothèques publiques des Pays-Bas', *Zentralblatt für Bibliothekswesen* 4: 185–214

Onofri, L. (1979) 'Sacralità, immaginazione e proposte politiche: La *Vita* di Niccolò V di Giannozzo Manetti', *HumLov* 28: 27–77

Orlandi, G. (ed.) (1975) *Aldo Manuzio Editore, Dediche, Prefazioni, Noti ai testi* (2 vols.), Milan

O'Rourke Boyle, M. (1977) *Erasmus on Language and Method in Theology*, Toronto and Buffalo

Pace, N. (1988) 'La traduzione di Niccolò Perotti delle *Historiae* di Polibio', *RPL* 11: 221–34

(1989) 'La tradizione di Niccolò Perotti delle *Historiae* di Polibio, II: a proposito dei codici di Polibio utilizzati dal Perotti per la traduzione del I e del II libro', *RPL* 12: 145–54

Pade, M. (1989) 'Guarino, his princely patron, and Plutarch's *Vita Alexandri ac Caesaris*: an ineditum in *Archivio di S. Pietro H 31*', *Analecta Romana Instituti Danici* 17–18: 133–47

(1991) 'The dedicatory letter as a genre: the prefaces of Guarino Veronese's translations of Plutarch', in *Acta Conventus Neo-Latini Torontonensis, Proceedings of the Seventh International Congress of Neo-Latin Studies: Toronto, 8 August to 13 August 1988*, ed. A. Dalzell, C. Fantazzi and R. J. Schoek, Medieval and Renaissance Texts and Studies 86, Binghamton, N.Y.: 559–68

(1995) 'The Latin translations of Plutarch's *Lives* in fifteenth-century Italy and their manuscript diffusion', in *The Classical Tradition in the Middle Ages and the Renaissance: Proceedings of the First European Science Foundation Workshop on 'The Reception of Classical Texts' (Florence: Certosa del Galluzzo, 26–27 June 1992)*, ed. C. Leonardi and B. M. Olsen, Biblioteca di Medioevo Latino 15, Spoleto: 170–83

Pagnotti, F. (1891) 'La vita di Niccolò V scritta da Giannozzo Manetti: studio preparatorio alla nuova edizione critica', *Archivio della R. Società romana di Storia Patria* 14: 411–36

Paschini, P. (1943) 'Un ellenista veneziano del Quattrocento: Giovanni Lorenzi', *Archivio Veneto*, ser. 5, 32–3: 114–46

Perossa, A. (ed.) (1960) *Giovanni Rucellai ed il suo Zibaldone I: 'Il zibaldone quaresimale'*, London

(ed.) (1970) *Collatio Novi testamenti*, Florence

Pertusi, A. (1962) 'Ἐρωτήματα: per la storia e le fonti delle prime grammatiche greche a stampa', *IMU* 5: 321–51

(1964) *Leonzio Pilato fra Petrarca e Boccaccio: le sue versioni omeriche negli autografi di Venezia e la cultura greca del primo umanesimo*, Civiltà veneziana 16, Venice

de Petris, A. (1975) 'Le teorie umanistiche del tradurre e l'*Apologeticus* di Giannozzo Manetti', *BiblH&R* 37: 15–32

(1976) 'L'*Adversus Judaeos et Gentes* di Giannozzo Manetti', *Rinascimento* n.s. 16: 193–205

(1977) 'Il *Dialogus Consolatorius* di Giannozzo Manetti e le sue fonti', *Giornale storico* 154: 76–106

de Petris, A. (ed.) (1979) *Vita Socratis et Senecae*, Florence

(1981) *Apologeticus*, Temi e testi 29, Rome

(1983) *Dialogus consolatorius*, Temi e testi 32, Rome

Pfeiffer, R. (1976) *History of Classical Scholarship from 1300 to 1850*, Oxford

di Pierro, C. (ed.) (1914–26) *Leonardo Bruni: Rerum suo tempore gestarum commentarius*, Rerum Italicarum Scriptores 19, part 3, Città di Castello / Bologna: 403–71

Plater, W. E. and H. J. White (1926) *A Grammar of the Vulgate: An Introduction to the Study of the Latinity of the Vulgate Bible*, Oxford, repr. 1997

Poliziano, A. (1553) *Angeli Politiani opera, quae quidem extitere hactenus, omnia*, Basle

Pomar, J. M. Fernández (1966) 'La colección de Uceda y los manuscritos griegos de Constantino Lascaris', *Emerita* 34: 211–88

Powicke, F. M. (1930) 'Robert Grosseteste and the *Nicomachean Ethics*', *Proceedings of the British Academy* 16: 85–104

Rabil, A. (1972) *Erasmus and the New Testament: The Mind of a Christian Humanist*, San Antonio

Reeve, A. (ed.) (1986) *Erasmus' Annotations on the New Testament: The Gospels, Facsimile of the Final Latin text (1535) with all Earlier Variants (1516, 1519, 1522 and 1527)*, intro. by M. A. Screech, London

(1990) *Erasmus' Annotations on the New Testament: Acts – Romans – I and II Corinthians, Facsimile of the Final Latin text with all Earlier Variants*, intro. by M. A. Screech, Studies in the History of Christian Thought 42, Leiden

(1993) *Erasmus' Annotations on the New Testament: Galatians to the Apocalypse, Facsimile of the Final Latin text with all Earlier Variants*, intro. by M. A. Screech, Studies in the History of Christian Thought 52, Leiden

Reeve, M. D. (1991) 'The rediscovery of classical texts in the Renaissance', in *Itinerari dei testi antichi*, ed. O. Pecere, Rome: 115–57

Reimherr, O., asst. F. E. Cranz (1992) 'Irenaeus Lugdunensis', in Kristeller, Cranz and Brown (1960–92) VII: 13–54

Resta, G. (1959) 'Antonio Cassarino e le sue traduzioni da Plutarco e Platone', *IMU* 2: 207–83

Reynolds, B. (1954) 'Bruni and Perotti present a Greek historian', *BiblH&R* 16: 108–18

Reynolds, L. D. (ed.) (1983) *Texts and Transmission: A Survey of the Latin Classics*, Oxford

Reynolds, L. D. and N. G. Wilson (1974) *Scribes and Scholars: A Guide to the Transmission of Greek and Latin Literature*, 2nd edn, Oxford

Rice, E. F. (ed.) (1972) *The Prefatory Epistles of Jacques Lefèvre d'Étaples and Related Texts*, New York and London

Roberts, J. T. (1987) 'Florentine perceptions of Athenian democracy', *M&H* n.s. 15: 25–41

Robinson, C. (ed.) (1969) *Luciani dialogi*, in *Opera omnia Desiderii Erasmi Roterodami recognita et adnotatione critica instructa notisque illustrata*, vol. I, part 1, Amsterdam and Oxford: 361–627

Robinson, R. P. (1921) 'The inventory of Niccolò Niccoli', *CPh* 16: 251–5

De' Rosmini, C. (1808) *Vita di Francesco Filelfo* (3 vols.), Milan

Ruiz-Calonja, J. (1950) 'Alfonso el Magnánimo y la traducción de la "Ilíada" por Lorenzo Valla', *Boletín de la Real Academia de buenas letras de Barcelona* 23: 109–15

Rummel, E. (1974) 'Erasmus and the Greek classics', *CWE* 29, Toronto: xxi–xxxiii

(1981) 'The use of Greek in Erasmus' letters', *HumLov* 30: 55–92

(1985) *Erasmus as a Translator of the Classics*, Toronto, Buffalo and London

(1986) *Erasmus' Annotations on the New Testament: from Philologist to Theologian*, Toronto

(1989a) 'Erasmus' conflict with Latomus: round two', *Archiv für Reformationsgeschichte* 80: 5–23

(1989b) *Erasmus and his Catholic Critics* (2 vols.), Nieuwkoop

(1991) '*Probati Auctores* as models of the Biblical translator', in *Acta Conventus Neo-Latini Torontonensis, Proceedings of the Seventh International Congress of Neo-Latin Studies: Toronto, 8 August to 13 August 1988*, ed. A. Dalzell, C. Fantazzi and R. J. Schoek, Medieval and Renaissance Texts and Studies 86, Binghamton, N.Y.: 121–7

(1992) '*Epistola Hermolai nova ac subditicia*: a declamation falsely attributed to Philipp Melanchthon', *Archiv für Reformationsgeschichte* 83: 302–5

Rupprich, H. (ed.) (1934) *Der Briefwechsel des Konrad Celtis*, München

Ruysschaert, J. (1971) 'L'envoi au roi Alphonse d'Aragon du "De dignitate et excellentia hominis" de Giannozzo Manetti', *Bibliofilía* 73: 229–34

Sabbadini, R. (1891) 'Briciole umanistiche: 1. Carlo Marsuppini. 2. Leonardo Bruni', *Giornale storico della letteratura italiana* 17: 212–28

(1896) *La scuola e gli studi di Guarino Guarini Veronese*, Catania

(1898) 'Dione Cassio nel secolo XV', *SIFC* 6: 397–406

(1900) 'Del tradurre i classichi antichi in Italia', *A&R* 3: 201–18

(1905) 'Una traduzione medievale del Πρὸς Δημόνικον di Isocrate e una umanistica', *Rendiconti dell'Istituto lombardo di scienze e lettere* 38: 674–87

(1905–14) *Le scoperte dei codici latini e greci ne' secoli XIV e XV* (2 vols.), Florence (Facsimile, Florence 1967, with additions and corrections by the author, ed. E. Garin, Biblioteca storica del Rinascimento n.s. 4)

Sabbadini, R. (ed.) (1915–19) *Epistolario di Guarino Veronese* (3 vols.), Miscellanea di storia veneta, ser. 3, 8, Venice

(1916a) ' "Maccheroni", "Tradurre" (per la "Crusca")', *Rendiconti del R. Istituto lombardo* ser. 2, 49: 219–24

(1916b) 'Ancora Pietro Marcello', *Nuovo archivio veneto* n.s. 31: 260–2

(1916c) 'Andrea Contrario', *Nuovo archivio veneto* n.s. 31: 378–433

(1924) *Giovanni da Ravenna, insigne figura d'umanista, 1343–1408*, Como

(1931) *Carteggio di Giovanni Aurispa*, Rome

Saffrey, H. D. (1971) 'Un humaniste dominicain, Jean Cuno de Nuremberg, précurseur d'Erasme à Bâle', *BiblH&R* 33: 19–62

(1976) 'Une exercice de latin philosophique, autographe du cardinal Bessarion', *Miscellanea marciana di studi bessarionei*, Padua: 371–9

Salter, F. M. and H. L. R. Edwards (eds) (1956–7) *The Bibliotheca Historica of Diodorus Siculus translated by John Skelton*, Early English Text Society (2 vols.), London

Sandeo, F. (ed.) (1611a) 'Oratio ad Alfonsum in nuptiali unici filii', in *De regibus Siciliae et Apuliae*, Hanau: 169–75

Sandeo, F. (ed.) (1611b) 'Oratio ad Alfonsum de laudibus pacis', in *De regibus Siciliae et Apuliae*, Hanau: 177–84

Sandys, J. E. (1908) *A History of Classical Scholarship*, vol. II: *From the Revival of Learning to the End of the Eighteenth Century in Italy, France, England and the Netherlands*, Cambridge

Santini, E. (1910) 'Leonardo Bruni Aretino e i suoi "Historiarum Florentini populi libri XII": contributo allo studio della storiografia umanistica fiorentina', *ASNP* 22, Pisa

Santini, E. (ed.) (1914–26) *Leonardo Bruni Aretino: Historiarum Florentini populi libri XII*, Rerum Italicarum Scriptores 19, part 3, Città di Castello / Bologna: 1–402

Santosuosso, A. (1986) 'Leonardo Bruni revisited: a reassessment of Hans Baron's thesis on the influence of the classics in the *Laudatio florentinae urbis*', in *Aspects of Late Medieval Government and Society: Essays Presented to J. R. Lander*, ed. J. G. Rowe, Toronto: 25–51

Schwarz, W. (1944) 'The meaning of *fidus interpres* in medieval translation', *JThS* 45: 73–8

(1945) 'The theory of translation in sixteenth-century Germany', *Modern Language Review* 4: 289–99

(1955) *Principles and Problems of Biblical Translation*, Cambridge

(1963) 'The history of principles of Bible translation in the western world', *Babel* 9: 5–22

Segarizzi, A. (ed.) (1899) *La catinia, le orazioni, e le epistole di Sicco Polenton, umanista trentino del secolo XV*, Biblioteca storica della letteratura italiana 5, Bergamo

Seigel, J. E. (1966) ' "Civic humanism" or Ciceronian rhetoric? The culture of Petrarch and Bruni', *P&P* 34: 3–48

(1968) 'Leonardo Bruni and the new Aristotle', in J. E. Seigel, *Rhetoric and Philosophy in Renaissance Humanism: The Union of Eloquence and Wisdom, Petrarch to Valla*, Princeton: 99–136

(1969) 'The teaching of Argyropoulos and the rhetoric of the first humanists', in *Action and Conviction in Early Modern Europe*, ed. T. Rabb and J. Seigel, Princeton: 237–60

Setton, K. (1956) 'The Byzantine background to the Italian Renaissance', *PAPhS* 100: 1–76

Skelton, J. (1956–7) *The Bibliotheca Historica of Diodorus Siculus Translated by John Skelton*, ed. F. M. Salter and H. L. R. Edwards (2 vols.), Early English Text Society o.s. 233 and 239, Oxford

Smalley, B. (1983) *The Study of the Bible in the Middle Ages*, Oxford

Smith, L. (ed.) (1934) *Epistolario di Pier Paolo Vergerio*, Rome

Solerti, A. (ed.) (1904) *Le vite di Dante, Petrarca e Boccaccio scritte fino al secolo decimosesto*, Milan

Sottili, A. (1966) 'Ambrogio Traversari, Francesco Pizolpasso, Giovanni Aurispa: traduzioni e letture', *RomForsch* 78: 42–63

Soudek, J. (1958) 'The genesis and tradition of Leonardo Bruni's annotated Latin version of the (pseudo-) Aristotelian *Economics*', *Scriptorium* 12: 260–8

   (1976) 'A fifteenth-century humanistic bestseller: the manuscript diffusion of Leonardo Bruni's annotated Latin version of the (pseudo-) Aristotelian *Economics*', in *Philosophy and Humanism: Renaissance Essays in Honour of P. O. Kristeller*, ed. E. P. Mahoney, Leiden: 130–43

Spengel, L. (ed.) (1867) *Aristotelis Ars rhetorica cum adnotatione Leonardi Spengel, accedit vetusta translatio latina* (2 vols.), Leipzig

Stadter, P. A. (1976) 'Arrianus, Flavius', in Kristeller, Cranz and Brown (1960–92): III: 1–20

Stevenson jr, H. (1886) *Codices palatini latini Bibliothecae Vaticanae descripti praeside I. B. Pitra, recensuit et digessit H. Stevenson iunior, recognovit I. B. de Rossi*, Rome

Stevenson sr, H. (1885) *Codices manuscripti palatini graeci Bibliothecae Vaticanae descripti praeside I. B. Pitra, recensuit et digessit H. Stevenson senior*, Rome

Stinger, C. L. (1977) *Humanism and the Church Fathers: Ambrogio Traversari and Christian Antiquity in the Italian Renaissance*, New York

Stornaiolo, C. (1895) *Codices urbinates graeci Bibliothecae Vaticanae*, Rome

   (1902–21) *Codices urbinates latini* (3 vols.), Rome

Surtz, E. and J. H. Hexter (eds) (1965) *The Complete Works of St Thomas More*, vol. IV, New Haven and London

Swete, H. B. (1902) *Introduction to the Old Testament in Greek*, Cambridge

Tarelli, C. C. (1943–7) 'Erasmus' manuscripts of the Gospels', *JThS* 44: 155–62 and 48: 207–8

Tasker, R. V. G. (1953) 'The Complutensian Polyglot', *Church Quarterly Review* 154: 197–210

Thiermann, P. (ed.) (1993) *Die Orationes Homeri des Leonardo Bruni Aretino: Kritische Edition der lateinischen und kastilianischen Übersetzung mit Prolegomena und Kommentar*, Leiden

Thompson, C. R. (1940) *The Translation of Lucian by Erasmus and St Thomas More*, Ithaca, N.Y.

Toynbee, P. (1919) 'Giannozzo Manetti, Leonardo Bruni, and Dante's letter to the Florentines (*epist.* vi)', *Modern Language Review* 14: 111–13

Trapp, J. B. (1990) 'The conformity of Greek with the vernacular: the history of a Renaissance theory of language', in J. B. Trapp, *Essays on the Renaissance and the Classical Tradition*, Norfolk, Va.: 8–21

Trinkaus, C. (1970) *In our Image and Likeness: Humanity and Divinity in Italian Humanist Thought* (2 vols.), London

(1976) 'Erasmus, Augustine and the nominalists', *Archiv für Reformations-geschichte* 67: 5–32

Troilo, S. (1932) 'Due traduttori dell' *Etica Nicomachea*: Roberto di Lincoln e Leonardo Bruni', *Atti del R. Istituto veneto di scienze, lettere ed arti* 91: 275–305

Ullman, B. L. (ed.) (1928) *Sicco Polenton, Scriptorum illustrium Latinae linguae libri XVIII*, Papers and Monographs of the American Academy in Rome 6, Rome

    (1946) 'Leonardo Bruni and humanistic historiography', *M&H* 4: 45–61, cited from B. L. Ullman, *Studies in the Italian Renaissance*, 2nd edn, Rome, 1973: 321–43

    (1963) *The Humanism of Coluccio Salutati*, Medioevo e Umanesimo 4, Padua

    (1973) 'The post-mortem adventures of Livy', in B. L. Ullman, *Studies in the Italian Renaissance*, 2nd edn, Storia e letteratura 51, Rome: 53–77

Ullman, B. L. and P. A. Stadter (1972) *The Public Library of Renaissance Florence: Niccolò Niccoli, Cosimo de'Medici and the Library of San Marco*, Padua

Valla, Lorenzo (1962) *Opera omnia*, intro. by E. Garin (2 vols.), *Monumenta politica et philosophica rariora ex optimis ed. phototypice expressa*, ser. 1, 5–6, facsimile of the edition printed at Basle in 1540, and of later editions of other works, Turin

Viti, Paolo (1992) *Leonardo Bruni e Firenze: studi sulle lettere pubbliche e private*, Humanistica 12, Rome

    (1996) *Opere letterarie e politiche di Leonardo Bruni*, Turin

Waszink, J. H. (ed.) (1969) *Euripidis Hecuba et Iphigenia latinae factae Erasmo interprete*, in *Opera omnia Desiderii Erasmi Roterodami recognita et adnotatione critica instructa notisque illustrata*, vol. 1, part 1, Amsterdam and Oxford: 193–359

Watson, A. G. (1984) *Catalogue of Dated and Datable Manuscripts c.435–1600 in Oxford Libraries* (2 vols.), Oxford

Weiss, R. (1951) 'The study of Greek in England during the fourteenth century', *Rinascimento* 2: 209–39, cited from Weiss (1977a) 80–107

    (1953a) 'The Greek culture of South Italy in the later Middle Ages', *Proceedings of the British Academy* 37: 23–50, cited from Weiss (1977a) 14–43

    (1953b) 'Notes on Petrarch and Homer', *Rinascimento* 4: 263–75, cited from Weiss (1977a) 150–65

    (1953c) 'Lo studio di Plutarco nel trecento', *P&P* 32: 321–42, cited from Weiss (1977a) 204–26

    (1955a) 'Lo studio del greco all'università di Parigi alla fine del medioevo', *Convivium* n.s. 2: 146–9, cited from Weiss (1977a) 60–4

    (1955b) 'Greek in Western Europe at the end of the Middle Ages', *Dublin Review* 119: 68–76, cited from Weiss (1977a) 3–12

(1955c) 'Iacopo Angeli da Scarperia (c.1360–1410–11)', in *Medioevo e Rinascimento: Studi in onore di Bruno Nardi* (2 vols.), Florence: 803–17, cited from Weiss (1977a) 255–77

(1967) *Humanism in England during the Fifteenth Century*, 3rd edn, Oxford

(1977a) *Medieval and Humanist Greek: Collected Essays*, Medioevo e umanesimo 8, Padua

(1977b) 'Gli inizi dello studio del greco a Firenze', in Weiss (1977a) 227–54

Wesseling, A. (ed.) (1978) *Antidotum primum: La prima apologia contro Poggio Bracciolini*, Respublica Literaria Neerlandica 4, Assen

Westfall, C. W. (1973) 'Biblical typology in the *Vita Nicolai V* by Giannozzo Manetti', in *Acta Conventus Neo-Latini Lovaniensis*, ed. J. IJsewijn and E. Kessler, Louvain

Wilamowitz-Moellendorff, U. von (1921) *Geschichte der Philologie: Einleitung in die Altertumswissenschaft* I, I, ed. A. Gercke and E. Norden, Leipzig

(1982) *History of Classical Scholarship*, an English translation by A. Harris of *Geschichte der Philologie*, London

Wilson, N. G. (1977) 'The book trade in Venice ca. 1400–1515', in *Venezia, centro di mediazione tra Oriente e Occidente (secoli XV–XVI): Aspetti e problemi*, ed. H. G. Beck, M. Manoussacas and A. Pertusi, Florence: 2, 381–97

(1992) *From Byzantium to Italy: Greek Studies in the Italian Renaissance*, London

Witt, R. (1978) 'Salutati and Plutarch', in *Essays presented to Myron P. Gilmore*, ed. S. Bertelli and G. Ramakus (2 vols.), Florence: 1: 335–46

Wittschier, H. W. (1968) *Giannozzo Manetti: Das Corpus der Orationes*, Studi italiani 10, Böhlau

Woodward, A. M. (1943) 'Greek history at the Renaissance', *JHS* 63: 1–14

Zaccaria, V. (1959) 'Pier Candido Decembrio traduttore della "Repubblica" di Platone', *IMU* 2: 179–206

(1967) 'Pier Candido Decembrio e Leonardo Bruni: notizie dall'epistolario del Decembrio', *StudMed*, ser. 3, 8: 504–54

Zippel, G. (1979) 'Carlo Marsuppini da Arezzo: notizie bibliografiche', in *Storia e cultura del rinascimento italiano*, Padua: 198–214

INDEX OF NAMES